MW00773028

HUP!

TRAINING FLUSHING SPANIELS THE AMERICAN WAY

James B. Spencer

Macmillan General Reference
A Simon & Schuster Macmillan Company
1633 Broadway
New York, NY 10019-6785

Macmillan Publishing Company is part of the Maxwell Communication Group of Companies.

Library of Congress Cataloging-in-Publication Data

Spencer, James B.
Hup! : training flushing spaniels the American way / James B. Spencer.
p. cm.
ISBN 0-87605-620-6
1. Spaniels—Training. I. Title.
SF429.S7S64 1992
636.7′52—dc20 91-47706
CIP

10 9 8 7 6 5 4 3 2

Printed in the United States of America

To Orion's Flicker MH,
my guide in Brigadoon.

Orion's Flicker, MH.

Some show-breds are good workers. This is Tawney Crawford's English Cocker "Stoney"—AM/CAN CH Ranzel Quarrystone, CDX, TD, MH, WDX, CAN CD. *Bill Crawford*

Contents

Preface

BRIGADOON

In early 1987 I sauntered unsuspectingly into the spaniel world—after twenty years in retrievers, preceded by ten years in pointing breeds, preceded by three years in Obedience Trial competition. All through those years I was curious about spaniels, but no one in my area had a working spaniel. Mostly I read about them. For years, I looked for a spaniel Field Trial within a reasonable distance. No luck.

Then, in 1985, Jim Reid, the outdoor columnist for the *Wichita Eagle,* wrote a piece about a local young man named Chad Betts. Chad not only had working spaniels, he also ran them in Field Trials, and—best of all—he was starting a spaniel club right here in my hometown.

I joined Chad's club, the Springer Spaniel Club of Central Kansas. Almost overnight, I was surrounded by working spaniels. But it was another two years before I had kennel space for one of my own. In the spring of 1987 I bought Flick, a field-bred English Springer, as a seven-week-old pup from Brenda Falkowski, who lives within three miles of my house. In 1990 I bought Rocky, another seven-week-old field-bred English Springer, from Dr. David Kettleson of Omaha, Nebraska.

Going from the high-tech world of electronic retriever training (which I never bought, never practiced) to the enchanting, enchanted world of spaniel training, I felt like Gene Kelly in the movie version of the musical *Brigadoon.* (Even my tactful wife will admit, if pressed, that I neither look nor dance like Gene Kelly—but, hey, no analogy is perfect.)

How refreshing to watch people praise and encourage their dogs again—as they did in my Camelot days among pointing dog and Obedience Trial trainers so many years ago. The spaniel training group became my Brigadoon, while the retriever group became my Midtown Manhattan.

I preferred Brigadoon. But then, so did Gene Kelly.

I have spent over four years there. Like Gene Kelly, I plan to stay for life. Brigadoon has been good to me, good for me. Now, in this book, I reciprocate. Most of what the Brigadooners have taught me about spaniel training came from word of mouth and example. They have written nothing down, at least not in book form. In gratitude for all their help, I am including in this book everything they have taught me about traditional spaniel training: quartering, steadying, brace work.

But I didn't enter Brigadoon empty-handed. I came bearing gifts, gifts that will appreciate in value as Brigadooners expand the horizons of their all-round hunting dogs.

In recent years, they have shown increasing interest in advanced retrieving. More and more of them are hunting doves and waterfowl with their spaniels. That means multiple marked retrieves, and blind retrieves. The new AKC hunting tests for spaniels require both water work and blind retrieves. This requirement is more a result than a cause of the developing interest in advanced retrieving in Brigadoon.

Spaniels can do this work, and do it very well. My Flick, whose full name is Orion's Flicker MH, has proved this most dramatically. The MH after his name stands for "Master Hunter," the highest level AKC hunting test title. Flick does water work, multiple marks, and blind retrieves so well that my retriever friends have suggested that I spray paint him orange and run him as a Golden!

Yes, Flick has proved that spaniels can do advanced retrieving. But that's not the point. What's important is that he does it without having suffered through the heavy-handed Midtown Manhattan training techniques. Flick doesn't "glow in the dark" from excessive use of the electronic collar. Flick doesn't tuck his tail between his legs and slink on blind retrieves. No, he bounces out there like . . . like . . . well, like a spaniel.

I formed my training attitudes long ago in my Camelot days among pointing dog and Obedience trainers. Twenty years in Midtown Manhattan couldn't change those attitudes. Not liking the way retriever trainers hammered the blind retrieve into their dogs, I looked for a kinder, gentler way. I picked up a technique here, a trick there, added a twist from somewhere else. I slowly assembled this hodgepodge into an integrated training program that keeps a dog's spirit up while conditioning him to run a true blind retrieve. Not the random run with a (surprise) happy ending that some Brigadooners accept as a blind retrieve. Not the plodding robot blind retrieve Midtown Manhattan retrieverites instill. In my approach, the dog learns to run happily *to* a "picture," not fearfully *from* the trainer.

There's more. Spaniel owners who do a lot of dove and waterfowl hunting are finding that force-breaking has some advantages. Not to teach spaniels to retrieve. No, they do that naturally. But force-breaking offers fringe benefits for water dogs, especially in the way it assures reliable delivery to hand. The dog comes ashore with a coatful of water. He may lay the bird down at the edge and shake. Then he may wander off, leaving the hunter the unpleasant job of slogging through deep mud to retrieve the abandoned bird. Force-breaking solves that problem.

In Midtown Manhattan, they force-break with the quick and rough "Hell Week" technique. Most Brigadooners would rather wade in mud after their ducks than put their spaniels through the misery of Hell Week. I agree. Even so, I force-broke Flick. I didn't use Hell Week. No, I used the very gentle David Sanborn technique, which I long ago brought to Midtown Manhattan from Camelot. The Sanborn method takes longer than Hell Week, but it's just as effective. More important, it's gentle enough for the most sensitive spaniel.

I do not claim that every spaniel should be force-broken. No, the spaniel that hunts only upland birds can get by nicely with natural retrieving. But the spaniel that does a lot of water work is another matter. However, even that spaniel doesn't deserve Hell Week. The Sanborn method I describe here is a practical, sensible alternative.

So, as I said, I didn't enter Brigadoon empty-handed. I brought with me gentle techniques for training spaniels to do things that Brigadooners are beginning to recognize as valuable: nonslip retrieving training techniques for both single and multiple marked retrieves; more important, blind retrieve training and force-breaking. All very gentle, very effective.

Maybe I brought a touch of Camelot with me to Brigadoon.

SECTION I

Acquiring Your Flushing Spaniel

OVERVIEW

Let me start off by congratulating you. You belong to that exclusive group of hunters who are in on the "secret"—that spaniels suit American hunting conditions better than any other type of sporting dog. You either own a spaniel or soon will. Whether you have achieved this distinction through empiric, cerebral, or fortuitous methods matters not the least to me. Congratulations!

In this section of the book, you will learn the expanded hunting role Americans have given to these marvelous dogs. You will also learn about the eight flushing spaniel breeds. And you will learn how to locate the ideal spaniel for you.

Chapter 1 explains the spaniel's job in American hunting. Over here, we expect our spaniels to do a bit of everything. More than a bit. We want our dogs to work effectively on almost every bird that comes in season. That means to quarter, flush, and retrieve various upland game birds (plus perhaps the odd rabbit). It also means we expect them to do nonslip retrieving of doves and waterfowl. Waterfowl, especially, call for some skill in blind retrieves.

Chapters 2 through 9 showcase the eight selected spaniel breeds: English Springer Spaniel, Welsh Springer Spaniel, English Cocker Spaniel, American Cocker Spaniel, Clumber Spaniel, Field Spaniel, Sussex Spaniel, and American Water Spaniel.

If you don't already have your spaniel, this section will help you locate the ideal one *for you*. No one breed will satisfy every potential owner. The more you know about each breed, the better your chances of picking the one that will please you most. So, if you must, skip first to the chapter on the breed you currently *think* you want. But after you read that one, read the chapters on the other breeds, too. You might be surprised.

If you already have your spaniel, these breed chapters will not only teach you more about your breed but will also help you appreciate the entire spaniel world. I think it was Cardinal Newman who defined an educated person as someone who knows a little about every field and a lot about one field—the Renaissance man concept. Dogdom needs more such people. Today we see too much one-breed myopia.

I had a difficult time selecting these eight breeds. Unlike the well-water-clear terms ''retriever'' and ''pointing dog,'' the word ''spaniel'' is too generic. It includes too many breeds, some sporting and some not. AKC registers Toy Spaniels that aren't hunters and were never meant to be. Clearly, those ''spaniels'' have no place in this book.

''Sporting spaniels'' clarifies matters some, but not enough. The Irish Water Spaniel (IWS) is a spaniel and a sporting breed. But AKC classifies it as a retriever and allows it to run only in AKC field trials and hunting tests for retrievers. The Brittany, still called ''Brittany Spaniel'' everywhere but in America, is a pointing dog, runs only in AKC pointing dog trials and tests. Great sporting dogs though they may be, neither the IWS nor the Brit belongs in this book.

Even ''flushing spaniel'' has some fuzzy edges. Although only the English Springer can run in AKC spaniel Field Trials, six breeds can run in AKC spaniel hunting tests: English Springer, Welsh Springer, English Cocker, American Cocker, Clumber, Field and Sussex Spaniels. All belong in this book. But what about the American Water Spaniel (AWS) and the Boykin Spaniel? Both are great upland flushers as well as waterfowl retrievers. Both are native American breeds, too, which inclines me to include them.

Although the AWS is an AKC breed, it cannot run in any AKC Field Trial or hunting test. Not those for spaniels. Not those for retrievers. Why? Because the sponsoring parent club, the American Water Spaniel Club, has not sought AKC classification for the AWS as either a retriever or a spaniel. The club has agonized over that decision for years but has never reached a conclusion. At this writing (1991) the club is scheduled to vote around the end of the year, but no one can predict whether it will go spaniel, go retriever, or stay unclassified. Even so, I decided to include the breed. Why? The American Water Spaniel Club sponsors ''field tests'' for the breed. These tests include both quartering/flushing work and nonslip retriever work. Thus the parent club considers the breed at least half flushing spaniel. That's good enough for me.

The Boykin Spaniel is not an AKC-recognized breed. The sponsoring parent club, the Boykin Spaniel Society, maintains its own registry. I have talked to many Boykin owners who consider the breed excellent as upland game flushers. However, I reluctantly decided to leave the breed out. The Boykin Spaniel Society sponsors their own Field Trials. The work is entirely nonslip retriever stuff. Much as I like the little dogs, and much as I want to include any

American-developed spaniel breed, I feel I must defer to the definition of the sponsoring parent club.

Look at it this way: If I included one breed that has been classified as a nonslip retriever, I would have to include all retriever breeds. Hunters use the various retrievers as upland flushing dogs, and they can learn how to train their dogs for this work in these pages. However, they will be better served, especially in the areas of priorities and phasing, with one of the many retriever books (among which are my three: *Training Retrievers for the Marshes & Meadows* [Fairfax, Virginia: Denlingers, 1990], *Hunting Retrievers: Hindsights, Foresights, & Insights* [Loveland, Colorado: Alpine, 1989], and *Retriever Training Tests* [New York: Arco, 1983, New York: Prentice Hall 1987]).

This book includes only the eight spaniel breeds classed as flushing spaniels, either by AKC or by the parent club. *I do not consider this a limitation.* It is an expansion on the ''breed scope'' of most spaniel training books, which cover only the English Springer Spaniel and maybe the English Cocker.

In describing these eight breeds, I have tried to show each breed in its entirety, from a hunter's point of view. I have concentrated on the features a hunter should be interested in as he selects a breed: physical characteristics, personality, temperament, maturity rate, trainability, and hunting methods. And I have presented each breed with as little personal bias as possible. To move away from my own knothole, I interviewed ''heavyweight'' fanciers of each breed. They have helped me avoid describing any breed characteristic as ''good'' or ''bad.'' I pretty much tell you what's there and what isn't and let you decide whether you like it or not.

Chapter 10, ''Finding the Right Spaniel for You,'' explains how to locate the right spaniel for your tastes, your hunting. It explains the seldom-considered option of starting with a trained dog, as well as the more common one, starting with a puppy. It tells you how to find sources for both. It advises you on housing and ends by giving you the argument for having your spaniel tattooed.

Flick delivers a rooster pheasant to the author.
Bill Ruble

Can English Cockers handle pheasants? Sure, says Mike Tillotson's "Molly" (Parson's Miss Molly, SH).

Welshies make outstanding hunting dogs, as Bill and Peggy Ruble's CH Statesman's Exuberance, SH shows.

1

The Spaniel's Job in America

OVER HERE in the colonies, we have developed a pragmatic civilization. We ask, ''Will it work?'' rather than, ''Is this the traditional, the proper, way to proceed?''

We are acquisitive. If we can't have it all, we want at least a little of each, so to speak. Small wonder, then, that the typical American shotgunner hunts nearly every bird that comes in season. Upland birds, like pheasant, quail, ruffed grouse, sharptails, prairie chickens, woodcock. Waterfowl, like ducks, geese, and shorebirds. And, of course, our Mr. In-Between, the dove. Most even like to pop an occasional rabbit.

We love dogs, especially the Sporting breeds. Every year AKC registers more dogs in its Sporting Group than in any of the other six Groups (Hound, Working, Terrier, Toy, Non-Sporting, and Herding). The AKC Sporting Group includes three types of bird-hunting breeds: pointing dogs, retrievers, and flushing spaniels. Each type has a specialty. A pointing dog ranges out, locates birds, and holds them (if they can be held) until the hunter approaches to flush and shoot them. A retriever remains at the hunter's side until he shoots a bird and commands the dog to retrieve it. This is called, for reasons I don't fully understand, ''nonslip retrieving.'' A spaniel hunts close to the hunter, flushes birds, and retrieves them when shot. Pointing dogs excel on birds that sit well for a point, like quail and woodcock. Retrievers excel in waterfowl hunting. Spaniels excel in handling upland birds that will not sit for a point, like pheasants and ruffed grouse.

But we Americans are not purists. Just as nature abhors a vacuum, we abhor specialization. We—almost compulsively—expand every specialization to a more general use. We seek more "bang for the buck" in everything. Small wonder then that American catch-as-catch-can hunters have never been satisfied with specialization in their dogs. Small wonder that we have pursued the "all-round" hunting dog as if it were the American Holy Grail. Every season thousands of pointing dogs shiver beside duck blinds and dutifully retrieve waterfowl. Every year retrievers hunt upland birds like spaniels, or even like pointing dogs! (Yes, we do have a "pointing Labrador" movement developing right now.)

Perhaps we have come closer to the Holy Grail than we realize. Anyone who (like me) has tried all three types of sporting dogs—putting them to the widest possible use in American hunting conditions—will tell you that the flushing spaniels come very close to being our mythical all-round hunting dog. True, they can't do absolutely everything. Only the American Water Spaniel can handle duck hunting in extremely cold weather. True also, no spaniel breed is ideal for geese in any weather. At the other end of the spectrum, they weren't designed for the big plantation quail hunting practiced in the Deep South. But those are all highly specialized forms of hunting. Typically, the guy or gal who hunts ducks late in the season doesn't hunt much else all year. Ditto for the goose hunter and the plantation quail hunter. These people aren't typical of American hunters. They don't hunt every bird that comes in season.

Most of us start each season in September filling the air around elusive doves with harmless loads of shot. Then we take in the early teal season. Next we switch to the resident upland game birds. We interrupt that occasionally to do a little ducking, some over decoys, some by jump shooting, until the weather gets too nasty. Then we go back into late-season upland bird hunting until the season closes. It's easier to keep warm while walking than while sitting in a drafty duck blind.

Neither a pointing dog nor a retriever can handle all of this as well as a spaniel can. The typical American hunts more in the uplands than in the marshes. The spaniel will handle that kind of workload better than will the retriever. Even the hunter who is more ducker than uplander might be better off with a spaniel, provided it is an American Water Spaniel. See what I mean? The spaniels come very close to being our Holy Grail.

In the Uplands

The spaniels have a natural tendency to "quarter" ahead of the hunter. That means they hunt back and forth in front of him, searching all birdy areas. Natural doesn't mean "automatic." No, owners must train their spaniels to quarter properly, but spaniels take to it more easily than do retrievers.

I hunted upland birds for many years with retrievers before getting my first spaniel. I enjoyed it immensely. However, I had to use my whistle to keep the typical retriever within gun range maybe twenty-five times as often as I do with a typical spaniel. My Flick sometimes goes all day with only one or two reminders. I've never had a retriever that would hunt that close so naturally.

Spaniels vary in style (animation, eagerness, verve) from breed to breed and from dog to dog within a breed. However, all the good ones have a pleasing way of doing their jobs. I love to watch them bounce this way and that, squirm under this snarl, jump over that one, as they hunt the cover for birds. My Flick is well named. That's what he does. He flicks and floats back and forth in front of me. Rocky is also well named. A bouncy little guy, he rock 'n' rolls through the cover. I enjoy even those days when we go birdless or nearly so, simply because I like to watch Flick and Rocky work. And, I must admit, my light game bag usually is more the fault of my poor shooting than of any lack of opportunities.

When a spaniel scents a bird, his entire body tells you about it. He becomes more animated, more intense. Some flush "hard" (boldly), diving immediately at the bird with a fly-or-die attitude. That is the preferred flush in America, where birds are relatively scarce and cover sometimes too light to hold running pheasants. Other spaniels have a "soft" or "English" flush. They pause when they scent the bird. Some flash-point and dive in. Others hold point until ordered to flush. That is the preferred flush in England, where they hunt only on lush estates, on which the resident gamekeeper tends both the cover and the bird supply for ideal hunting conditions. Some in this country prefer a soft flush, especially for birds that sit reasonably well, or in extremely heavy cover.

Although the pointing breeds excel on birds that sit tight, the flushing spaniel has a significant advantage in extremely tough cover. It charges into the nastiest brambles to put the birds in the air for the waiting hunter. The pointing dog poses politely outside and waits for the hunter to wade in for the flush.

The spaniel retrieves shot birds. Naturally, too. The steady spaniel hups (sits) immediately after the flush, marks the fall, and retrieves on command. The break-and-chase model is off to the races with the flush and pounces on the bird almost as soon as it comes down. Many prefer the breaking dog, but it has a couple of drawbacks. First, it can keep the hunter from shooting if the bird flies low. Second, it can disturb a lot of cover unnecessarily when the hunter fails to down a flushed bird.

Clearly, spaniels make better pheasant dogs than either pointing or retriever breeds. Pheasants aren't the gentlemanly birds a pointing dog needs to show his stuff. They run. They flush wild. They do everything but shoot back. The spaniel will push a runner hard to put it in the air quickly, which means within gun range. So will a retriever, but not with the same slash and dash.

I prefer spaniels for midwestern quail, too. Year in and year out, my home state of Kansas ranks in the top two or three states in quail production, frequently coming in first. We hunt these birds mostly on small farms, not on large plantations. We hunt them on foot, not from the back of a horse. Our quail run more than they did thirty years ago. They run early in the season because it's too warm to hold them. They run late in the season because they have been hunted too hard. They sit tight for only the middle of the season. Although I enjoy watching a pointing dog lock up as much as anyone, I get more shots at quail through an entire season with a spaniel.

For ruffed grouse, the spaniel's natural quartering tendency gives it a distinct advantage over the pointing dog that may pass large areas of cover, and over the retriever that may be too difficult to keep close. For woodcock, the spaniel's willingness to flush birds from tight spots comes in handy. I must admit, however, that a pointing dog can be nice for timberdoodles.

Most of the prairie chicken hunting I've done has been similar to duck hunting. We build blinds from hay bales in grain fields and wait for the birds to come in to feed mornings and evenings. This is dry land nonslip retriever work that a spaniel can do as well as a retriever. We sometimes walk chickens up during the middle of the day. They don't sit well for a point, nor will they tolerate noisy handling. Spaniels excel here, too.

Opinions differ on whether rabbits constitute proper game for spaniels. The English shoot rabbits over their spaniels, but many Americans have a hang-up against it. Mostly it's our pointing dog background that alarms us. If a spaniel hunts within gun range, popping rabbits in front of it will do it no harm. A steady dog provides more shooting than a breaker, which can be uncomfortably close to the fleeing rabbit.

In the Marshes

Most of us start the hunting season in September with dove shooting. When the temperature drops, the doves go south. So this is warm-weather shooting. Usually it's pretty hot hereabouts. For anyone with a dog, that means hunting only near water. Why? Because too many dogs have overheated and died while walking doves up along hedgerows, and so forth. Keep your dove dog wet to keep him alive.

A properly trained spaniel can retrieve doves shot around a pond as well as a retriever. Most spaniels take to water quite well, and they retrieve naturally. Actually, a pointing dog that will swim and retrieve does fine here, too. Every dog that swims and retrieves is what I call an "and doves" dog. They hunt whatever else the boss hunts, "and doves."

The early teal season, which is the only time most of us get to shoot bluewing teal, comes sometime in September, when it's still warm enough for any dog to retrieve from water. If a retriever has any advantage here, it is in its more placid temperament, its greater patience while sitting by the blind. Some would claim retrievers are less visible, too. However, if an all-black dog doesn't bother incoming birds, why should a partially white one? Either may draw the birds' attention to the blind area. That is only a problem if the hunters are moving around (or are otherwise conspicuous), or if they have left too much human debris lying around. Thus, in my opinion, any "and doves" dog is also an "and teal" dog.

I have never hunted shorebirds (rail, etc.). Probably never will. But I have read about it, and I can see no reason why a spaniel wouldn't be ideal. Most people do this hunting early in the year, around the edges of marshes, frequently from a small skiff. The spaniel's smaller size would be an advantage here.

During the first part of the regular duck season, conditions are usually mild enough for a spaniel to retrieve birds shot over decoys, whether from a shore blind or a boat. In a boat, a spaniel has a size advantage over a retriever.

During the later segments of the duck season, the water may be too cold for all spaniels except the American Water Spaniel, at least for shooting ducks over decoys, which requires sitting still between retrieves. The typical spaniel can join in for jump shooting ducks until the ice drives the birds south. In jump shooting, the dog gets to move around between retrieves, so he can shake out and warm up. If you have only a spaniel, and that one not an AWS, jump shooting will get you your share of those fat, red-legged late-season mallards that barbecue up so nicely on the grill.

Goose hunting? Even among retrievers, a good goose dog is rare. Like knuckleball pitchers, they're born, not made. Most of the good ones are born to Chesapeake parents. A goose dog must be willing and able to whip a huge, cantankerous crippled Canada goose before he can retrieve it. No job for even the most willing spaniel. True, some American Water Spaniels do a passable job on a now-and-again basis, but I wouldn't recommend any flushing spaniel to the dedicated goose hunter.

Nonslip Retrieving and the Blind Retrieve

Because we use our spaniels for limited water retrieving, we train them to do basic nonslip marked retrieving, in which the dog starts each retrieve sitting at heel. This prepares the dog for sitting by the blind in duck hunting with decoys.

Because no dog sees every fall, especially from a large flock of waterfowl, we also train our spaniels to do the true blind retrieve, at least in its rudimentary form.

Like the chaps across the Atlantic, American hunters do not need a true blind retrieve in the uplands. When a dog fails to see a bird fall there, the hunter can collect it in a couple of ways. To limit the amount of cover disturbed in the process, he can walk his dog to the area of the fall and command it search for the downed bird in a simple "hunt-dead" exercise. Or, as a poor second choice, he can stand in place, send his dog off in the general direction, let it hunt an area the size of New Jersey, and hope it stumbles on the bird before sundown. Some spaniel people call that a blind retrieve. It is not. It is, at best, a random run with a hopefully (surprise) happy ending.

However, neither approach works in water. Humanoids don't walk well on water, and random swims (unlike random runs) seldom have happy endings. When an unmarked bird falls in or across water, the hunter needs a true blind retrieve, in which he keeps the dog under complete and continuous control from the time he sends it until it picks up the bird. The handler first "lines" the dog in the right direction. The dog carries that line for a reasonable distance. If the dog drifts off-line, the handler toots his whistle to stop it. The dog stops, turns, and looks at the handler for directions. The handler "casts" the dog in the appropriate direction with an arm signal. The dog carries the cast for a reasonable distance. And so on until the dog winds the bird. This is a totally controlled retrieve. It is also highly interactive. It requires more teamwork than anything else in handling a hunting dog.

Although the true blind retrieve is not necessary in the uplands, it does come in handy. The hunter can pick up unmarked falls there without walking long distances, and without relying on random runs.

Spaniels are also good in water, especially American Water Spaniels, like Dr. Gary Forshee's youngster here.

2

The English Springer Spaniel: *A Popular Pair*

TELL THE AVERAGE American hunter that you hunt with a *flushing spaniel*, and it's five to one his response will be something like this: ''Gee, I envy you. I've always wanted to shoot over a *Springer*.''

Many use ''Springer'' as a synonym for ''flushing spaniel,'' much as many use ''Lab'' for ''retriever.'' Few bother to qualify it with ''English.'' Maddening as it may be to Welsh Springer Spaniel fanciers, ''Springer'' means English Springer Spaniel to almost everyone who doesn't own a Welshie.

The English Springer Spaniel has earned this place in the hunter's mind. It dominates field sports for flushing spaniels in this country as well as in England and elsewhere throughout the world. The nearest challenger, the English Cocker Spaniel, has never approached the Springer's popularity with hunters and field trialers.

Funny thing is, this appears to be two breeds, not one. Technically, it is one breed which has been split into two types: one for field, and the other for show. AKC registers both types as a single breed. No one considers pups from, say, a show dam and a field sire to be ''crossbred'' or even ''interbred.'' No, they are ''purebred,'' eligible for AKC registration.

Still, the field Springer differs remarkably from the show type in every physical characteristic that defines a breed as a breed: size, coat, markings, head shape, ears, even tail-dock. No one could mistake one for the other.

The show-bred English Springer is a handsome animal. This is Rollie and Pam Speck's CH Ruffwind's Wish Upon a Star.

The field-bred English Springer can also be a handsome animal, although it looks little like the show-breds. This is "Flick," with his six MH qualifying score rosettes.

Theresa Spencer

The two Springers resulted from two divergent competitions: dog shows and Field Trials. Dog show folks breed Springers that can win on the bench. Field Trialers breed Springers that can win in Field Trials. As competition in each activity increased, breeders found it less and less possible to breed Springers capable of winning in both. Winning in either one is plenty tough enough.

According to AKC registration statistics, the English Springer Spaniel ranks second in popularity among the spaniel breeds, behind the American Cocker. Considered as two separate breeds, they would still rank second and third, substantially ahead of other spaniels. I would guess the field type outnumbers the show type. I cannot verify that guess because AKC doesn't maintain separate registration statistics.

Show Springers are canine bodybuilders, beautifully proportioned and uniform in size and markings. Males stand about 20 inches at the withers and weigh about 50 pounds. Females are slightly smaller. They are more heavily boned than field Springers.

The field-breds are athletes. Wiry and agile, they can be as small as English Cockers and as large as retrievers. For example, my Rocky stands 17 inches and weighs 37 pounds, and my Flicker stands 23 inches and weighs 63 pounds. I told a show Springer acquaintance that my Springers average 20 inches and 50 pounds, just like his. Looking at my two dogs, he said, "Right. And the average married person has one testicle and one ovary."

The show Springer coat lies flat and has long feathering on the ears, legs, and underside. The underside feathers almost reach the floor.

The field Springer's coat is usually curly and coarse, but not excessively long. It might be as short as the coat of a field-bred English Setter or as long as that of a Golden Retriever.

The show Springer's markings are typically liver and white or black and white. Tricolors (tan points in a liver and white or black and white coat) and roans are okay, but rare. In the more common colors (liver/white, black/white), the darker color dominates. The dog has a large "saddle" of liver or black on its body. The ears and most of the head are dark. White usually appears only on the muzzle, front, neck, underside, rear, and legs.

The field Springer's markings might be any combination of liver or black and white, perhaps with tan points (tricolor). White frequently dominates. Many hunters (including me) prefer plenty of white, both for visibility and for its extra flash. Flicker is about 90 percent white with moderate liver ticking all over. He has liver around his eyes, skull, and ears, plus a liver patch at the base of his tail. My tricolored Rocky is about two-thirds white, with several largish liver spots. He has tan points above his eyes, on his muzzle, and on his rear legs.

The show Springer's head could have been sculpted by da Vinci. It's breathtaking with its square muzzle, nicely pronounced stop, soft expression, skull neither too wide nor too narrow, and long ears set on quite low.

The field Springer's head might be anything. The skulls vary from as wide as a Chesapeake's to as narrow as a Cocker's. The muzzles vary from square to snipey. The stops vary from as deep as a Cocker's to as "Roman" as a Flat-

Coated Retriever's. The expression varies from soft to fiery. The ears start too high and stop too soon. By show standards, Flick's head is a disaster. Too wide on top. Ears too short and set too high. Muzzle not a bit square. "Quizzical" expression. Yet when he bounces toward me carrying a fresh-shot rooster pheasant, he's gorgeous all over, even his head.

The tail-docks differ. Show Springers retain only about one-third of the tails they were born with. Just enough to give the show handler a good grip when posing the dog. Some claim this short tail best balances the rest of the dog aesthetically. I don't know. It's all in what you're used to.

Field Springers sport about two-thirds of their original tails. A hunter "reads" his dog by watching its tail. The longer dock offers more "reading material." A white tip helps even more. Rocky's breeder docked his tail extra long, specifically to give me a white tip. I'm glad he did.

Form follows function. The show Springer is gorgeous when standing still or moving at a show gait. The field Springer doesn't reach its "beauty" zenith until it is fairly flying back and forth in front of you while hunting. Picture the typical field Springer at work: slashing and bounding left and right, left and right, ears flying, tail snapping and cracking; diving in to flush a pheasant; leaping high as the bird lifts off; dashing out to make the retrieve; bouncing joyfully back with the bird. The stockier show Springer can't approach the agility and speed of this broken field runner.

Beauty is only partially in the eyes of the beholder. It is also partially in the activity of the beheld.

Show and field Springers share a charming temperament. At least they should. I have only seen two field-breds that were less then cordial, and only one of those had an inclination to bite. But some show lines (certainly not all, not even most) exhibit unpleasant temperaments: shyness, aggressiveness, territorial inclination, unwillingness to please. Then, too, a few show-breds exhibit "rage syndrome." No one has figured out exactly what this is. Maybe a form of epilepsy, maybe some other type of seizure. The affected dog will exhibit a normal temperament most of the time but occasionally go into a frenzy of rage, in which it attacks anything that moves (including its owner). When the seizure (or whatever) ends, the dog seems to have no recollection of it. Many show breeders deny the very existence of rage syndrome, but I've talked to two people who suffered attacks from such dogs. My nonscientific conclusion is: This is something, and something to be concerned about. Denial won't make it go away.

However, the proper Springer temperament is a joy to work with, a joy to live with, and a joy to be around.

Springers bubble with energy, the field-breds more so than the show-breds. Even so, either type, as a house dog, adapts to family patterns, family wishes. It may lie around unnoticed much of the time. But let any family member call its name, and it will bounce up and prance around expectantly. Always ready to go. Always ready to play. Always ready for a training session.

If ignored too long, the house Springer will make its presence known. It may just wiggle up to someone and nuzzle his/her hand. The dog may pounce and freeze—fanny up, chest on the floor, front legs outstretched—and look expectantly. It may bring someone a toy. But it will get attention somehow.

A typical Springer may have a favorite person, but it is not a one-person dog. It loves everyone: family, friends, strangers who visit the house, the mailman, everyone. Watchdog? Naw, just not territorially inclined. Oh, it will bark at an intruder, but that's about it. If a burglar gets in, that's okay with the resident Springer. Especially if the person does a little petting before getting down to business.

A Springer gets along with other dogs, too. They make up quickly and love to play. Flicker has been trying to teach my Chesapeake, Beaver, how to play for three years now. Slow, grinding work, but he's making progress. Chesapeakes take life very seriously.

Anyone who can train any dog can train a Springer. They're bright and want desperately to please. They love training sessions, as long as the trainer is not heavy-handed. A soft breed, Springers respond best to those who lead them through each exercise, praising lavishly at every opportunity. Corrections? Sure, but only for deliberate offenses, not for accidents and misunderstandings. Deliberate Springer disobediences are rare.

Because they are so energetic, they master "active" exercises more easily than "passive" ones. Especially field-breds. They want to move, to do something (anything). Inactivity bores them. Thus, they learn to heel, to come, to jump, to retrieve, and so on, more easily than they learn to stay. Many Springers scoot around excitedly while sitting at heel. Or "dance" slightly with their feet on the SIT-STAY. The dog doesn't move; it just picks up and puts down one front paw, then the other. You can work through these problems if they bother you (as they do Obedience Trial competitors). Or you can live with them if your interest is just basic obedience for home and field.

Flick has a slight case of "nervous feet" on his SIT-STAYS. He doesn't change his position. But when I walk around the yard with him on a SIT-STAY, he sometimes picks up and replaces one front foot or the other. I doubt he realizes it. Because of my early Obedience trial background, this mannerism bothers me. But not much. Certainly not enough to get me to shorten up and straighten it out. You must be close to the dog to make an effective correction: a sharp "No!" just before you reposition the errant foot, followed by "Good boy." No, I live with this problem instead of correcting it. For my purposes, it's trivial, even though I always notice it.

Field-bred Springers mature, both physically and mentally, more rapidly than other spaniels, including show-bred Springers. They normally demonstrate birdiness quite early. Even just-weaned pups enjoy romps in cover, where all the wonderful smells are. They also show a strong retrieving instinct quite young.

Field-bred Springers usually take to water readily, and quite young if given the chance. No one should try to make a foul-weather duck dog out of a Springer. It lacks the body fat and water-repellent coat for such work. But every working Springer should be able to swim out into a farm pond or across a stream to retrieve a downed upland game bird. Or retrieve doves and early season ducks from water.

When Flick was young, I overworked him in the water. I lengthened his retrieves too far and too fast. I also reran him too many times per session. One day he sat me down and explained that he wasn't a Chesapeake, never would be, and in fact didn't even want to be. He communicated these things to me most eloquently by refusing to enter the water when I sent him. Hard to miss a message like that.

I took him off water work for a month or so, then started over again. It took time, but he learned to like water work again. In moderation. Even today, I seldom rerun him immediately on a water retrieve (as I do retrievers). The point is: The Springer can do some water work, but it isn't a water dog in the sense that a Chesapeake is.

In the uplands, the field-bred Springer sets the standard by which most hunters judge all flushing dogs. Rightly or wrongly. The only other breed that approaches the Springer standard afield is the field-bred English Cocker.

The field-bred Springer moves faster through its quartering pattern than any other breed (including show-bred Springers). They fly. They don't just want to find birds; they are frantic to do so. Desire, intensity, agility, and speed have been selectively bred into these dogs by Field Trialers because that's what wins.

Ditto for the field-bred Springer's hard flush. No hesitation here. No flash-pointing. Just a kamikaze dive into the bird-holding patch of cover, often followed by a spectacular leap as the bird takes off. Again, only the field-bred English Cocker can approach the flush of this dog.

Granted, not every hunter wants such a flush. Some prefer a soft (or English) flush, in which the dog hesitates or even points before flushing the bird. This gives the hunter some warning that a bird is about to get up. English Field Trial judges prefer soft flushes. English cover is quite heavy, so pheasants don't run like they do in this country. Besides, the English gamekeeper keeps the estate grounds well stocked with birds. If one gets away, another will pop up soon.

In America, many hunters find cover sparser, birds scarcer. This is especially true of pheasant hunters, who often hunt all day and find only one or two birds. If a soft flush lets the day's one pheasant scurry off on foot, it may get away. Thus the American preference for the field-bred English Springer's wham-bam flush.

Quail, grouse, and woodcock hunters have fewer problems with running birds, so many of them prefer a soft flush.

The field-bred Springer normally marks shot birds down quite well. Not like retrievers, but better than pointing dogs and better than most other spaniels. Even when the Springer fails to find a downed bird immediately, it has unbelievable persistence in hunting the area of the fall. Typical spaniels, regardless of breed, persevere longer than typical retrievers when seeking downed birds. The typical field-bred Springer hunts a much larger area than the typical retriever, but it covers the ground so quickly, uses the wind so well, and stays with the job so untiringly that few birds get away unretrieved.

Most field-bred Springers have tender mouths, some to a fault. The most common Springer mouth problem is gripping the bird tentatively, thus dropping and picking it up repeatedly. Flick does this sometimes. Having had firmer-mouthed dogs (not spaniels, incidentally) eat birds now and then, I don't look unkindly on Flick's sometimes too-gentle mouth.

The show-bred Springer may or may not hunt successfully. Some dogs, even some lines, have retained their field abilities after many generations of straight show breeding. Other lines haven't. Those that do hunt typically do it at a more moderate pace than the field-breds. More like a Welsh Springer.

Few show-breds have a "banzai" flush, either. Most have a soft flush. Even those with a hard flush don't match what you see from the best of the field-breds. For all but pheasant hunters, this is a matter of taste. For pheasant hunters, except in the heaviest cover, the harder the flush, the more likely the birds will be to fly rather than run. In very heavy cover, pheasants flush like aviary gentlemen to the softest flush.

The huntable show-bred typically retrieves well enough for most hunters, even if it lacks the speed and perseverance of the field-bred. If it will retrieve from land, it will also retrieve from water, if properly introduced.

Of course, the show-bred's coat gives the hunter his major headache afield. Few people hunt in areas devoid of burrs. Where burrs are a problem, they will fill that luxurious show coat like fans fill the stadium for the Super Bowl. In serious burr country, the hunter may have to stop every thirty minutes to dig burrs out. Each stop could take more than thirty minutes, too.

Some who hunt show-breds trim their coats quite short, so that burrs stay on the surface where they can be easily plucked off. Others oil the coat heavily, so burrs can be easily pulled out. Still others do both: trim the coat moderately and apply oil. The point is, you don't have to let the burr problem ruin your hunting experiences with your dog.

For the prospective buyer, the English Springer Spaniel is two breeds. For those attracted to them, choosing between them is like choosing between any other two breeds. It depends on which you like better and what you want to do with your dog. The field-breds dominate all spaniel field activities (field trials and hunting tests), but "ain't all that purty." The show-breds are gorgeous but may or may not hunt. However, the relatively new hunting test movement offers show breeders a wonderful opportunity to prove their stock as hunters. Some are taking advantage of this and are doing quite well. Thus the show fancier can, with careful searching, find a dog with known working parents, and maybe grandparents.

A "triple threat" Welshie (show, obedience, field): CH Statesman's Sporting Chance, CD, SH, owned by Bill and Peggy Ruble.

"Breezey" delivers a quail to Peggy Ruble.

3

The Welsh Springer Spaniel: *Canine Knight of the Round Table*

LIKE MANY, I have long believed that each nation develops dog breeds with character traits similar to those of its people. Americans breed independent, dominant dogs. Germans breed energetic, trainable dogs. Frenchmen breed joyful, unpredictable dogs. And so on.

Thus, to understand the Welsh Springer Spaniel, we should understand the Welsh people. Who are they? Or, more important, who were they when they became a people?

During the legendary centuries (approximately A.D. 350 to A.D. 650) when England was ruled by the very real King Arthur and his like-minded successors, the true British people inhabited most of what we now call England. They were harassed constantly by the Picts and Scots from the north, and probably by Celtic freebooters from across the Irish Sea.

To even the odds faced by small and widely dispersed British populations, the Arthurian kings allowed the immigration of thousands of Angles and Saxons from Germany, with an agreement that the latter would help the British against the Picts and Scots. He settled them in isolated pockets throughout Britain. The Anglo-Saxons, as they became known, were less than second-class citizens within the British realm. Even so, their condition was so much better than it had been in Germany that they flocked over at every British invitation. Eventually the size of the Anglo-Saxon population in Britain approximated that of the British themselves.

When the first wave of the Plague hit Britain (around A.D. 550), it decimated the British, who were heavily involved in trade with the Continent, but hardly touched the isolated Anglo-Saxons. Predictably, the Anglo-Saxons turned on their British masters. Unable to defeat and subjugate the remaining hardy Britishers, they gradually drove them into a region so mountainous and rugged that it was considered unfit for human habitation. The true British still live there today. The "uninhabitable" region is called Wales.

Britain gradually became England (land of the Angles) and the British became the Welsh (because they lived in Wales). In 1066 the Normans conquered England and again reduced the Anglo-Saxons to second-class citizenship. However, the Normans avoided Wales. They realized that the difficulties of a campaign against such a hardy people in such forbidding surroundings far outweighed any small gains they might realize.

Thus has it always been. Wales and the Welsh have been left alone to maintain and develop their true British culture in peace and seclusion. The Welsh Springer Spaniel, therefore, must be considered the dog that Arthur and his knights would have developed if they had had shotguns and hunted birds for food and recreation.

Some romantics feel that Arthur has always watched over his entire realm, not just Wales. For example, in the late 1400s, when Henry VII tried to legitimize the Tudor claim on the throne by naming his eldest son Arthur, the old Arthur would have none of it. Young Arthur died before his father, and England was scourged with Henry VIII instead. In modern vernacular, there just ain't no messing with Arthur, so let's take a careful, respectful look at his dog.

Physically, the Welsh Springer Spaniel is attractive in a workaday manner. A self-sustaining survivor rather than a beauty-shop creation, his coat doesn't wave softly in the breeze or drag on the ground. His movements are efficient rather than flashy. His size varies to suit the needs of his master. If it weren't for his bright red and white colors and sorrowful facial expression, few would notice him.

He may be as small as an English Cocker or as large as a Labrador Retriever. Until 1989 the AKC breed Standard didn't mention size. Now it calls for males to stand 18 to 19 inches and females 17 to 18 inches at the withers. Weight is to be "in proportion to height and overall balance." That tells you very little, for "overall balance" means different things for different breeds (like the Basset Hound and the Whippet, for example). Actually, Welsh Springers in the 17- to 19-inch range should weigh between 35 and 45 pounds. They should be somewhat lower and longer than show-type English Springers.

"Historically," breeder Susan Healy of Tallahassee, Florida told me, "people have bred Welsh to whatever size they need for their specific hunting. Size varies widely in American Welsh Springers. In the South, where they hunt mostly dove and quail, the dogs tend to be quite small. In the North, where people hunt mostly pheasants and grouse, the dogs are larger. A few even breed them very large for field goose shooting. They're gritty dogs and will retrieve geese if asked to."

When I asked her about the new size recommendation in the Standard, she said, "It will be a long, long time before that has much impact. Even in dog shows the oversized or undersized Welshie that is otherwise excellent will have no trouble finishing its championship for many years to come."

As with most breeds, the head indicates the character. The overall geometry of the Welshman's head is so practical for a hunting dog that one hardly notices it. No flopping flews. No deep stop. No bulging eyeballs. No long, heavily feathered, and low-set ears dragging the ground. Just a nice businesslike head. Only the doleful expression stands out. When I first looked into the sad brown eyes of a Welshie, I thought, "Here is a dog that could con me into or out of anything anytime."

The coat is as practical as the head. Long and heavy enough to protect the dog as he wiggles through the nastiest cover, it is short and light enough to be easily maintained. Sure, the owner may have to pull out a few burrs, but he won't have to barber and groom the dog regularly to keep him operational. Even the feathering behind the legs and on the stubby tail is not long enough to be a problem.

The breed's only physical extravagance is the gorgeous color mixture of red and white. The red approximates that of the Irish setter, running from a bright chestnut to a deep mahogany with the midrange more like a deep and brilliant orange. Individual dogs may come in almost any pattern of red and white, and many dogs are ticked. The head is usually mostly red.

Most Welsh carry only about one-third to one-half of their original tails. The rest is docked in the first week of life.

The temperament of the Welsh Springer is about what you would expect of a dog developed by the Arthurian British. Devoted to his family, and especially to the one special person he considers his master or mistress, he is reserved with strangers. However, he reads people's intentions well and soon accepts friends as friends. Enemies are a different story. Although not aggressive, he protects his territory and family. A good watchdog, intent on keeping his family informed, he may become a problem barker if not properly trained early in life.

"When the meter reader is in the neighborhood," Susan Healy says, "my Welshies keep me posted on just how close he is by how they bark. When they say he is at the gate, I go out and let him in. No way would he get in if I didn't. No way."

His devotion to family makes him a poor kennel dog, although he can spend some of his life in the kennel as long as he gets plenty of house time, too. An energetic dog, he wants to participate in every family activity. He likes other canine company, too. If several Welshies are kept together, they tend to become a pack. Where one goes, all go. What one does, all do.

Mentally they mature rather slowly. "Some of ours have taken puppyhood to the max," breeder Susan Riese of Atlanta, Georgia says, "acting like puppies until past their second birthdays."

On the other hand, they require training fairly early in life. If the owner doesn't establish control over the pup, the grown dog may become a self-hunter, a dog that ignores the boss and hunts only for himself.

They are a soft breed to train. Most Welshies require a light touch and plenty of praise and encouragement. Heavy-handedness will ruin a Welsh faster and more surely than anything else, especially if that heavy-handedness comes from the one person on earth the dog truly adores. The Welsh, like all soft dogs, will sometimes become stubborn and turn the boss off—especially during training with birds—but the trainer need only shake the dog up enough to regain his attention. After that he should resume the gentle approach, even if he doesn't feel all that happy about things himself. A knowing trainer will praise at every opportunity, even when that means praising through gritted teeth.

"To correct a Welsh, you need something less threatening than a wet noodle," Susan Healy says.

They learn quickly and retain well. They are workers at heart and insist on having something to do, preferably something that involves their people.

"If you don't give him a job, he will make one up for himself," Susan Riese says. "And not always one you would like him to take on, like opening all the gates, dumping water pails, and so forth."

Stamina rather than style characterizes the Welshie's approach to hunting. Although he lacks the hackle-raising slash and sweep that win Field Trials, he can hunt all day at his deliberate pace. A Welsh works as hard at sundown as he does at sunrise.

Bill Ruble of Erie, Kansas told me, "I shoot a hundred to a hundred and fifty quail a year over my dogs. I've used pointing dogs and other spaniels in the past, but none of them will go all day for me like my Welshmen do."

I can attest to their tirelessness, for I hunted quail with Bill one day in early December 1989. His two Welshies, Chance and Breezy, hunted until I was ready to drop—although the much younger Bill was still lifting his feet instead of dragging them when we quit.

The Welshie hunts with "laid-back determination." Although he never seems to hurry, he never seems to relax, either. He doesn't potter around aimlessly. No, he hunts diligently, even though he moves slowly enough to stay within easy gun range without much handling. Perhaps his outstanding nose tells him so many wildlife tales that he must be cautious to make sure he gets the entire story from each waft of scent.

They do have outstanding noses. When I hunted with Bill, I was amazed at the distances at which Breezy and Chance detected quail sitting tightly in dense cover. They would lope along cautiously down a hedgerow for a long time, then whirl suddenly and drive deep into the cover and disappear from sight. Up would come a covey or a single bird. I got so I set myself to shoot every time one of those dogs disappeared into the cover. I was seldom disappointed.

Peggy Ruble, Bill's wife, told me, "Many years ago I took my first Welshie to a field day before he had had any training. They were planting pigeons for the dogs to flush. When I unsnapped my dog's leash, he went totally out of control.

He headed into the wind, jumped a fence, and just took off, while I screamed and hollered for him to come back. He ignored me and finally flushed a flock of partridge way over in the next field. Everyone was flabbergasted at his nose. He scented those birds from hundreds of yards."

Gary Riese, Susan's husband, told me, "When Bill Ruble and I took our dogs to South Dakota in the fall of 1989, everyone told us it was too hot and dry to find any birds. The advice we got was: 'Better not miss, for you won't get many chances.' Nonsense. Our Welshies filled the air with pheasants all day. We missed plenty and still limited out."

The Welshie performs in the water much as he does on land: deliberately and persistently. Typically he lacks the big entry of some of the other spaniels. Instead of that breathtaking long leap, he slips gently into the water. He may even look worried as he swims, but he tends to look a little worried all the time anyhow. Nevertheless he retrieves anything the boss drops in the drink, and does it over and over.

He makes a nice dove dog. He is calm enough to sit still during the sometimes long periods of inactivity. He retrieves tenderly enough to deliver these delicate birds unharmed. He has the endurance to keep it up during those occasional hunts when birds are falling almost continuously for a large party of hunters.

However, the breed, like most "land" spaniels, lacks the body build and coat of a serious duck dog. He can do limited duty during the early part of the season. Even then he deserves special consideration. He should be allowed to run around and dry off after each retrieve. He should be kept in the blind out of the wind.

"Once up in Wisconsin," Gary Riese told me, "we left our dogs at home when we went duck hunting. The mallards were really working and we shot several, but didn't find any of them in the heavy marsh cover. Finally, I went home and got one of my Welshmen. We didn't lose any more birds, and he even hunted up some of the ones we had lost earlier."

Clearly, the Welsh Springer Spaniel makes an outstanding dog for today's catch-as-catch-can hunter/family person. Why then do we see so few of them?

Perhaps the breed's biggest problem is its name: Welsh *Springer* Spaniel. This name inspires, almost demands, comparisons with the English Springer Spaniel. Because of the English Springer's spectacular performances in Field Trials, those comparisons are always unfavorable to the Welsh.

"If you get a Welsh Springer," I was told years ago, "all you get is a slow English Springer."

The spaniels without "Springer" in their names seldom suffer such derogatory comparisons. Ask about the Clumber or Sussex, and you will hear about the "gentleman's shooting dog." Ask about the English Cocker, and you will hear about "a lot of dog in a small package." Ask about the American Water Spaniel, and you will hear about the "great little all-rounder." And so on. But ask about the Welsh Springer, and all you will hear about is the English Springer.

Too bad. Not that the English Springer isn't a great spaniel. It is. I have a pair myself and wouldn't part with either. However, like every breed, the English Springer isn't for everyone. The country has thousands of hunters who would be better off with Welshies. Because they are easier to train, easier to handle. Because they are less acrobatic around the house. Because they can hunt all day at the pace they set. And, most of all, because they have personalities that would appeal to many who are now unfamiliar with the breed.

Peggy Ruble told me that the parent club, the Welsh Springer Spaniel Club of America, has discussed changing the breed name because of the persistent unfavorable comparisons with the English Springer Spaniel.

"We should probably shorten it to 'Welsh Spaniel,' " she says. "After all, it is a separate breed, not just the Welsh version of some mythical Springer breed."

Welsh Spaniel. I like that. However, even as I repeat it to myself, I hear the faint sounds of horses riding from out of the distant past. I close my eyes and see Arthur, Lancelot, Gawain, and the other knights of the Round Table riding fast into today.

"By God, man!" Arthur shouts as he reigns up his huge horse. "You know what that dog is? Do you really know? It's the *British* Spaniel. Let the lowly Anglo-Saxons have their common *Angl-ish* Springer Spaniels. Let them take them back to Germany with them, for all I care. That little red and white dog is something special. It belongs to *my* Britain. So, by God, let it be called the 'British spaniel.' Hear me, man, the British spaniel!"

Who am I to argue with King Arthur about what is and what isn't British?

4

The English Cocker Spaniel: *The Merry Mighty Mouse*

I FIRST SAW an English Cocker work in the fall of 1989. It was at an AKC hunt test near Wichita, Kansas. Having chaired the hunt test committee and typed up the program personally, I knew that Walt Cline, a man of the cloth from Nebraska, would be running the dog in the Senior Stake. I looked forward to watching it.

I'm too traditional, too easily distracted by departures from tradition. As Walt heeled his fuzzy little black dog to the line, I hardly noticed the dog because I was so busy checking and rechecking Walt for some sign of a whistle. Everyone knows you can't work a spaniel (or pointing dog or retriever) without a whistle. Most of us carry two, in case one breaks in midtoot. Not Walt Cline. Not even one.

"Damned shame," I thought. "The guy has driven all the way down here for nothing. In these strange surroundings, with all the people and other dogs, his little Limey's sure to go out of control. I hope he doesn't get too embarrassed. Bet he'll have a whistle next time."

Mmmm boy, was I wrong. Walt and his English Cocker communicated in a way I had never seen before. No sound. No arm waving. Just an occasional glance at each other.

The dog hunted the course as well as any dog entered, better than most. He lacked the speed of the English Springers, but he had intensity. Speed is a function of size. Style comes from heart and desire. If the English Springer's

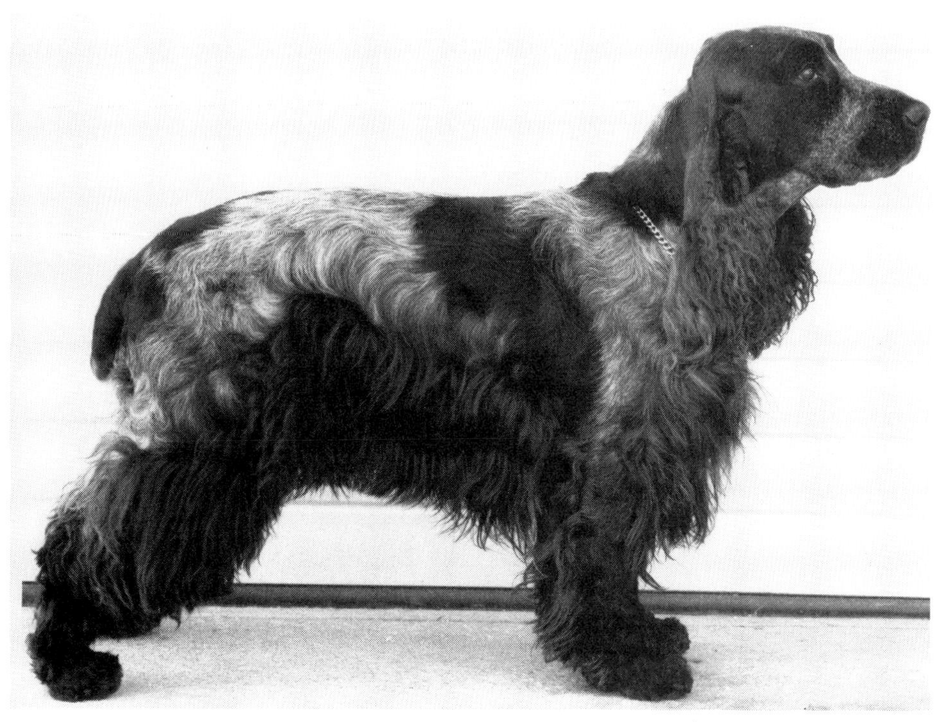

CH Moonlite's Allusive Atwood CD, owned by Brenda and Kyle Smith.

The field-bred English Cocker looks like a different breed, but it can really do the work. This is Mike Tillotson's Parsonage's Miss Molly, SH.

style is dashing, that of the English Cocker is merry. The tail is a blur, the movement bouncy, the attitude almost one of ecstasy.

This little black dog didn't hunt in a perfect windshield-wiper pattern. Still, he covered the course thoroughly and passed no birds. He hunted objectives. After checking one out, he would look up for another. Seeing one, he would bounce that way quickly, then slow down to hunt. And so on.

Nor did the dog reach out too far. Hunting experience had taught him the effective range of an upland game gun. Camaraderie had taught him to sense Walt's whereabouts. If the dog saw an objective that was too far ahead, he filed the information away for the future and looked for something closer. Amazing.

Walt trusted the dog. When it slowed to hunt an objective carefully, Walt stopped. When the dog looked back as if to say, "Nothing much around here," Walt sped up. The dog took that as permission to move out a bit. They moved like a pair of choreographed dancers. Neither led. Neither followed. They just moved together.

The dog put his birds up boldly, and then chased merrily. His retrieves were short, because he wasn't far behind when the bird tumbled to the gun. Dogs in the Senior Stake need not be steady-to-flush.

The little ball of black fuzz did the water mark as well as any, too. He earned a qualifying score in that hunt test. If AKC allowed placements, he would have earned one.

And Walt didn't even have a whistle! That still amazes me. I haven't pitched out my own ample supply of lanyards and tooters. But I have come to realize that a few handler/dog teams use telepathy instead.

Not every English Cocker works like Walt's. Not every English Cocker looks like Walt's. The breed is split into show dogs and field dogs. Walt's is a field dog.

Both types come in the same variety of colors: solids (black, red, blond, liver), black and tan, parti-colors (white with spots and ticking of the other colors), roans (salt-and-pepper mixtures of white and another color). There the similarity ends.

If you saw a show and a field English Cocker side by side, you would think they were two different breeds. The differences are that significant. Show dogs average larger, standing 15 to 17 inches at the withers (highest point of shoulders) and weighing 26 to 34 pounds. The less standardized field dogs may fall in that range, perhaps even a bit larger, but are more often smaller, down around 14 to 16 inches and 22 to 25 pounds. The show dog has a long, narrow *settery* head with low-set, long ears. The field dog's head is smaller, less aristocratic. The tail-dock differs, too. Show dogs carry about one-third of their tail while field dogs carry two-thirds. Show dogs have long, flowing coats. Not as extreme as the American Cocker's, but long enough to need trimming before hunting. Field dogs have shorter, more practical coats.

This split may seem baffling at first. Show/field splits usually happen in popular breeds for which AKC offers Field Trials as well as dog shows—the Labrador, the English Springer, the Golden. The English Setter. The Pointer.

In this country, the English Cocker doesn't fit this pattern. It's not a popular breed. With only 1000 to 1500 registered per year, it ranks down in the middle of AKC's 130+ breeds. Although the breed appears at practically every dog show, it has had no Field Trials in America since 1965.

How then did the split occur? It occurred in England, where the breed is very popular, and where the Kennel Club conducts Field Trials as well as shows for Cockers. We have been importing both types for decades.

The English call the breed the "Cocker Spaniel," not the "English Cocker Spaniel." Our "Cocker Spaniel" is their "American Cocker Spaniel."

We had Field Trials for Cockers (both breeds) from 1924 through 1965. Through those years American trialers imported and bred field-type English Cockers just as American show folks imported and bred the show-type. Thus, the breed has always suffered the same split here as it has throughout the rest of the world.

After Field Trials were discontinued in 1965, Americans all but stopped importing and breeding field-types. Only a few have kept the field strains alive here. Lionel Bond of Arden, New York, who was the original manager of Roland Harriman's Cinar Kennel back in the thirties, has continued to breed an occasional litter of pure field stock. In the late 1970s, Vance Van Laanen of Green Bay, Wisconsin brought in some field-types and started breeding them. He started to reintroduce Cocker Field Trials, but backed off when they began to resemble Springer trials too closely. Mr. Van Laanen wanted something different for his English Cockers. He has since contributed significantly to the design of the AKC hunt test format for spaniels. Stan and Lisa Wrobel of Greenleaf, Wisconsin, whose foundation stock came from Mr. Van Laanen, breed field-type English Cockers. Ditto for Walt Cline of Morrill, Nebraska.

The field-type English Cocker, although rare, has many traits the American hunter could enjoy. They make excellent pets as well as hunting dogs. Good family dogs. Good house dogs.

"They're the most affectionate dogs I've ever owned," Vance Van Laanen told me. Before settling on the English Cocker, Vance spent many years training, trialing, and hunting Labradors, English Springers, and German Shorthairs. "Cockers want to be with you all the time, preferably in your lap. They can really get to you, too. I don't care who you are."

They mature early and learn what you want them to do afield almost without training.

"I hunt woodcock in really heavy cover," Vance said. "No way I could keep a dog in sight if it didn't help me. Yet after I've taken a typical English Cocker out about half a dozen times, it learns to stop and wait for me when it gets out of sight. I don't teach that. The dogs just pick it up. I've never had a Lab, a Springer, or a Shorthair do that.

"They pick up what I train them to do more quickly than any other breed I've worked with. The only problem I have is in getting a Cocker to sit still while I walk away from it. Most of them start scooting after me as soon as I move away. They don't get up. They just scoot on their fannies, tails wagging in a blur. Teaching them to just sit there takes time. Other than that, they learn everything double-quick.''

Where visibility allows it, an English Cocker works its ground faster than any Spaniel except the English Springer. They work tight cover better than the English Springer. Being so small, they can wiggle under and through any tangle to push a bird out.

Most of them love water and have breathtaking entries. A photographer's dream, the English Cocker not only leaps long and high, it also hangs in air, stretched out in a perfect pose, long enough for the most ordinary photographer to snap a gem. Retrievers, even those with spectacular entries, are not so obliging. They don't pose and hang like English Cockers.

Vance Van Laanen summed it up like this: ''For the average hunter in the upper Midwest, the English Cocker is ideal. I'm talking about the guy who hunts whatever's open. Grouse, woodcock, pheasant, and maybe an occasional duck. They're not right for the dedicated waterfowler, the guy who hunts on big water in nasty weather. He needs a Lab or Chessy. But for anyone else in this part of the country, the English Cocker's hard to equal, let alone beat.''

Vance spoke of the field-type English Cocker. I have good news for you about the show-type also. Contrary to the popular myth in sporting literature, show breeders have not eliminated all the brains and hunting instincts from their English Cockers. True, most show breeders have made no effort to maintain field ability. Most have never tested for it in their stock. And, sadly, many have made misleading claims to the contrary, especially when trying to dispose of pups that are not show quality.

But here and there a fancier of the show-type English Cocker is demonstrating that some of these gorgeous animals can do a day's work afield. Here's what Tawney Crawford of Yelm, Washington said about the breed, especially her blue-roan dog, ''Stoney'' (Am. & Can. Ch. Ranzfel Quarrystone, Can. CD, Am. TD, CDX, WDX, JH, SH, MH). (For an explanation of these titles, see appendix 2, ''Reading Spaniel Pedigrees.'')

''Stoney is incredibly consistent in the field. Never blows up on me. His pace is moderate compared to an English Springer's. He always runs, never trots, but he couldn't keep up with the typical English Springer. To me, Springers are fun to watch but too much dog to hunt with. They're kamikaze dogs.

''The English Cocker seems to have a better nose than the Springer. Maybe it's just that they move slower, so don't pass birds so easily. The Cocker also works really heavy cover better, mostly because it is small enough to crawl in and under things easier. It also has outstanding stamina.

''I used to hunt with pointing dogs. They pointed outside of the heavy stuff—like the Scotch broom out here in Washington—leaving me the job of going in for the flush. My Cockers dive in and put the bird in the air for me.

''I like the looks of the long show coat. I don't see it as a problem for the hunter. I just cut it off before running my dog in the field.

''Some Cockers flush hard, others soft. My Stoney is on the soft side. I'm not overly impressed with hard-flushing spaniels.''

Clearly, in spite of all the neglect, some—certainly not all, probably not even most—English Cockers from many generations of pure show breeding have retained their hunting instincts. In recent years, a few breeders and owners (like Tawney Crawford) have been proving this by handling their dogs to after-the-name field titles in the noncompetitive working certificate programs sponsored by the English Cocker Spaniel Club of America and in the noncompetitive AKC hunting test program. (See chapter 24, "Hunting Tests," and chapter 25, "Working Certificate Tests," for more information on these programs.)

Today, if you are a hunter seeking an English Cocker, you can separate the wheat from the chaff easily. Just look in the pedigree for titles that mean something to you, and ignore those that don't. The good ones all follow the name: WD, WDX, JH, SH, MH. (See appendix 2, "Reading Spaniel Pedigrees," for more information on these titles.) Whether field or show stock, good working stock should have a good sprinkling of these titles.

How do you recognize show breeding? Simple. Many of the dogs in the pedigree will have show titles before their names: "Ch." (show champion), sometimes "Am. & Can. Ch." (American and Canadian show champion). Such a title only means that three or more judges liked the dog's looks in the show ring. That shouldn't impress you much one way or the other. If the same dogs carry the right after-the-name titles, wonderful. If not, you should look for a stronger field pedigree.

Some English Cockers flush hard. Tawney Crawford says her "Stoney" has a soft flush. This picture makes one wonder. *Bill Crawford*

5

The American Cocker: *A Work of Art That* Might *Work for You*

FEW TODAY regard the American Cocker Spaniel as a hunter. Cocker-bashing has long been fashionable throughout the sporting press. Much of what has been said is true. However, a few American Cockers do indeed hunt and do it rather well. For the thousands of hunters who love the little devils as pets, that may be news, but it should be welcome news.

The Cocker emerged as one string from the bird's-nest tangle of nineteenth-century spaniels. By the 1920s it had split in two. Cocker breeders in America took off on a tangent of their own. The English held firm to the "original" type (more or less), which has continued to suit them, and every other nation in the world.

In 1936 Americans who preferred the English type formed a club and convinced AKC to establish their dogs as a distinct "variety" within our Cocker breed. In 1946 they persuaded AKC to designate it a separate breed. Since then, we have had two Cocker breeds: the "Cocker Spaniel" and the "English Cocker Spaniel." Throughout the rest of the world, the process happened in reverse, so the names are reversed. Our "Cocker" is their "American Cocker." Our "English Cocker" is their "Cocker."

Initially the American Cocker was a hunting dog, sometimes a Field Trial dog, as well as a show-ring darling. Field Trials for Cockers, never extensive here, died in the mid-1960s. Sporadic revival attempts through the 1970s and

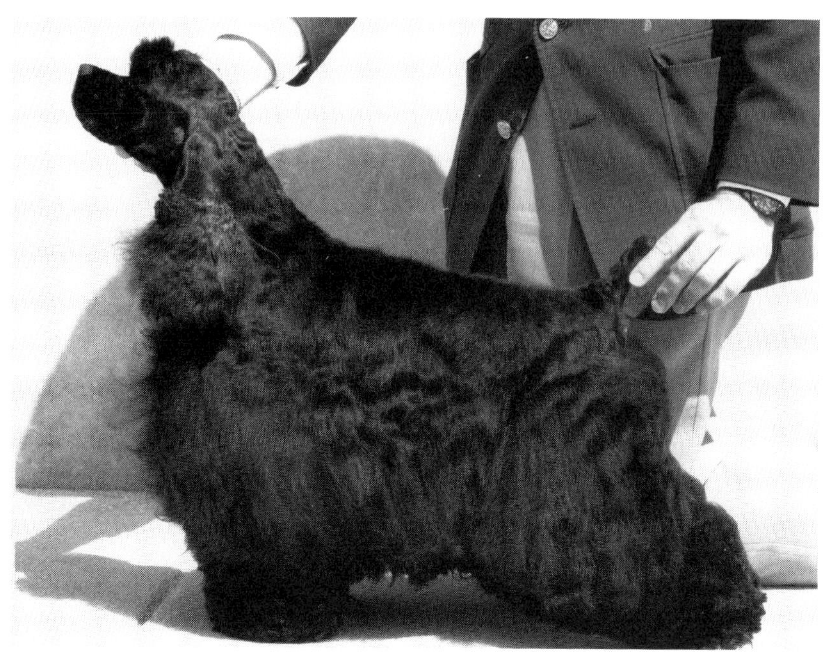

A black, show-type, American Cocker, WIB's Alpha and Omega, owned by Donna Helmiek, handled by Jeff Wright.

When the Cocker was primarily a hunting dog, it looked like "Zach" here, owned by Sally Cannata.

1980s failed. Small wonder, then, that American Cocker breeders of field persuasion have gone the way of the heath hen. Well, almost.

The dog show and pet markets have boomed for decades. The Cocker became this country's most popular breed in 1936, when 12,714 were registered with AKC. It held first place for seventeen years before yielding to the Beagle in 1953. From 1953 through 1982, it fell from the top ten only once (twelfth in 1975). In 1983 it regained the number one ranking, which it has held every year since (through the last year for which data is available, 1990). No other breed has ranked number one for so many total years (twenty-four). In 1990, 105,642 American Cockers were registered, almost ten times as many as in 1936. 1936's 12,714 would rank down in twenty-eighth place in 1990. That's how much purebred dog popularity has grown.

Although these numbers say nothing about the breed's hunting ability, they do attest to its broad appeal to Americans. Why? Several reasons: size, temperament, trainability, physical attractiveness.

Before discussing Cocker charisma, one caveat: with over one hundred thousand pups registered per year, many (most, really) are from inferior stock bred by ignorant and/or unscrupulous breeders. Too many American Cockers have poor temperaments (shyness, fear-biting, excitement-urinating, aggressiveness) and/or hereditary health problems (hip and eye defects, epilepsy). You should run, not walk, away from puppy mills, pet-stock breeders, and uninformed casual breeders (''I wanted my children to witness the miracle of birth'').

About four years ago, my daughter Sally decided to ''just look'' at a litter of backyard Cockers. They were in horrible shape. Trouble was, she couldn't walk away from them. She had to rescue at least one. She picked out probably the sickest pup, paid for it (!), and took it back to her apartment. She spent I know not how much on veterinary care to rid the pup of worms and other parasites and to restore it to health. She still has that dog, ''Zack,'' a medium-sized red cocker with a short coat that would be ideal for hunting. Sally doesn't hunt. Zack loves to retrieve tennis balls and such, so who knows? He might be a good hunter. Zack is an independent little rascal that would be a handful to train and control.

He still has significant health problems, too. Periodically, he suffers a series of seizures. Epilepsy? The vet's not sure, but it's something like that. Much as we all love Zack, he was no bargain, even at his bargain price.

I have heard that a few hard-to-find people still breed hunting Cockers. You know, with a coat like Zack's, but more trainable and more healthy, too. I have never met one, but I keep hearing about them. Reminds me of a conversation I had many years ago with a friend from Arkansas that went something like this:

''Arkansas is a Democrat state, isn't it?'' I asked.

''Not totally,'' he answered.

''How many registered Republicans live there?''

''Don't know exactly. I heard of one over in Little Rock once. Loaded the entire family in the car and drove over just to see him.''

''And?''

"Just my luck. He wasn't home that day, so we didn't get to see him. We're still on the lookout for another one."

Since straight field breeders are so rare and so elusive, you will probably have to seek your hunting pup from the small group of show-dog breeders who prove their stock in the field. You should avoid the large group of show breeders who do not. More on finding the right kind of show breeder after taking a look at the smallest of the spaniel family.

The American Cocker stands 14 to 15 inches at the withers (highest point of shoulders) and weighs 22 to 25 pounds. That is a nice size for a family dog, especially in these days of high-rise apartments and sports cars. It's also big enough for upland game hunting.

Many think the words "merry" and "Cocker" are inseparable. However, "merry" better describes the English Cocker. The American's temperament varies from carefree to truculent. Not surprising for a small dog with a large-dog self-image. Other words/expressions to fill out the description: charming; bright; outgoing; energetic; anxious to please; affectionate; sociable; everybody's buddy; watchdog washout. The Cocker needs almost constant interaction, and copious physical contact, with people. It is energetic enough to play with the kids all day, yet laid back enough to spend its evenings on Mom's lap or by Pop's chair. It reads people and responds to the family's routine and rhythm.

The breed matures early, physically and mentally, and trains easily. Whether the owner hunts the dog, pursues Obedience titles, keeps it as a house pet, or does all three, he will find the dog learns quickly and complies happily, enthusiastically. A Cocker with hunting instincts will hunt the way the boss wants—if the boss is even moderately consistent in his expectations.

A soft breed, it neither requires nor accepts heavy-handed training. Forget whips and switches. Never slap it. To the American Cocker, your hands are for petting, not hitting. For minor infractions, a harsh word with eye contact will do. For the rare major crime, a *light* shaking might be in order. Mostly, just lead the dog through what you want, with plenty of praise, until it understands.

In the show ring, the American Cocker is a living sculpture. The head has a well-squared muzzle, a deep stop, a nicely rounded cranial area, and long, long ears. The relatively short back slopes attractively from the withers to the tail. When it moves around the ring, it floats. Head high, tail a blur, coat flowing softly.

For show purposes, the colors are divided into three "varieties": blacks (including black and tans), all solid colors other than black (ASCOB), and parti-colors. ASCOB includes creams, silvers, buffs, golds, reds and chocolates. Parti-colors include two-color combinations, roans, and tricolors (any parti-color with tan points). If you can't find a color you like here, you won't find it in any other breed either.

However, coat length is a problem for the hunter. To win in dog shows, the American Cocker needs a coat that sweeps the floor—impractical and even contrary to the breed Standard. Originally the breed had a practical working coat with just enough feathering to protect it in cover. The coat has become longer and heavier over the years because dog-show judges have slobbered and swooned over such tresses.

Today the hunter who fancies the American Cocker must decide whether he/she can put up with all that hair. It requires frequent grooming plus serious barbering before hunting season. Those who want to preserve as much beauty as possible take the coat down neatly with electric clippers. Those who don't care about appearances hack it off with ordinary scissors.

"A proper Cocker coat is not as much of a problem as many think," Ruth Tabaka of Seattle, Washington says. "The coat should be fairly coarse without a wooly undercoat. I've taken my champion hunting one day and into the show ring the next. Here in western Washington, we don't have burrs and thistles. Before hunting in eastern Washington, I clip his coat down."

During the off-season, the hunter should give his Cocker reasonably frequent baths, brushings, and combings. Not just for appearances, but for cleanliness, to eliminate mats, and to control parasites. Serious dog grooming is not every hunter's snifter of brandy. Some take their dogs to professional groomers periodically.

The sloping topline that wows dog show judges wasn't designed for all-day hunting. A level back has more endurance. However, American Cockers being so small, any hunter who fancies them can keep two and rotate them through the day. That's a good idea for upland hunting with any breed.

Nor is the gorgeous head problem free for the hunter. It is so nicely proportioned, so "well chiseled" (as show people say), so expressive, that it takes your breath away. However, the mouth is small, limiting the payload the dog can tote. Sure, it's big enough for most upland birds: doves, quail, woodcock, chukars, ruffed grouse. But what about pheasants?

"My Cocker retrieves dead pheasants just fine," Debbie Dodge of Spanaway, Washington says. "She has even worked out a way to handle cripples. She pounces on them and holds them down until I get there. Works for us."

So, for less-than-dead pheasants, determined Cockers rely on cunning. Even so, the confirmed pheasant hunter—the one who hunts little else—should realize that the American Cocker operates at a distinct disadvantage on such large (and often hostile) birds.

Nor is the breed right for serious ducking. The typical American Cocker loves water, frequently flying in with a long leap that many retrievers could envy. It can retrieve ducks in mild weather and light seas. However, no one should expect this breed to retrieve ducks under typical late-season conditions. Geese? Never. I've heard those stories about a Cocker "rassling" and tug-o'-warring a crippled giant Canada back to the blind, but I don't think that's fair to either dog or goose.

In summary, the properly bred and trimmed American Cocker can hunt most upland birds, including pheasants. It can retrieve doves and fair-weather ducks. It trains easily and is a joy as a family pet. If you are attracted to the breed, and if you will do (or hire done) the needed barbering and grooming, the American Cocker might do everything you want done, and more.

"Retrieve a pheasant? Who, me?" asks Debbie St. Myers' show-type, Deidree Shannon Dodge, UDT, SH, WDX. *Debbie St. Myers*

"Why certainly, Boss. No problem as long as it's dead." *Debbie St. Myers*

To find your pup, ideally, you should be acquainted with a nearby breeder who hunts his American Cockers. That way, you can shoot over your prospect's immediate forebears before pulling out your checkbook and uncapping your pen. Sadly, few enjoy such a position today. That means you will have to buy from a distant breeder. You may have to pan a lot of fool's gold before you find a real nugget.

With distant breeders, you should rely heavily on references. You should also learn to read pedigrees. (See appendix 2, ''Reading Spaniel Pedigrees.'') In studying a pedigree, rely on the after-the-name noncompetitive field titles: WD and WDX earned in working dog tests sponsored by the American Spaniel Club; and JH, SH, MH earned in AKC spaniel hunting tests.

Working Certificate tests have been around since the late 1970s. Today (1991) about thirty-five or forty American Cockers have WDs and about twenty have WDXs. AKC spaniel hunting tests started in July 1988, so fewer of these titles can be found. At this time, about a dozen American Cockers have earned JH titles. Six have earned SHs. Others are partway through each title. I know of none with the MH—yet.

If you think these numbers are small, tell me this: before reading this chapter, did you think there were any?

If you're strongly attracted to the little devils, why not jump in? You might help bring the breed back to respectability among hunters.

"Shannon" hits the water enthusiastically. *Debbie St. Myers*

CH Cypress Woods Grenade, JH, owned by Jane Reeves.
Laura Reeves

A young Clumber flushes a pigeon.

Physically, a Clumber is awesome.

6

The Clumber Spaniel: *The Mellow Hunter's Helper*

MY FIRST EXPERIENCE afield with a Clumber taught me a lot about the main virtue of this breed—a breed that incidentally better represents the English people (and certainly looks more like Winston Churchill) than the esteemed Bulldog.

It was 9:00 A.M. on Saturday, April 9, 1988. It was cold, rainy, blustery, in the best British tradition. However, I wasn't in Britain. I was on the grounds of Cheney Lake, about twenty miles west of Wichita, Kansas. Longtime English Springer breeder and Field Trialer Cliff Hankins and I were judging the Plan B Sanctioned Hunting Test conducted by the Clumber Spaniel Club of America in conjunction with its 1988 National Specialty. Cliff and I stood at the line waiting for the first Junior Stake entry. Boyd Rawlins and David Wilkie had planted birds on the course and were fully four hundred yards ahead of us. The marshal, indefatigable Chad Betts, was everywhere, doing everything to make the test run smoothly. AKC's Ham Rowan and Jack Hansen stood a little to the rear, hoping the rain would let up so they could shoot some videotape. Larry Mueller stood beside them, protecting his 35mm camera from the drizzle.

Finally, a smiling Darrell Reeves lumbered to the line with a young Clumber male. After the usual judges/handler amenities, he said, "Well, let's see what this youngster will do," and turned the pup loose.

Everything I had heard and read about the breed prepared me for a slow, plodding—even sleepy—performance. You know: waddle this way awhile, then waddle the other way awhile; sniff around a bit; shuffle here and there.

Not so. While the pup blew the hunting test, he showed the character of the breed so well that I will never forget it. He hit the ground hunting hard, with his nose to the ground. While his stubby tail vibrated his entire back half, his little legs propelled him at a quite respectable pace.

Then he hit scent . . .

To appreciate the rest of this story, you have to understand the breed a lot better than I did as I stood there in my frightfully British thornproof coat and britches, with rain dripping from my nose, watching the dog's disappearing rear.

The Clumber is a breed of the English Midlands, first found in the possession of the second duke of Newcastle in the late eighteenth century. Dr. Bryant Freeman of Lawrence, Kansas has one of only four existing 1792 pictures showing the duke with four Clumbers. Legend has it that the duke received them many years earlier as a gift from the French duc de Noailles. If that is true, old *duc de* must have shipped him all of them, for none have ever been found in France (except more recent imports from England).

For a long time the Clumber remained the exclusive property of Newcastle before spreading among other titled Midland families. Various canine historians have made much of the fact that the breed was kept away from the common folks for many decades. However, those were the days of the Industrial Revolution, when entire families worked one hundred or more hours a week for subsistence wages in mines and factories that would have shocked the Marquis de Sade. Few ordinary blokes developed much interest in hunting and dog training—or anything else besides sleep and a little gin (which was kept artificially cheap to prevent popular uprisings and artificially bitter to control drunkenness).

Around 1860 British naval officers (then from noble families) brought Clumbers to Canada. From there they gradually drifted southward into the United States, where they achieved enough popularity to be among the original ten breeds recognized by the fledging AKC in 1884. Spaniel Field Trials began in 1899, and Clumbers dominated them for several years. Tastes changed. Professional trainers found the English Springer more biddable and stylish. The Clumber all but vanished in America by 1920.

Dr. Freeman told me that the Du Pont family maintained the only Clumber kennel in this country through the 1930s and into early 1940s. Their dogs were shown in dog shows by liveried handlers, but they would not sell Clumbers. According to Dr. Freeman, they did now and again give one to a peer. When Frank and Imogene Ruckstuhl of Santa Fe, New Mexico decided to obtain Clumbers, they had to import them from England. So did Milton and Eunice Gies of New York. These importations eventually made the breed again available in this country. In February of 1972 the Gieses, the Ruckstuhls, Dr. Freeman, and a few others gathered at the Westminster Dog Show to found the Clumber Spaniel Club of America. Since then, the breed has slowly gained in popularity, both among dog-show folks and hunters.

It may well be that the hunter will again popularize the Clumber here, especially now that there are hunting tests where the breed can show its talents. This is not a Field Trial breed, not a professional trainer's breed. However, it has traits and abilities that suit it well to today's hunting conditions, especially for the person who hunts a little of everything and doesn't spend near enough time training.

Physically, the Clumber is awesome. Standing only 17 to 19 inches at the withers, they weigh from 65 to 85 pounds. In other words, the breed is no taller than an English Springer but weighs as much as most Labradors. The powerful body allows the Clumber to plow through heavy cover and makes it buoyant in water. The short legs allow it to crawl under impenetrable cover and tend to keep it within gun range, even when it is really hustling.

The coat is ideal for American catch-as-catch-can hunting: everything from doves to upland birds to waterfowl (except in really severe weather, of course). The outercoat is long enough to protect the animal, but short enough to be easily cared for. Burrs and mud are not the problem they are with many long-haired breeds. Beneath the highly visible white (with a few lemon or orange markings) outercoat is a wooly undercoat, which protects the dog from the cold.

The ponderous head is so British that one wonders whether the duc de Noailles was a closet Englishman. The expression of the face—and of the stubby tail—tells the discerning observer much about the remarkably English character of the breed: reserved, mellow, friendly, yet determined.

Dr. Freeman describes the breed as "conservative." He says, "A Clumber adjusts slowly to new experiences. If you were to offer one a steak, he would not gulp it right down, at least not the first time. He would sniff it, walk around it, study it, lick it a time or two, then walk away and lie down to watch it. Eventually, he would take a small bite, then another, and so on. Of course, the second time, he would devour it quickly."

Darrell Reeves says the Clumber is the best dog around the house he has ever had (and he has had many pointing and retrieving breeds).

"They sleep a lot. They are affectionate. They get along with other dogs—although they are a bit tough on cats. A Clumber will bark at a stranger, if it happens to wake up. Not good watchdogs, really. Too friendly. Oh, a little reserved at first, but usually make up with anyone."

And yet they can be very animated. I noticed this while judging the hunting test. While their short legs tend to keep them within gun range, they definitely hunt hard and enthusiastically. Tail popping back and forth. Head throwing this way and that. Body, especially the rear quarters, rolling vigorously. Legs driving.

Jane Reeves (Darrell's wife) ran a bitch in the Junior Stake that was a pleasure to watch. The dog was remarkably animated from the time she was cast off until she finished the course. She hunted intelligently to both sides, wherever there was suitable cover. She retrieved nicely and entered the water eagerly in the second series.

Every Clumber there seemed to love water. Although they slip in with little splash, they show genuine enthusiasm. Their buoyant bodies allow them to swim totally relaxed, like a fisherman bobbing around in one of those inner-tube float affairs. Clumbers are not fast swimmers, but they are steady and determined.

It was that British determination which first sold Darrell Reeves on the breed, after many years with setters and Labradors. His wife Jane bought a Clumber, "Chappie," primarily for showing. Jane and Darrell took Chappie—no training, no exposure to birds—along on a pheasant hunt in which Darrell's Lab was the intended canine star. Jane shot the first rooster when both dogs were elsewhere. Darrell brought the Lab over to help find the bird and Chappie tagged along.

While Jane, Darrell, and the Lab searched the area of the fall, Chappie just shuffled around, not understanding what they were doing. However, he suddenly hit bird scent. Down went his nose, and his little legs churned beneath him as he tracked the cripple this way and that. Darrell noticed, and followed Chappie. He encouraged the Lab to pick up the trail, too, but the Lab wouldn't stay with it very long, preferring to outguess the bird. Not Chappie. He tracked doggedly, following every curve and angle the bird took to escape.

One hundred yards. A cut to the left. Two hundred yards. A series of turns. Two hundred and fifty yards. A 180-degree reversal. Three hundred yards. Another sharp change of direction. Three hundred and fifty yards. Finally, after tracking the bird four hundred yards, Chappie pounced on it. He didn't understand about retrieving yet, so he just held the bird prisoner until Darrell arrived to pick it up.

"Best trackers I have ever seen," Darrell told me. "They don't try to outguess the bird, like my Labs have always done. They don't push the bird too hard. They are just relentless."

That first Junior Stake Clumber showed me that, and what a show he put on for us.

Darrell hunts his Clumbers on ruffed grouse and mountain quail. The breed's determined tracking puts plenty of both kinds of birds in the back of his vest.

"Mountain quail are runners," he says. "If a dog pushes them too fast, they flush wild and all at once. A Clumber stays after them, but doesn't panic them. They get up within gun range, and in small groups. Sometimes after the main covey has flushed, my Clumber will rework the area and locate several tight-sitting singles."

Darrell described his technique for hunting ruffed grouse, a bird he said runs a lot in his area (Oregon). He follows the dog until it hits the trail of a moving grouse. Then Darrell catches up, staying about ten yards to whichever side offers the better shot. Eventually, the Clumber will flush the bird, although it may be a long and crooked way from where the dog first scented it.

"Other breeds I've had just wouldn't track so thoroughly—or they would tear off and flush the bird way out of gun range."

Most of the Clumbers Cliff and I judged in the hunting test worked the cover painstakingly. They were highly animated, stylish in their own Winston Churchill way. Yet I had the feeling that "they didn't have their ears on." In other words, they were in their own world, oblivious to gallery, judges, and even handlers. However, their natural thoroughness and their short legs kept them hunting plenty close enough without any whistle tooting. They also retrieved quite well, showing none of the breed's reputed roughness on birds.

I asked Darrell Reeves if I saw correctly, if the typical Clumber does tend to turn his handlers off and hunt as he pleases. He confirmed my observation but pointed out that they were developed structurally and temperamentally so that the handler didn't need to control and direct the dog much.

"Are they easy to train?" I asked.

"No. In fact, you can't do much with force. They are stubborn and have a high threshold of pain. I tried to force-break one once, but no matter how I pinched his ear, he just sat there and ignored it. Didn't open his mouth. Didn't try to bite me. Didn't yelp. Didn't do anything a Lab would do. I finally gave up and went back to play-retrieving."

"What if you get one that won't take to play-retrieving?"

"I had one of those once. He wouldn't bring a bird back to me. He'd run out and shake it to make sure it was dead, then drop it and come back."

"What did you do?"

"I tricked him. I tied a long string to a dead bird and had Jane twitch it every time the dog dropped it. Kinda funny. He ran out, picked it up, and dropped it. Jane twitched it with the string. The dog pounced on it again, but dropped it after a couple of steps. Jane twitched the bird once more and the dog again pounced on it, and so on. Each time the dog brought it a little closer. When he got it all the way in, I made a big fuss over him. He looked at me as if to say, 'You mean this is all you want? No problem, boss,' and he retrieved okay after that.

"Had I tried to force-break that dog, I would've got nowhere. With Clumbers it takes subterfuge, not force. Goodies help, too. I train with goodies a lot."

Dr. Freeman agrees that the Clumber is not the most trainable breed. "There are quite a few with CDs (lowest level Obedience Trial title), several with CDXs (next level up), and one that is working for its UD (highest level).

"The biggest trouble with the breed in Obedience Trials is that they 'anticipate' all the time. Once a Clumber thinks he knows what you want him to do, he won't wait for the command. He just does it. He sees the jumps in the ring, so he runs over and jumps them, instead of waiting to be sent.

"They are outstanding at tracking (another formal AKC event), however. Great noses and track naturally."

No matter where you start a discussion with a Clumber owner, you quickly get to this tracking thing. That is one of the breed's strongest features, one that will help the hunter in the uplands, especially in pheasant country. It will also help the waterfowler who hunts in a marsh with plenty of cover for crippled birds to hide in.

Unfortunately, it didn't help that first Junior Stake Clumber that Darrell Reeves ran. You see, almost as soon as Darrell turned him loose, he hit the track of Boyd Rawlins and David Wilkie, the bird planters. The young dog took off on their trail, ignoring Darrell's whistles, commands, and pleadings. In an amazingly short time, the young pup was four hundred yards away, begging Boyd to pick him up and let him get inside the bird bag. Boyd complied halfway. He picked the pup up, petted it awhile, and then handed it to Chad Betts, who carried it off the course to a point where Darrell could get it.

Later, Darrell chuckled almost continuously as he explained what had happened. This pup had had absolutely no field experience, and very little obedience training. Darrell had entered the youngster mostly to support the Clumber Spaniel Club of America, and also just to see what an absolutely green pup would do in a hunting test. (Darrell ran several other Clumbers that did quite well, and his wife Jane ran one that was outstanding.)

With no experience, and no idea what he was supposed to do, the young Clumber followed his strongest instinct. He tracked the only scent he could find, much as Chappie had tracked the crippled pheasant. Since this pup was the first dog to run in the test, the only scent he could find on the soggy course was that put down by the bird planters.

Clumbers track so naturally that some believe that a Basset may have successfully wooed one of the bitches used in the development of the Clumber. There are physical and mental similarities between the breeds.

Regardless, the Clumber is a wonderful tracker, yet one that doesn't put birds up out of gun range, one the more mellow upland hunter can enjoy. True, it would have taken at least a middle-aged athlete to keep up with that pup tracking the bird planters, but he was following a very strong and very straight scent trail, with no other distracting scents (because of the drizzle). A bird in ordinary hunting cover would not be so easy to follow.

7

The Field Spaniel: *Lovelier the Second Time Around*

THE FIELD SPANIEL has been developed twice. Once in the late 1800s. Again in the 1960s. They mostly floundered around the first time. They got it right the second time, although it may be one of the best-kept secrets in the sporting-dog world.

The first time it happened, they didn't document it as well as they could have, so we have some trouble separating romance from reality. We know who "they" were well enough. Breed historians have named them. For our purposes, it's enough to know that they were the British nobility and economic aristocracy. Back in the late 1800s, during the height of the Industrial Revolution in England, who else had the time or money for hunting, dog shows, and dog breeding?

Unfortunately, the breed name, Field Spaniel, gets in our way when we try to pin down the precise origin of the breed. For many preceding centuries, writers grouped spaniels into two broad categories: water spaniels and land spaniels. Being writers, they sought synonyms with which to make their tomes more palatable to readers. So, from the earliest times they used the terms "land spaniel" and "field spaniel" interchangeably, having no way of knowing the confusion they would create. Today, anyone can "prove" any breed development theory he/she likes by equivocating the meaning of "field spaniel" in early writings.

However, most respected breed historians tell us that the "Fieldie" was developed late in the nineteenth century for the specific purpose of wowing early dog show judges. At the time there were black spaniels and big spaniels, but no spaniels that were both black and big. Figuring it was worth a shot, they developed just such a dog.

That doesn't mean that the early Field Spaniel was a show dog in the modern sense. In the late 1800s shows were new, a novelty for the leisure class. But hunting was old. Every respectable sporting-dog breeder hunted. Breeding dogs to show but not hunt was unthinkable. Granted, their new interest in dog shows may well have stimulated the concurrent interest in separating the spaniels into several distinct—and clearly identifiable—breeds. As hunters, they cared little that the large dogs from one litter were called "Springers" while the small ones were called "Cockers." In other litters, the large ones were "Fields" and the small ones "Cockers." However, as dog show exhibitors, they wanted separate classes for each type of dog. How else can a judge apply a written "Standard of physical perfection" to all the dogs before him? Dog shows made it necessary to sort out the spaniels.

Dog show judges then (as now) were often unduly influenced by smoke and mirrors. A big black spaniel just might dazzle them, especially in the big-league categories: Group and Best in Show. Therefore, certain spaniel fanciers developed the Fieldie. They found they had to accept liver and roan as well as black, but then the real world is seldom pure.

It worked so well that the Fieldie became a very popular show dog. Early fanciers hunted the Fieldie too, and documented his performance quite honestly. The book on the breed was that the trainer had to establish control early or never, that the dog had to bond strongly with the trainer "and no one else," that it learned slowly, that it wasn't too anxious to please, and that it was an indifferent retriever. In other words, a dedicated trainer could make something of the dog, but it wouldn't be easy. Back then, most breeders employed dedicated trainers, so the breed's working temperament was not a serious problem.

Besides, the breed knocked 'em dead in dog shows, and dog show wins were the junk bonds of the day. Sadly, success in any purely competitive activity leads inevitably to abuse. Dog shows go through fads, few of which make sense. Most are little more than arbitrary criteria to guide judges through difficult decisions between dogs of relatively equal quality. Whatever the current fad, breeders must breed such dogs and thereby win, or hang it up. What wins, especially in a sport as subjective as dog shows, depends on the collective whims of the judges of the day.

Apparently the judges of the early years of this century liked their dogs long and low to the ground. How else to explain the fact that the breed rapidly approached the dimensions of, say, a Basset Hound? Oh, I have another thought on that subject, and I will mention it later. Even so, judges must have been "putting up" weenie-dog Fieldies, for that was what serious breeders bred.

Predictably, long and low gave way to newer fads faster than Field Spaniel breeders could adjust. The breed lost popularity, drifted toward oblivion. By the

Chambord's That's Life, owned by Winifred McCann and Jeanniene Pyles.

A liver-and-tan Fieldie, CH Blackbriar's B OK-D, owned by Sandra Burt-Jones and Clara Brinkelman.

early 1920s, the doggy press was carrying obits for the breed. Fortunately, they were premature.

In the early 1960s, serious breeders in England rebuilt the breed. They crossed the few remaining Fieldies with other spaniel breeds, mostly English Springers. The Kennel Club in England (unlike AKC) allows interbreds to be registered, so this redevelopment was done openly and is well documented. They didn't return to the long, low conformation that destroyed the breed before. No, the modern Field Spaniel looks like a working spaniel.

Although the folks who rebuilt the Fieldie intended it to be, again, the darling of the dog show set, they crossed with breeds having outstanding hunting credentials. So the new Field Spaniel, serendipitously, can and does hunt.

"I can't believe how good they are," says Rudy Garafola, a dedicated pheasant hunter of San Martin, California. Before getting his first Field Spaniel in the early 1980s, Rudy had hunted pheasants for many years with German Shorthairs and Labradors. "I've always shot a lot of pheasants, and I've never had dogs that work them like my Fieldies do."

"Their noses are the best I've ever seen," says Jeanette Spurlock, a breed and Obedience judge of Nixa, Missouri. "I had Pointers for years before I got my first Field Spaniel in the early 1970s. Fieldies just don't pass birds. They take a little more time going through a field, but they get them all."

When I hear these people talk about the rebuilt Field Spaniel, I hear Sinatra singing, "Love is lovelier the second time around." The Field Spaniel is lovelier, both physically and as a hunter, the second time around.

The new Field Spaniel is a handsome animal. Standing about 18 inches at the withers, and weighing 45 to 55 pounds, it is nicely balanced, a little lower and heavier boned than the English Springer but taller and shorter coupled than the Sussex and Clumber.

Remarkably, the Fieldie sports a practical hunting coat. The flat or wavy outercoat overlays an insulating undercoat. Even though the dog show set designed the breed, they did not (thank heaven) give it more coat than a working spaniel needs. The color may be black, liver (anything from a light golden liver to a deep chocolate), or roan. Any of these may have tan points over the eyes, on the cheeks, feet, and pasterns. Other colors occur, and work just fine in the uplands, even though they are frowned on in the show ring.

The coat sheds water well enough to make the Fieldie a respectable water dog, at least in moderate conditions.

"When I give any of my Field Spaniels a bath," says breeder/exhibitor Becki Jo Wolkenheim of Wales, Wisconsin, "soaking the coat takes forever. It sheds water like a duck."

The breed's most distinguishing (and attractive) feature is its head. "Well chiseled" is how Becki Jo Wolkenheim describes it. To me, it looks like the head of an Irish Setter, or a field-type English Setter, but with longer ears. The muzzle is proportionately longer than that of any other spaniel breed, except the English Cocker. I see great similarities between the head of the Fieldie and the English Cocker. Becki Jo says the differences are easy to pick out, at least for those ''in'' either breed. To me, they're both gorgeous, and I have no interest in minute differences.

The Field Spaniel has long ears and big feet. Jeanette Spurlock says that's what first attracted her to the breed. ''The breeder showed me two puppies and two adults. You know how puppies are all ears and feet. Well, in Fieldies, the adults are the same way. I just fell in love with them.''

The breed has a new temperament, unlike the rather difficult original Fieldie. The slow-maturing modern Fieldie is a soft, affectionate breed that enjoys constant human company. Playful rather than hostile, it gets along well with other dogs. It is too friendly—neither aggressive nor territorial—to be a good watchdog. Yet it is reserved with strangers. It's not shy or fearful. It just wants a little time to get used to a new person before having much physical contact with him/her.

''When a visitor pets one of my Fieldies too soon,'' says Becki Jo Wolkenheim, ''the dog looks up as if to say, 'How dare you!' Yet a few minutes later the same dog will be all over the visitor, insisting on being petted.''

They are active and energetic around the house—''Not for the person wanting a rug or couch-potato,'' Becki Jo says.

''All its life, a Fieldie acts like a three-year-old kid in a fur coat,'' Jeanette Spurlock says.

Field Spaniels have a sense of humor that is not always immediately appreciated by their owners.

''If I leave the hamper down the basement open, my dogs will drag dirty laundry all over the house,'' says Becki Jo.

''At a dog show once, when we were showing in Group, my Fieldie rolled over on his back and barked at the judge. Not a good way to win in serious competition,'' says Jeanette.

''Once when a friend of mine had her minister over for dinner,'' Jeanette goes on, ''her Fieldie ran through the house dragging a bra by the strap.''

Field Spaniels are not noisy around the house. When I talked to Jeanette Spurlock on the phone—for about half an hour—she had seven of them in the living room with her. I never heard a sound.

''However, they snore,'' Jeanette says. ''They make more noise than any human snorer you ever heard. If they sleep in your bedroom, they'll keep you awake. They snore so loud that many new owners take them to the vet, thinking something must be wrong with them.''

These rebuilt Fieldies train up better and easier than the original. They want nothing more than to please the boss, are easily trained and controlled, and love to retrieve. They also take to the water like a retriever.

''My Fieldies are very bright and eager to please,'' says Becki Jo Wolkenheim, who competes at the highest level in Obedience Trials. ''They learn so quickly that I have to think of new ways for them to do things all the time to keep them from becoming bored.''

''Some of the Shorthairs and Labs I hunted with were pretty hardheaded,'' says Rudy Garafola. ''Not so with my Fieldies. They train very easily. I steady them to wing and shot so they don't get in the way when I shoot. They pick this up very quickly.

"And talk about retrieving! The first retrieve my original Fieldie, 'Freddie Bletnikoff,' made was a two-hundred-yarder on a running pheasant. Guess I named him right, eh?"

Remembering that the original Field Spaniels were said to be unreliable retrievers, I asked Rudy whether he force-breaks his.

"No, every Fieldie I've had retrieves naturally," he replied.

"I hate the term 'natural retriever,' " says Becki Jo. That's not unusual among Obedience Trial people, who almost always force-break their dogs. "But the average Fieldie will do what most people mean when they say 'natural retrieving.' My son shoots the dummy launcher for his Fieldie almost every evening. That dog will retrieve it as long as my son will shoot it. I still force-train mine, though, for reliability."

They are extremely soft mouthed. Once when Becki Jo's son was shooting the dummy launcher for his Fieldie, his sister's Schipperke broke loose and got to the dummy first. No problem. The Fieldie simply picked up the little dog and brought it back to Becki's son. The Schipperke never made a sound, in fact seemed to enjoy the ride. It held onto the dummy, too, so they may have invented a new sport with Olympic possibilities: team retrieving.

Fieldies love water. Rudy Garafola hunts pheasants in an area where irrigation canals are common. He frequently drops a bird across the water.

"My Fieldies hit the water so hard they about splash the canal dry," he says.

"Once I shot a duck in a pond," Jeanette Spurlock says. "It wasn't dead, so when my Fieldie approached, the duck dove. The dog went right after it, diving completely out of sight. After several ups and downs, he finally caught the duck underwater and brought it in to me."

The Field Spaniel has a moderate pace when working the uplands. Slower than the English Springer, faster than the Sussex. Perhaps about the same as the Welshie. Keeping him within a reasonable distance is easy.

"I whistle through my teeth to control my dogs," Rudy Garafola says. "My dogs pay attention and stay close enough that way. I teach them to quarter with a long rope before I take them out. After that, I just whistle at them whenever they start to get too far off. They're easy to handle."

That they stay close says a lot about their temperament and trainability. I have seen dogs of extremely slow general pace cover four hundred yards in a flash when properly motivated. If the Field Spaniel hunts close to the boss, it's because he wants to please the boss. Even a young, athletic person can't catch a dog of moderate size that doesn't want to be caught.

This improved temperament may be the single most important reason that the rebuilt Field Spaniel has been so well received by those who have tried the breed.

I mentioned above that I have another thought on why the early breeders bred the dogs longer and lower. Remembering that the early dog was said to be difficult to train, here's a question to ponder, even if we can never answer it fully: Did the breeders in the early days of this century breed the dog longer and lower, longer and lower, just to win dog shows, or did they do it—at least partially—to make the dog easier to control in the field? Shorter legs and a longer back would certainly impede the dog's progress.

Okay, so the Field Spaniel is lovelier the second time around. Perhaps the honeymoon should end and the happy couple (dogs and breeders) should return to society again. This country is full of hunters who would be happier with Field Spaniels than with any other dogs—if they just knew about the breed. Fieldies would suit upland hunters who work small areas of heavy cover, hunters who want their birds flushed close to the gun and retrieved to hand. Fieldies would suit upland hunters who hunt areas with ponds and streams and need a dog that likes water. Fieldies would suit upland hunters who also hunt doves and maybe a few early season ducks.

Most of all, Fieldies would suit upland hunters with families. Hubby, wife, and kids could all enjoy having this active dog around the house, sharing their individual and collective lives. All but the most serious would enjoy the Fieldie's occasional practical jokes, too. That minister probably still chuckles when he remembers the lady's embarrassment at seeing her Field Spaniel drag a bra triumphantly through the house, like a horse pulling a Roman chariot.

The Field Spaniel needs hunters and families as badly as many of them need the breed. Let's hope they get together in larger and larger numbers.

Rudy Garafola with his "Freddie" and one of its long-distant pheasants.
Photo courtesy of Rudy Garafola

"Snuffy," owned by Pluis Davern.

"Snuffy" delivers a pigeon to Pluis Davern.

8

The Sussex Spaniel: *The Overlooked Limey*

THIS BREED, which was developed in the southern English shire (county) of Sussex, has never achieved great popularity anywhere. Certainly not in the United States.

Maybe we are missing something here. The Sussex is small and calm enough for apartment living, devoted enough to be a family pet, protective enough to keep the uninvited away, unusual (and attractive) enough to garner its share of oohs and aahs, and naturally talented enough to help Dad fill his game bag each fall without much formal training.

What more can today's urban family want? Perhaps folks would give this wonderful spaniel a chance if they knew a little about it.

Physically, the Sussex can fit nicely into any family situation, from the tiniest apartment to the suburban estate. Compactly built, it is heavily boned, muscular, short of leg, and long of body. It has strength and stamina rather than speed and agility.

"A good Sussex is long, low, and level," breeder/exhibitor Linda Legare of Randolph, Minnesota says. "It stands about 15 inches at the withers and weighs between 35 and 45 pounds. I've seen them as short as 12½ inches and as tall as 19, as light as 30 pounds and as heavy as 60. The undersized ones tend to lose mobility, especially in cover. The oversized ones usually lack the breed characteristics, the overall appearance that fanciers value so much."

Around the house, they tend to be couch-potatoes, sleeping most of the time. However, the typical Sussex has a sense of humor, and uses it to relate to the person it accepts as boss. For example, Linda Legare told me that one of her Sussex hides the laundry and makes her look for it. The dog follows along to see how she is doing.

"Mine sleep a lot," bird hunter and Obedience Trial competitor Frank Komatar of West Valley City, Utah says of his four Sussex. "One female plays a little game with anything she finds on the floor. She sneaks up on it like a cat, pauses, and then pounces on it. If she can, she tosses it in the air and starts the game over again."

Perhaps the first-time observer most notices the striking golden liver color. Breeders work hard to maintain the distinct golden tint in their stock. Dogs with too light or dark coats are heavily penalized in the show ring and eliminated from the programs of serious breeders. The Sussex should be "self-colored" (solid colored), but a little white on the chest or chin is acceptable, although not desirable.

The Sussex has a double coat. A protectively coarse outercoat overlays an insulating wooly undercoat. Although the legs, tail, and ears are moderately feathered, the overall coat length suits a dog that makes its living flushing birds from dense cover. Long enough and heavy enough to protect the dog. Short enough and flat enough for easy maintenance.

"The outer coat is seallike," Linda Legare says. "Not as short as a Labrador Retriever's coat, but the same texture."

Breeders dock the tails so that they mature between five to seven inches. The Sussex tail is seldom still, except when the dog is asleep. The breed's merriness shows primarily in its often blurred tail.

The head, which is another distinguishing breed characteristic, is heavy but not massive. The rather low-set ears are large and moderately well feathered. The brows are heavy, protecting the eyes in tough cover. The doleful eyes are hazel, and the nose is liver. The pendulous flews on the squarish muzzle balance the rest of the head nicely, giving an expression that implies stoic determination. This expression and the rapidly wagging tail contradict each other, which may be appropriate for this breed.

The temperament may seem an unintelligible mass of contradictions to the novice, but the more experienced will recognize similarities with such breeds as the Chesapeake Bay Retriever, the Gordon Setter, and the American Water Spaniel. The Sussex temperament doesn't duplicate any of these, but it has the same tendency toward contradictions.

Both males and females are protective and territorial. Either will defend its people and turf almost gleefully, whether they need it or not. One breed fancier told me that at dog shows she has seen crated Sussex so intent on repelling the "intruders" walking by that their owners had to cover their crates to prevent them from hurting themselves. Obviously, not all Sussex are that territorial, but the breed does have stronger than average protective instincts. For some prospective owners, that may be a problem. For others, especially in these days of violent crime even in the nicest part of town, it can be a wonderful trait.

"Mine bark ferociously when someone knocks at the door and wouldn't let anyone in if I weren't there to tell them everything's okay," Frank Komatar says. "However, once visitors are in the house and seated, the dogs bug them for attention. They love to be petted. They're not much for wallowing with kids. Mine will accept a little petting from strange kids, but that's about it."

They do not accept other dogs within their territory. When more than one Sussex of the same sex lives in the house, they may fight.

"I wouldn't recommend keeping two males in the house together," Frank Komatar says. "I do, but one of mine has been neutered, which seems to help. My two females are a problem sometimes. When I pet either one of them, the other growls."

The Sussex male can be an aggressive, even a dominant animal. If owned by a timid person, the dog may control the relationship. However, the person who establishes him/herself as the leader from the start will find the Sussex a devoted follower. The Sussex female is less aggressive and less dominant with people but can be more inclined to fight with other dogs.

"One of my females will not tolerate a 'guest' dog around the place. My ex-wife once brought her Sheltie over, but my female Sussex chased it off the property."

Thus the Sussex should probably be looked on as a dog for the one-dog family. Nor does it do well as a kennel dog. It seems to need a strong bond with one person and considerable attention from other family members to develop properly.

"I've seen a few examples of 'sharp' temperaments," professional gundog trainer Pluis Davern of Soquel, California says. "In almost every case, the dog was a kennel dog. Sussex should be house dogs. That's the only way their merry dispositions have a chance to develop."

For all its aggressive inclinations, a Sussex of either sex can be extremely soft and sensitive to the person with whom it has bonded.

"They are very tenderhearted in training," Linda Legare says. "They don't take physical punishment well. They'll cry like you've killed them. To train them you have to use subterfuge. You have to build their confidence all the time. Sometimes you feel like you're begging them to do things. They just don't train like other dogs."

Like most soft dogs, the Sussex wants to please its master. However, it shows just a trace of independence, even stubbornness.

"They're as anxious to please as Golden Retrievers," Pluis Davern says. "They have an even happier outlook on life than Goldens. They are extremely merry. Yet they are more aloof somehow."

"They want to please," Linda Legare says, "but they want to do it in their own time."

"They are soft, and learn rather slowly," Frank Komatar says. "In training them for Obedience Trials, I've found that new exercises bewilder them at first. I have to encourage them a lot. And, now and then, they can be stubborn."

Yet in spite of their softness, Sussex are a merry breed. Their constantly wagging tails tell what goes on within the Sussex psyche most of the time. Linda Legare says they are "almost silly."

"As a professional trainer, I have found the breed outgoing and extremely merry," Pluis Davern says. "That's why I decided to get one of my own. I call them the 'tail-propelled dogs.' "

Okay, they're territorial, sensitive, and merry—contradictory as that may seem. There's more. The really good news for the average hunter is that the Sussex makes a good journeyman bird finder/flusher without much formal training. The breed is a natural in the field.

"I hate the word 'natural' for hunting dogs," Pluis Davern says. "It implies that no training is required. I don't believe a completely natural hunting dog exists, but the Sussex is as close as any I've worked with."

Frank Komatar hunts chukar, Hungarian partridge, and grouse in his native Utah with his four Sussex. He also travels to Iowa about once a year to hunt pheasant. The only formal field training he gives his dogs is a little work on a long check cord to teach them to take his whistle and arm signals well enough so he can keep them within gun range. Frank competes in the advanced classes at Obedience Trials, so he is a capable trainer. He just hasn't found it necessary to give his Sussex much training to get them to do everything he wants done in the field.

Their size, build, and outstanding noses make them slow workers, not much inclined to hunt out of gun range. They work readily through the nastiest cover. "They work under cover that most dogs must drive through or jump over," Frank Komatar says.

They are a low-energy, high-stamina dog. Although they don't hunt fast, they hunt all day without tiring.

"I have four," Frank Komatar says, "but I prefer to hunt with just one dog. I can take any of mine out at sunrise and hunt till sunset without tiring it. I may be worn out, tramping up and down the mountains after chukars, but not my dogs."

A good Sussex works as if possessed. Extremely birdy, with its outstanding nose naturally close to the ground, the Sussex goes into a world by itself while hunting. It can wiggle through and under the most impenetrable tangles as it tracks a running bird. Its tail is a blur when on hot scent.

"My dogs' tails confuse some of my hunting buddies," Frank Komatar says. "They always think the dog is on a bird. Their tails go fast all the time, but when they hit bird scent, it really blurs. I can read them just fine, but they fool my buddies sometimes."

Fortunately, the breed's short legs won't let it outfoot the boss, especially in the heavy cover the breed was developed for. Being in its own world, it would be difficult to control if it had legs like an English Springer Spaniel.

With its low-slung body, outstanding nose, and English tenacity, the Sussex will put up just about every bird it scents. It may take some time, and some distance. But the dog will persevere until the bird tires of the constant pursuit and flushes. If the boss will just let the dog work, follow it quietly, and be ready to shoot when the tail indicates a flush is imminent, he will get a shot.

Some Sussex "give tongue" (bark) when they approach a bird. Not all, of course, but some. When the dog is digging birds out of extremely heavy cover, where the hunter may not be able to see the dog much of the time, barking just before a flush can be an advantage.

"About half of mine give tongue," Frank Komatar says. "I have one that really yaps just before he flushes a flock of chukars. Chukars tend to run uphill, so the dog may trail them a long way. When this dog starts to bark, I get ready to shoot. Kinda nice."

Some Sussex flush hard. Some flush soft—that is, hesitate before diving in after the bird. In spaniel field trials a soft flush is heavily penalized, but for the ordinary hunter it may have an advantage. It allows him to get ready to shoot.

"My two males really get with it when they flush," Frank Komatar says. "Dive in on the fly and put the bird up. My females approach birds more cautiously. One experimented for a while with an interesting technique. When she got near a bird, she stood up on her hind legs and then dove straight down on it. She caught two pheasants that way. But just as I was getting to like this method, she stopped doing it."

If the hunter knocks the bird down, the Sussex may or may not retrieve it. If not, it will at least locate the bird and stand over it until the shooter arrives to pick it up.

Natural retrieving instincts vary widely in the breed. Linda Legare says that most of her dogs are natural retrievers.

Pluis Davern has had middle-of-the-road experience with hers. She says, "Mine has some retrieving instinct. Initially he ran out, picked up the bird, and brought it partway back. I have found that it takes the forced-retrieve, the induced-retrieve, or whatever euphemism you prefer for force-breaking, to make a reliable retriever of many Sussex."

"None of mine retrieve," says Frank Komatar. "No interest in dead birds. Sure, they'll locate them so I can pick them up, but they won't retrieve dead birds. I once hunted with a guy up in Minnesota and his Sussex wouldn't retrieve either."

Frank competes in the advanced classes of Obedience Trials with his Sussex. These classes require that the dogs retrieve the wooden dumbbells, so Frank has force-broken his dogs to do that. He said it was slow, arduous training. He has never bothered extending it to birds for field work, feeling that having his dogs locate dead birds for him is all he needs.

The Sussex that retrieves naturally or through force-breaking will retrieve from water, too, after it discovers that it can swim. The breed doesn't seek water naturally but adjusts to it reasonably well. As in many things with the Sussex, the trainer may have to use subterfuge.

"I use clipped-wing pigeons to induce them to swim," Pluis Davern says. "I toss the bird a few feet out in the water. It flops around invitingly. The dog jumps in and gets it before he realizes he's swimming. After a few clips, the dog will go in for dummies, too.''

Even the finest retrieving Sussex is not a proper duck dog. It lacks the coat and body build for serious waterfowl work in cold weather and heavy seas. However, it can retrieve all the doves the average party can legally shoot each day. It can also retrieve any upland bird that falls in a lake or across a creek. It can even do light-duty on ducks, early in the season, when the air and water aren't too cold.

Why haven't more people taken to this breed? Beats me. It can do all that most American upland hunters could ever ask of a dog, and do it naturally, with little formal training. It is also a charming house pet that will protect the family when necessary. Nice little dog.

"Snuffy" likes the water. *Pluis Davern*

9

The American Water Spaniel: *Yankee Doodle Dandy*

THE AMERICAN WATER SPANIEL (AWS) is as American as George M. Cohan, and just as capable of "doing it all" in his particular line of work.

A marvelous little all-weather ducker, the AWS can also bust the nastiest cover in the uplands to flush and retrieve birds for the boss. The dog's small size and placid temperament make him ideal in a duck skiff, where he can slip into and out of the water without upsetting or soaking the skipper. His methodical thoroughness in the uplands makes him a delightful companion for the gunner over thirty-five years of age.

Developed in the last century in the Great Lakes region, and now the state dog of Wisconsin, this native breed possesses so many talents that the national breed club, American Water Spaniel Club (AWSC), has struggled for years trying to decide whether to seek AKC classification as a retriever or as a flushing spaniel. The breed must be classified as one or the other before it can participate in AKC Field Trials and hunting tests. The breed needs the exposure these activities, especially AKC hunting tests, would give it among dog-loving hunters. Trouble is, the AWSC membership is badly split—four ways. Some members favor classification as a spaniel. Some favor classification as a retriever. Others, fearing that either would eventually damage the breed's dual abilities, have until very recently held out for dual classification. Still others prefer no classification at all.

The AKC recently denied the AWSC dual classification, and for good reasons. AKC field titles (FC, AFC, JH, SH, MH) do not indicate whether they were earned in spaniel, retriever, or pointing breed events. The breed classification does that. If AKC granted dual classification to the AWS, it would have to make similar grants for other breeds. That would lead to chaos, especially in hunting tests. Labrador owners might seek triple classification, since many use their dogs as upland flushers and some even have Labs that point their birds.

Although the AWS cannot run in AKC Field Trials or hunting tests, it can run in two different non-AKC hunting tests for retrievers. The UKC affiliate, the Hunting Retriever Club, sponsors a fine program. So does North American Hunting Retriever Association (NAHRA), although it has no registry affiliation. However, like it or not, AKC controls the market in both spaniels and retrievers. If the hunters are ever to discover the American Water Spaniel, they will have to see them perform in AKC activities, especially AKC hunting tests.

I heard just recently that AWSC will vote on the remaining three options (retriever classification, spaniel classification, or no classification) in late 1991 or early 1992. No one can predict what the outcome will be.

After years of experience with both spaniels and retrievers, I feel the AWS should be classified as a spaniel. Its abilities would make it a strong participant in AKC spaniel hunting tests. Spaniel hunting tests require water work at every level, even a simple water blind at the highest level. Frankly, AKC spaniel hunting tests appear to have been designed more for the AWS than for any other spaniel breed. The AWS's small size would work against it in AKC retriever hunting tests.

Okay, let's look at this spunky little Yankee water dog that has more talents than one AKC classification can encompass to everyone's satisfaction.

A welterweight among spaniels, the typical AWS weighs about 40 pounds and stands some 18 inches at the withers. This small stature, more that of a big Cocker or small Springer, clearly says "spaniel." However, his long tail says "waterfowler." I gained great respect for the usefulness of a long tail on any quadruped with all four feet off the ground when I one day watched a tailless squirrel struggle cautiously through the trees in our backyard while his fully tailed buddies did aerial acrobatics around him.

The AWS coat also says "dual dog." It can be anything from the flat, harsh, slightly wavy coat of the field-bred English Springer to the tight, hard curls of the Curly Coated Retriever. The less curl there is, the more dense the undercoat. Most AWS coats fall somewhere in the middle, much like that of the Irish Water Spaniel. Regardless of coat type, the outercoat is relatively short, only about one-half inch longer than that of the Labrador.

This coat protects the dog quite well in the normally cold water of the upper Midwest, its region of origin. It also protects him from briars and brambles in the uplands. However, it does pick up burrs, and they do work their way into the undercoat, where they are a real challenge to the owner. While owners cannot avoid the chore of pulling burrs at the end of the day—before cleaning their

Kelly's Chocolate Magic, owned by Dr. Gary Forshee.

Kelly's Chocolate Magic hits the water big-time . . .

. . . and swims through the decoys.

birds, their guns, and their aching anatomies—most have found ways to minimize it. Sharon Beaupre of Cambridge, Minnesota, lightly trims her dog's coat before opening day—not enough to expose the dog to the elements, but just enough to make him less of a burr magnet. Dr. Gary Forshee of Bonner Springs, Kansas, puts a light coat of cheap hair oil ("the cheaper and greasier the better") on his AWS so the burrs don't twist into the undercoat. This lubrication also facilitates their removal.

The character of the AWS is pure American. In fact, my one-word description of the breed is "opportunistic."

Perhaps the most distinctive AWS quality is their peculiarly American intelligence. Call them clever, crafty, or whatever, they can carpe diem better than any dog that walks, swims, and barks.

For example, in the early days of the heartworm problem, Tom Olson of Milaca, Minnesota began giving his AWS daily caracide pills. The dog accepted each one, feigned chewing until Tom turned away, and then hid the pill behind an out-of-the-way chair. One day Tom found about thirty pills back there and realized he had been outsmarted.

Vaughn Brockman of Menomonie, Wisconsin, had an AWS, Sergeant Barney Good Times, back in the 1960s that became a legend among Vaughn's hunting and nonhunting friends for his craftiness. In an effort to control Barney's range in the uplands, Vaughn bought an electronic collar, one of those early models that only worked when the dog was grounded. The dealer assured Vaughn that he could solve the problem forever with no more than three jolts. Clearly, he had no experience with AWS in general and Barney in particular. Within the first three jolts, Barney realized that the discomfort went away when he jumped, and also when he put a lot of distance between himself and the boss. Vaughn still laughs when he tells of watching Barney make long kangaroo leaps, one after another, as he hustled out of the transmitter's range. That was exactly the opposite of what Vaughn had in mind, and therefore precisely what Barney had to do to win.

AWS's are possessive, so they make excellent watchdogs for those who allow this trait to develop. However, if the owner shows that he disapproves of this kind of behavior, the average AWS will desist.

A very personal dog, the AWS becomes attached to one family, and especially to one member of that family. He focuses his life on that one person, bonds only with him/her, and manipulates the other family members as required. For this reason, that one person should train the dog. AWS do not respond well to professional training, unless the pro can establish a strong bond with the animal first—which takes time and therefore costs money.

As a youngster, Vaughn Brockman sent Sergeant Barney Good Times to a pro, from whom Barney learned plenty in his own crafty way. From the first day, Barney steadfastly refused to acknowledge the pro's existence, much less accept his training. After three weeks of futility, the pro called and told owner Vaughn Brockman to come and get his worthless dog. When Vaughn arrived, the pro gave him a demonstration with Barney. However, instead of refusing to work, Barney did everything right! Reluctantly, the pro agreed to keep the dog for another try. Three weeks later, he called Vaughn again and told him that all Barney would do was sit and watch the other dogs work. When Vaughn picked Barney up, this time without a demonstration, the pro told him that he hoped that he would never see another AWS in his life. During the following hunting season, Vaughn found that Barney had learned plenty just sitting and watching the other dogs work.

"In fact," Vaughn chuckles, "Barney hunted like a fully trained dog ever after!"

Pro Tom Dokken of Northfield, Minnesota has trained many AWS over the past few years, so he has some interesting insights into the breed's personality. He says they mature more slowly than Labradors and learn more slowly, too. Tom takes a typical Lab through his basic program in three months but has to spend four or five months cajoling a typical AWS through it. He feels that he succeeds more frequently with AWS's that have been well socialized at home before he sees them, that he bonds more easily with such dogs. Tom prefers starting an AWS at about five months old, when the dog is still quite maleable.

The AWS is physically tough, durable, and healthy. Dr. Gary Forshee, who has been training and hunting them for twelve years, told me he has yet to spend a buck at his vet's for anything but elective procedures and repair of hunting injuries. None of his AWS's has ever come down with any of the many current canine maladies. Douglas Doyle of Stanfordville, New York told me that his vet calls the AWS the toughest breed he has ever treated.

Mentally tough, too, the AWS has enough aggressiveness for an occasional crippled honker. While the goose-hunting specialist needs a bigger retriever, the catch-as-catch-can hunter who shoots an occasional goose can depend on an AWS to bring it in to him somehow. Vaughn Brockman once tried unsuccessfully to keep a nine-month-old female puppy from going after a bluffing and blustering crippled Greater Canada. The youngster broke and charged the puffed-up, hissing honker, hitting it full tilt in the chest. This bowled the bird over and knocked it senseless, making it easy for the little dog to grab its neck and drag it back. Driving through a bird and then picking it up on the way back seems to be a trait more common in American dogs. I have seen Chessies do this often, but I can't remember ever seeing any other retriever breed do it.

Douglas Doyle, who hunts a little of everything with his AWS's, told me that his dogs retrieve about a half dozen geese a year. I asked if they are all stone-dead. "Are yours all stone-dead?" he answered. Good point.

The breed is tough in other ways, too. While swimming back with a duck, one of Douglas Doyle's dogs was sucked into a culvert full of rushing water. The dog thrashed its way through the culvert and out the other side—with the duck still in its mouth. Nor did it hesitate to leap back into the water the next time the boss dropped a bird.

For all his mental and physical toughness, the AWS has a strong sense of fair play, which the smart owner will never violate. In this, the breed resembles two other American breeds with which I am familiar: the Chesapeake Bay Retriever and the Boston Terrier.

The AWS will accept punishment in training, as long as it understands what it did wrong. However, the dog won't put up with mistreatment, which violates its sense of fair play. If the trainer establishes proper rapport with the AWS and takes the time to lead it through the training, punishment will seldom be needed. The AWS really wants to please that one human with whom it is bonded.

If the trainer, even that special person, abuses the AWS—by too severe punishment or incomprehensible punishment or even excessive neglect—the dog will quit, refuse to work, turn him off. A surprisingly few repetitions will convert this into a permanent condition, creating a dog that may never trust another human being, a canine robot that goes through the motions of living with none of the spaniel merriment.

The AWS may use its opportunistic intelligence to deal with mild punishment it feels is unjustified. For example, in one family the husband handled all canine corrections. Whenever the dog felt justice had not been properly served on a specific occasion, it would sneak into the bedroom, pull the husband's pillow—never the wife's—off the bed, and lift its leg on it. The man could hardly ignore such eloquent complaints, so he and the dog gradually negotiated a mutually acceptable code of "canine criminal law."

The AWS will figure ways to deal with every person in the household, especially those who dislike dogs. Years ago an AWS-owning parish priest in Wisconsin had an assistant who didn't share his enthusiasm for dogs. The AWS sensed—and resented—this attitude, of course, so it haughtily ignored the offending assistant. However, on occasion it would avenge itself by keeping this priest awake at night. The dog would wait quietly outside the assistant's bedroom window until about five minutes after the light went out. Then the dog would yodel softly, just loud enough to be heard in the one room. When the light came back on, the dog would be quiet again, waiting until about five minutes after it went out again before resuming the serenade. That way the priest would just get to sleep each time before being woken up again. The dog would repeat this for several hours. The assistant was happy to be transferred to another parish—and the AWS probably took his departure as a "personal" triumph, as proof of who really was in charge.

The breed does have a tendency to yodel. The AWS in the story above used to join its owner in singing High Mass on Sundays—from the safety of the rectory window. Yodeling becomes an operatic art form with some AWS's. A true Caruso of the breed sits down, points its muzzle to the heavens, opens its jaw, closes its lips until its mouth is a small round hole, and then moans softly. In an urban setting, such unearthly sounds in the middle of the night can reduce neighborly harmony to a dangerously low level. However, the AWS will accept early training in "Hush!" thereby never developing its full operatic range.

Many American Water Spaniels "grin." This looks like a snarl, for the dog curls his lip up, uncovering his teeth. However, it also wags and dances all over, showing delight at seeing a family member or at the prospect of going hunting. The dog's total demeanor shows that it is grinning, not snarling. Many Chesapeakes show happiness this way, too.

The AWS is a delightful dog, a character if you will. However, it has never regained its pre–World War II popularity, even in the upper Midwest. Since the end of the Big One, highly publicized imports have dominated the American hunting dog scene to the detriment of our homebreds, especially the American Water Spaniel. Too bad, for no other breed can do so many things the American hunter needs done. The AWS was developed right here long before we started adapting British and European breeds to our needs.

This may change in the near future, especially if AWSC seeks AKC classification as a spaniel and starts running the breed in spaniel hunting tests, where they can best show their dual ability. Many modern American hunters live in situations which don't allow more than one dog, situations which favor the smaller dog: apartments, condos, urban and suburban houses with tiny yards. The American Water Spaniel fits into any of these environments, in fact into any environment suitable for human habitation. Besides, the AWS will hunt anything a feather-chaser can stuff in his game bag. Some even use them for rabbits.

Douglas Doyle sums it like this: "I can hunt everything I want to hunt in my area (New York) with an American Water Spaniel, and do it on less dog food."

But the American Water Spaniel is much more than a do-it-all meat dog that is cheap to keep. A delight around the house, it has the charming ability to smile at its owner and communicate, if not speak, George M. Cohan's immortal line: "My mother thanks you. My father thanks you. My sister thanks you. And I thank you!"

"Just wait 'til I grow up!"

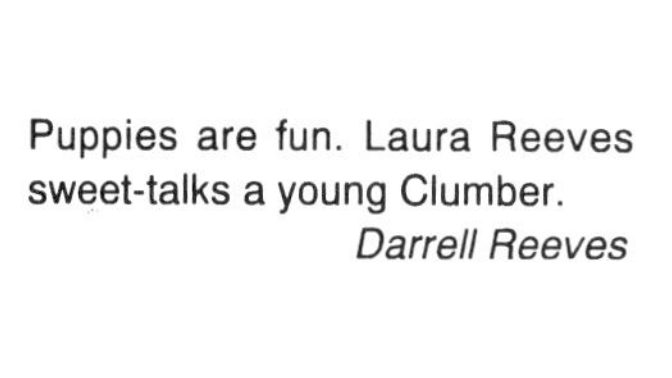

Puppies are fun. Laura Reeves sweet-talks a young Clumber.
Darrell Reeves

10

Finding the Right Spaniel For You

THE FIRST RULE of successful dog acquisition is: *Stay away from litters of puppies until you have done three things:*

1. Selected a breed.
2. Decided whether to buy a puppy or trained dog.
3. Selected a source (breeder for a puppy, trainer for trained dog).

If you ignore this rule, you will probably buy a puppy from the first litter you visit. That all but dashes your chance of getting an ideal dog for your particular situation. It also transfers control of the process from you to the most appealing of a bunch of squirmy young canines.

Selecting Your Breed

First, select the best breed for you. Not necessarily the one experts tout as the "perfect" for your type of hunting. At best, such experts have personal experience with only one or two breeds. At worst, they are merely repeating what they have read or heard from other experts, who in turn may have been repeating what they received from still other experts, and so on.

Once you understand the options, let your heart rule your head. Go with your tummy. As you read the chapters on the eight spaniel breeds, one or two may have appealed to you more than the others. If one breed stands out in your mind, go with it. If two breeds finish neck and neck, reread the two chapters, and maybe a winner will emerge. If not, get acquainted with people who have adults (not puppies) of each breed. To find them, ask the secretary of the local Field Trial or hunting test club, the local kennel club, the local Obedience Trial club. If you strike out in those places, contact the secretaries of the two national breed clubs (see appendix 3, "Important Contacts").

Preferably, you should talk to owners who actually hunt with their dogs. If no local owners hunt, talk to distant hunters by telephone. Ask them about the breed's hunting strengths and weaknesses, its level of trainability, and what it's like to live with.

After such investigations into both breeds, you will probably like one better than the other. Good. That's the right one for you. Breed selection should be an emotional process based on your personal feelings, not on some pseudointellectual analysis of relative hunting skills. Shooting one bird over a dog you love will please you more than limiting out with one to which you are indifferent.

Consider a Trained Dog

Few first-time buyers consider a trained dog. Too bad, for they would derive more benefits from such an animal than would those adding a second spaniel or replacing one that has died.

Trained dogs come in two basic types: fully trained and started. Neither is well defined. The fully trained dog may or may not be steadied, may or may not do blind retrieves, may or may not like water. As a minimum, it should hunt enthusiastically, quarter reasonably well, flush in an acceptable (to the buyer) manner, not be gun-shy, retrieve shot birds, and not chase flyaways uncontrollably. The started dog can be anything from a yearling that has shown good potential to a dog that approaches the requirements for a fully trained dog.

The trained dog removes the risk from the acquisition process. The buyer knows exactly what the dog can and cannot do before he spends his money. If he is dealing with a reputable trainer, he will receive (as part of the purchase) adequate instructions about how to handle the dog and how to keep its training up, plus all the follow-on advice he needs.

The trained dog is ready to hunt as soon as the season opens. Of course, the person who decides on a breed other than the field-bred English Springer Spaniel may have to look a long time to find a trained dog for sale. Even trained Springers aren't always available on demand.

The trained dog's major drawback is price. A minimally started dog will probably cost twice as much as a pup. Fully trained dogs start at about four times the price of a pup. They spiral up, depending on the dog's level of training and ability, to five-figure prices. If these figures seem high, remember that money is a replenishable resource. Time is not. You will waste a year or more with a dud pup before seeing that you threw snake eyes. You may do that with several puppies in a row. Those years are gone.

Puppies Are Fun

Still, a lot can be said for buying a puppy. Granted, it's a gamble, no matter how royally bred the litter may be. But realistically, it may be the only affordable option for the average middle-class paterfamilias (or materfamilias). My wife and I raised five children, so I know about skimping. The needs of a family can make money scarce, even if it is replenishable.

Economy is not the only reason some choose the puppy option. Many of us prefer the excitement of bringing a pup along, watching it develop, working through its problems. We get a special sense of pride from this. Hunting with a dog you have trained yourself is like catching fish on flies you tied yourself.

Even for the person who starts with a trained dog, a pup makes a good follow-on dog. He can train it himself with minimal risk. If the first pup doesn't work out, he can try another, and another, and so on until he gets the right one. During all that time, he has his trained dog to hunt with.

Finding a Source

If you opt for a trained dog, contact breeders and professional trainers in your selected breed. If you don't know any, inquire about them from the secretary of the national breed club.

If you opt for a puppy, look for a breeder with a reputation for producing the kind of stock you seek. The secretary of your national breed club can help you locate several potential breeders.

The secretary of your national breed club can also inform you about the hereditary health problems to which your breed is most vulnerable. Some breeds have serious hip problems. Others suffer from eye problems. Some have a relatively high incidence of poor temperament. You need to know about these.

When you contact breeders, ask for references, including some whose dogs have matured enough to be trained and hunted. And contact these references. Ask what they like and dislike about their dogs, what health and temperament problems they have encountered, and so on. Ask also if they know of others who have bought dogs from that particular breeder. You may get some names the breeder would rather you didn't have.

After you select a source, request pedigrees of planned litters or available trained dogs. Study appendix 2, "Reading Spaniel Pedigrees," and apply what you learn to the pedigrees you receive. For puppies, the pedigree gives you an idea of how big a risk you are taking. For a trained dog, the pedigree indicates the dog's approximate value as breeding stock (which is one of the pricing factors).

Selecting an Individual Dog

Even with a trained dog, rapport should be your major consideration. I have known many outstanding dogs that I could not enjoy hunting with, much less living with, because of traits in their personalities. Before buying a dog, spend enough time with it to assure yourself that it will be a "marriage made in heaven," not a "hunting dog from hell" situation for you. Ideally, before buying a trained dog, you should have a pro (not the one through whom you are buying) evaluate the dog for thirty days. During that period, you should visit the pro's place often enough to become well acquainted with the dog.

Never buy a trained dog without first seeing it work. Especially not by mail. At least one sharp operator works a nationwide mail-order scam with "started" and "trained" hunting dogs. He picks up sporting dogs at local shelters and advertises them nationally. When some innocent buys one by mail, the operator ships whatever he has on hand in the requested breed. The "fleecee" soon complains that the dog is worthless. The operator agrees to replace it. The replacement dog is not better, so he offers another replacement, and so on until the fleecee gives up. Of course, the victim pays all shipping costs both ways, so the operator is out nothing with all these replacements. He profited from the original sale and can continue shipping one worthless mutt after another until the buyer runs out of money, patience, or both.

If you opt for a pup, you may now start playing with puppies. Go with your tummy again. Rapport is the major ingredient in a dog/trainer relationship. Select the pup with which you have the strongest rapport. That will be the best one for you. It may not be the best one for your hunting buddy, but it's right for you. That's the nice thing about a litter of pups. Every pup is the best one for someone.

You will hear Field Trialers recommend that you find a good litter and just reach in and grab a pup. Field Trialers seek competitive dogs, dogs that can win. They can learn to love any dog that wins. But you are looking for a hunting buddy, a companion afield and at home. You can do better than the blind grab. Play with all the pups in the litter until you identify the one with which you have the strongest rapport.

Whether you seek a pup or a trained dog, insist that you receive the AKC registration form at the time of the sale. AKC controls all spaniel activities, so a spaniel not registered (or registerable) with AKC is not worth much. Don't accept any explanation for the lack of AKC registration papers. If, for example, "It's not back from AKC yet," wait until it arrives before buying. Don't accept registration with another registry as "just as good." The Field Dog Stud Book (FDSB) is the major registry for Field Trial pointers and setters, but not for spaniels. The United Kennel Club (UKC) is the major registry for Coonhounds and several other breeds, but not for spaniels.

The AKC is the major registry for spaniels. The AKC may, as many experienced dog folks say, have charm and charisma similar to General Motors, IBM, or any other muscle-flexing eight-hundred-pound gorilla. But, lovable or not, AKC controls all off-season dog games for spaniels. Insist on AKC registration.

Housing for Your Spaniel

If you plan to maintain only one dog, you should keep it in the house with you. That way, it will have your company and that of your family. If you put it

The author's kennel runs in winter. Canvas gate-covers stop the north wind, with help from the jon-boat alongside. Notice how close to the house these runs are.

One of the author's weatherproof doghouses.

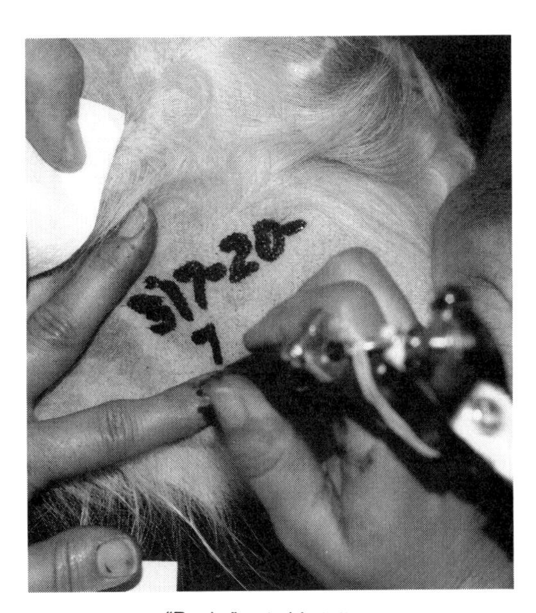

"Rocky" gets his tattoo.

outside, even in an ideal kennel, it will suffer loneliness. I remember years ago watching helplessly as a delightful Brittany went stir-crazy because it was kenneled alone in a backyard run. The owner fed and watered it as he should have, cleaned up after it often enough for good sanitation. But, except during hunting season, he paid no attention to the dog. I talked to the poor animal over the fence frequently. In a couple of years, I saw it change from a happy, glad-to-see-ya animal to a cold-eyed, suspicious slinker.

If you must keep the dog outside, get two dogs. They will keep each other company. Besides, alternating two spaniels while hunting gives you fresh "dog power" all day.

Keep your two spaniels in adjacent kennel runs, where they can interact without being able to harm each other if they disagree on some point of canine etiquette. I prefer runs about twenty feet long and four feet wide with a concrete floor and chain link fencing (including a top). I place a double-built wooden doghouse of appropriate size in each run. During winter, I cover the gates, which are on the north end, with canvas to stop the wind.

I placed my runs right next to the house, by the back door. I have never understood why so many people put them way out in back. I don't like to wade through snowdrifts in winter to take care of my dogs. Ditto for heavy summer rainstorms. I can get to my dogs comfortably in any weather. When my dogs bark, I hear them before my neighbors do. I can keep them quieter that way.

Tattooing Foils Dognappers

Research laboratories pay two dollars per pound for live animals delivered to their doors, and they don't ask too many questions. After all, this country has always had more strays than we can count.

Not surprisingly, we have full-time dognappers who make very good livings satisfying this demand. The typical professional dognapper picks up strays, of course, but if he can't get enough animals that way, he will steal dogs from backyards, even from locked kennel runs. In this day of two-income families, many neighborhoods are deserted during working hours. If a dognapper finds a dog in a locked kennel run, he saws through the lock.

Laboratories will not accept tattooed dogs. A tattooed dog can be traced. Thus a professional dognapper leaves tattooed dogs alone. If he gets one accidentally, he turns it loose before arriving at the laboratory. Unless, of course, the dog carries its tattoo on its ear, in which case he might cut the entire ear off!

To foil dognappers, have your dog tattooed on the inside of one upper thigh. To find a tattooist, contact your veterinarian or one of the tattoo registries (see appendix 3, "Important Contacts").

As an added precaution, you might have little metal signs (TATTOOED DOG) made for your kennel gates. That would discourage dognappers from taking your dogs and discarding them miles away.

SECTION II

Training Your Spaniel

Bob Finch

OVERVIEW

Welcome

At this point, you either have your spaniel or you are in the process of acquiring one. Let's say you have just brought him home. This section tells you how to train him for American hunting conditions.

We Yanks teach our spaniels all the standard stuff like quartering, flushing, and retrieving shot birds in the uplands. We also teach them some rather sophisticated nonslip retrieving, like multiple marks and blind retrieves.

Here I speak of the true blind retrieve, not a random run with a happy ending. The dog that hunts the entire countryside looking for a bird it didn't see fall may eventually stumble on it. In spite of persistent rumors to the contrary, that is not a blind retrieve. In a true blind retrieve, the handler controls his dog continuously. He sends the pooch off in a certain direction, and the dog "carries that line" until he finds the bird or until the handler stops him with a whistle signal. When stopped, the dog turns to hup facing the handler and awaits further direction. The handler then "casts" the dog in some direction by some combination of arm and voice (or whistle) signal. The dog "continues that cast" until he finds the bird or is stopped and redirected again. And so on.

In this section I tell you how to train your spaniel to do all these wonderful things.

I hope that as you sit there reading, perhaps with your spaniel pup beside you, you dream of the wonderful things the youngster will one day do. Perhaps you see him bouncing through the heavy cover along the edge of a cut and snow-powdered grainfield. He dives in and puts a huge rooster pheasant in the air.

Your spaniel leaps, one, two, three times trying to catch it as it climbs. Then he hups quickly and waits for you to shoot and send him to retrieve. You shoot and connect, but not as well as you planned. The bird sails maybe seventy-five yards before tumbling. You send your spaniel to retrieve, and he quickly disappears in the cover. You wait anxiously for his return. Will he find the bird? When you are about to give up, he bounces back out of the near cover carrying the pheasant. Its long tail stretches from one side of your spaniel's mouth. Its iridescent head bobs from the other. Wow! What a dog!

Perhaps you see him squirming through typical grouse tangles (other birds live in "cover"; grouse live in "tangles"). He puts up a bird you don't even see. You fire at the whirring wing sound and listen for a *kerplop* on the ground. Did it or didn't it? You send your spaniel to find out. In less than a minute he returns with the grouse that you shot, even though you have never seen it before. Again, wow!

Perhaps you see your spaniel beside you in a boat during early ducking season. You spread your decoys, and wait, and wait, and wait. Just as you are about to nod off, you hear duck talk all around you. You come up shooting and knock down a brace of bluewing teal. You send your spaniel, who only marked one of them. No problem. You and he work together to pick up the other one as a blind retrieve. Once again, wow!

Such dreams are important to your training program. Remember them often and they will keep you going when you hit a training snag (as everyone does). When your other responsibilities take you away from training for a while, your dreams will bring you back as soon as possible. Keep dreaming and you'll keep training.

Your Training Program

Training is a continuous process, not a series of disconnected parts or phases. Nor is it what mathematicians call "linear." You do not complete all of one phase before starting the next. Sometimes you work on several phases in a single session. Sometimes you work on multiple phases in parallel for a sustained period of time. Be aware of this, but don't fret about it. Throughout these training chapters, I explain when you should be doing what.

I have divided the training program into eleven parts and devoted a chapter to each: Puppy Training; Obedience; Quartering; The Single Marked Retrieve; Steadying to Wing and Shot; Brace Work; Force-Breaking—Gently; The Multiple Marked Retrieve; The Blind Retrieve: Preliminary Training; and the Blind Retrieve: The Real Thing; and Keeping Your Spaniel Trained.

In each chapter, the training coverage is preceded with a background section, which includes: What Is It?; Why Do It?; Prerequisites; Equipment; Schedule; and Handling Techniques.

To get the big picture, read the entire book first, maybe a couple of times. Then you will understand how each chapter fits into the overall plan.

Most beginners worry too much about time. When starting each phase of training, they ask, "How long will it take to complete this one?" Maybe this is the "time is money" philosophy spilling over into our recreational lives. Perhaps it's the influence of football and basketball, in which the clock is so important.

In each chapter, there is an approximation of how long the training might take. These are estimates, not stopwatch setters. Take whatever comfort you can in them, but don't take them *too* seriously. No one will take your dog away from you if you run behind. *And no one will give you a prize if you lap the field.*

You would be happier if you would forget about the clock, even the calendar, when you lay out your training plans. Put yourself in a baseball frame of mind. The inning is over when you get the third out. Each training phase is complete when your dog can do the work. Not before.

Spaniels are not machines. They are sensitive animals. While they lack human intelligence (forcing us to condition them rather than reason with them), they share our emotions. They experience fear; they become bewildered; they feel joy; they love; and they hate. They also have physical traits like ours. They feel invigorated or tired. I'm sure they have headaches and backaches, but they can't complain verbally. They have good days and bad days. Any training program which ignores those emotional and physical characteristics to meet some fanciful schedule will ruin ten dogs for every one it "makes."

Different breeds mature at different rates. The English Springer and English Cocker mature more rapidly than the other breeds. A fast maturity rate is not an unmixed blessing, nor is a slow maturity rate a serious problem. The slower breeds generally retain their training better, whereas the faster ones require frequent refreshers throughout their lives.

Different dogs within a breed mature at different rates. Not every English Springer races through his training like those that have made the breed so popular.

Some trainers train faster than others, too. I am one of the slower ones. I value style, slash, and dash so much in my dogs that I do everything I can to retain it. You can't put it back after you have destroyed it. Thus, I take more time, underwork my dogs to keep them eager, and use as many positive motivators as I can.

So how long will it take you to train your spaniel? The answer comes in two parts, both admittedly vague. First: It will take as long as it takes; it depends on your dog; it depends on you. Second: You will never really complete it; you should train your spaniel all through his active life.

Even after you complete his initial training, you should continue working him until he's ready for social security. He will always need a little work here or there. If you run him in Field Trials or hunting tests, you must train hard all the time to keep him really sharp. Besides, he loves to work, and you love to work him. So, what's your hurry?

More relevant schedule questions are: How often should I train? And how long should each session be?

Training spaniels for American hunting is "labor-intensive." The dog must do more things under more conditions than almost any dog on earth. You must teach him so many more things that are not natural, like obedience, steadiness to wing and shot, and especially the blind retrieve. Even quartering and marked retrieves, which are mostly natural, require continuous work.

Clearly, the more time you spend training your spaniel—without overworking him—the better he will become. However, since you probably work for a living, you cannot spend all your waking hours creating a flushing and retrieving wonder. Besides, you probably have family and other social obligations that limit your training time even more. So, instead of talking about optimal time commitments, let's talk about what you can reasonably do with the time you do have.

Puppy training, obedience, and the optional force-breaking require frequent short sessions. Two or three brief periods per day are ideal. Since you do all or most of this training at home, you should be able to approximate that amount of time.

Field work (quartering, marked and blind retrieves) requires that you leave home. If you can get in several evening sessions per week plus one or two each weekend, you will make excellent progress. To prevent overworking your dog, limit him to two activities per session. One quartering session and one retrieving session, for example.

If you work a daytime job, you must limit your evening training to the months of daylight saving time, April through October. Weekend training often gives way to hunting during the fall—as it should. If you live somewhere in the northern part of the country, snow limits your training through the winter. So you may have to make do with six or seven months' serious training per year. More would be better, but the realities of life must prevail.

Handling Techniques

Operating a spaniel is an interactive process. You should train yourself as well as your dog. Your handling techniques must be clear and consistent if you are to communicate with the other half of the team.

You must be clear and consistent in directing your spaniel as he quarters. Actually, after he is trained, the less handling you do—as long as he covers the ground and stays close enough—the better. He will be able to concentrate on finding birds instead of worrying about what you are doing. However, when he misses a good patch of cover, or when he gets too far from you, you must handle him.

In your blind retrieve work, you must be clear and consistent in the way you set your dog up, the way you send him, the way you blow the whistle, the way you give arm signals, even the way you take a bird from him.

As I mentioned above, in each chapter, I explain the handling techniques you should use for the work involved. I admit there are alternative approaches, but what I present here is clear and consistent—and has worked for lots of folks with lots of spaniels.

If you will think of your handling techniques as ways to communicate with your spaniel, you will make few mistakes. You're the quarterback. He's the rest of the team. You call the plays. You give the snap count. The rest of the team keys off every sound you utter, every move you make. If you are clear and consistent, the rest of the team will do the right thing. If you are erratic and unpredictable, you will experience one broken play after another.

Your Training Group

It is extremely difficult to train a spaniel alone. In quartering, it's nice to have two assistants to walk your flanks, roll in birds and shoot for your dog. When you get to brace work, you need four assistants (plus at least one other dog). In marked retrieves, you can't throw far enough to challenge your dog's marking ability. Helpers are nice here, too, although you can do a lot of the work with a dummy launcher if you absolutely must.

For most trainers, the best answer is a training group of three to six committed spaniel fans, each with no more than two dogs. Any more people or dogs-per-person makes it difficult to work every dog during evening sessions.

Where do you find such a group? First, talk to the breeder from whom you bought your pup. If he can't help you, check out the local spaniel Field Trial club, the local hunting test club, or the local breed club. If none of these exist in your area, advertise in the classified of your local paper or company house organ.

Training Grounds

Your backyard will suffice for most of your obedience training and force-breaking.

You can start every type of retrieving work (single marks, multiple marks, blind retrieves) on bare ground in town—school yards, parks, vacant lots. In fact, that's the very best place for starting each of these, as you will see.

However, you will do most of your work in cover. Thus, you need suitable training grounds out in the country. Suitable grounds consists of large land areas with lots of the terrain and cover variations. Suitable grounds must also include adequate water. Frequently one large lake offers less than several small ponds, especially if the ponds have cover, stickups, points, island, and cover in the water.

Most spaniel Field Trial clubs and hunting test clubs have leases on grounds that members can use for training. If there is such a club in your area, join it.

However, you need more than one place to train. Dogs trained exclusively in one place frequently act as if they have never been trained when taken somewhere else.

If there is a retriever club in your area with leased land, join it too if they will let you train spaniels on their lease. Ditto for any pointing breed club.

I have gained access to excellent land and water by simply showing the landowner what I do with my dogs. They watch awhile, see that my dogs are under control, and tell me to come out anytime—free.

Many states have public lands that are open to dog training at certain times of the year. Contact your Fish and Game Commission for locations and schedules.

However and wherever you get the training grounds you need, use common sense when you go there. Remember you are a guest, even if you are paying a steep fee to lease the place. Close the gates you open. Don't knock fences down. All the do's and don'ts of hunting and fishing apply.

One retriever Field Trial club in my area lost a lease through the unbelievable stupidity of two members. It was a hot and dry summer. The pasture grass was beige and brittle. The ponds were low. At dusk on July 4, these two members brought their wives and kids out to the lease and started shooting fireworks! Fortunately, the farmer threw them out before they ignited the entire county. Asked about it later, one of the culprits said, "Hell, we lease the place. We ought to be able to do anything we want out there." The farmer relieved them (and the rest of the club) of any further opportunity to experiment on his land.

The Professional Trainer

Most amateurs fall into one of two schools of thought about pros: "all" and "nothing at all." I don't agree with either.

Members of the "all" school feel totally incompetent to train spaniels. They turn the entire job over to a pro, and only see the dog during hunting season or at Field Trials. Their attitude is, "Hey, I don't have time to train a dog. Yeah, I wish I knew ole Tangle-Coat better, but look at all the trophies and titles he has. Wouldn't have them if I hadn't put him with a pro."

Members of the "nothing at all" school feel it would be a disgrace to get help from a pro. "I can train my own dog, thank you. Don't need any help. So what if he punches out and flushes birds out of gun range. So what if he fails to find most of the birds I send him to retrieve. He flushes a few where I get a shot, and he finds some of them. That's plenty good enough for a hunting dog."

In my frequently disputed and often erroneous opinion, the pro's greatest usefulness among hunters lies between those two positions. You train your dog, but when you run into a particularly baffling problem, you confer with your pro (and pay him for his services, naturally).

That is the approach I have always taken, and the one I recommend to you. No one knows everything about spaniels, so you should feel no shame if you occasionally hit a snag you can't work out. Pros go to other pros for help now and then, just as golf pros do.

Here and there during the training program I present in this section, I tell you that if your dog behaves in such-and-such a way, you should take him to a pro for an evaluation. That is good advice every time I offer it. It is advice I would follow myself.

Reflect on what I have said here awhile before you read the next chapter. Spend the rest of the evening playing with the pup, and read again tomorrow after work.

However, don't try the read-a-page/train-a-page approach, nor even the read-a-chapter/train-a-chapter. Neither works. Instead, read the entire training section, maybe more than once, to get a complete picture of where you are going and how you will make the trip. Only then should you go back and start studying and applying the material in each chapter.

You may have noticed that I have not discussed what it takes to be a dog trainer. There are a couple of reasons for this.

First, every time I read such a passage in a book, I get a deep feeling of insecurity. The preternatural traits so many writers prescribe just to teach a dog to flush and fetch a bird intimidate me, even now, after I have done it over and over for years.

Second, I think any healthy and rational person can train a spaniel if he/she wants to. You only need to *know* two things: the techniques in an integrated training program; and your individual dog. I give you the former. Your dog tells you all about himself every moment you are with him. If you pay attention, you cannot avoid understanding him.

Granted, some people have more talent as dog trainers than others. They have more insight, more creativity, and probably much more interest than the general population. Some athletes play in the major leagues, some in the various levels of the minors, and some peak out in slow-pitch softball. Yet they are all ballplayers.

If you want to train a spaniel, you can train a spaniel. *Vaya con Dios.*

Rocky's "fancy" puppy delivery to the author. *Rita Betts*

11

Puppy Training

BACKGROUND

What Is It?

During the first several weeks after bringing your puppy home, you can teach him a number of things: his name; the commands NO and HUSH. You can also introduce him to play-retrieving, cover, water, birds, and gunfire.

Why Do It?

In this training, you not only build the foundation for all your pup's later work afield, you also build the foundation for your relationship with him. That relationship should be friendly—buddy-buddy, really—but, trust me, one of you will be the boss. If you want that to be you, establish yourself in that position early, when it's easy. That doesn't mean dominating the puppy unmercifully. It doesn't mean being unkind or unfeeling. It just means maintaining control in a friendly but firm way. Adopt the attitude that you are a benevolent monarch. You are the boss, but you assume full responsibility for your puppy's welfare.

Prerequisites

The only prerequisites are a healthy pup of seven to twelve weeks, and a strong desire on your part to learn how to train him.

Equipment and Facilities

You need a collar for your pup. Actually, you need a series of them in graduated sizes to accommodate his increasing neck size. I prefer the little nylon strap collars with plain buckles on them. They are cheap and sturdy.

You should have a light puppy lead. This can be a simple nylon affair, maybe four or five feet long. You should also have a ''flex-lead,'' which releases and rewinds a long lead in a manner similar to that of an automatic fly reel. This will come in handy for taking your pup for walks, and for encouraging a good return in play-retrieving.

You need a puppy-sized retrieving dummy, or better yet, a series of them in graduated sizes. My wife makes mine from pillow ticking and foam rubber chunks. Several mail-order catalogs offer these dummies in a variety of materials.

You need two plastic whistles. Why two? In case you blow the side out of one in midtoot. Why plastic? In cold weather a metal whistle will stick to your lips and tear the skin when you remove it from your mouth. Most spaniel Field Trialers use the traditional pealess horn spaniel whistles. Other spaniel owners use the more common dog whistles, like the Acme Thunderer, the Roy Gonia, and the Fox 40. Take your pick.

Carry your whistles on a lanyard around your neck. Lanyards come in many styles, from the inexpensive nylon cord models up to high-dollar affairs in braided leather, beaded macrame, even braided horsehair. Eventually you will stash several lanyards with whistles around the place. I have one in my hunting bag, one hanging on the mirror in my truck, one by the back door, and two with my training equipment. Two retired lanyards hang on the wall with the other memorabilia from outstanding dogs that live only in my memory.

You need a .22 blank pistol for introducing your pup to gunfire.

You need a source for pigeons. Contact any local Field Trial club (spaniel, retriever, pointing dog) for the name of a commercial bird supplier. For puppy training, you only need dead pigeons. Go to a local fun trial (any type) and ask for some of the birds that are shot during the day. Stick them in your freezer, and thaw them out as you need them. You can refreeze and rethaw them several times before they become unusable.

You need fields with cover and terrain variations. And you need a small creek.

Schedule

You should start this training almost as soon as you bring the puppy home. If possible, work with him every day. This training flows naturally into obedience training (chapter 12) and quartering (chapter 13). Your youngster may be four months old—or he may be eight months old—before you complete this puppy training and move on. Depends on him. Depends on you.

Puppy collar (bottom), flex-lead, short web lead, longer braided leather lead (top).

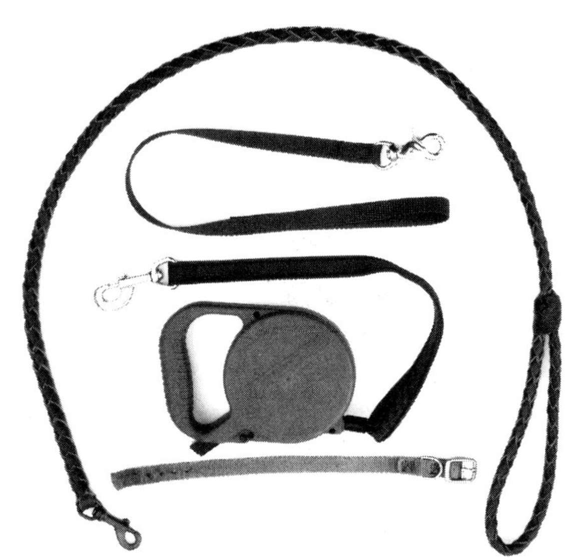

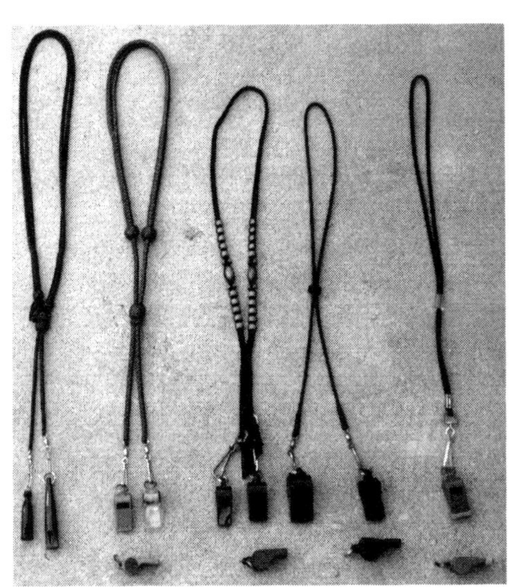

Whistles & lanyard. From left: braided leather lanyard with two different horn spaniel whistles, braided leather lanyard with orange and clear Roy Gonia whistles, macrame lanyard with small and medium Acme whistles, braided leather lanyard with large Acme and Fox 40 whistles, cord lanyard with Gonia commander whistle. Whistles across bottom show sideviews of whistles above.

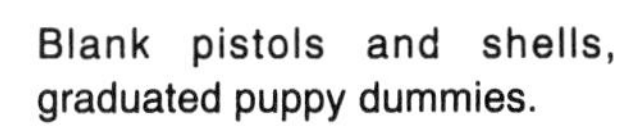

Blank pistols and shells, graduated puppy dummies.

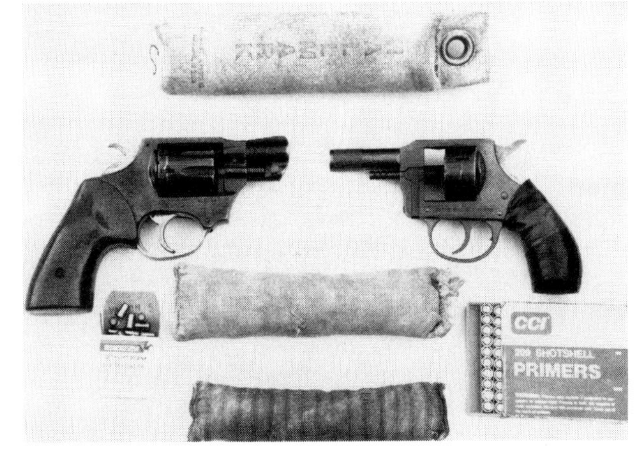

Handling Techniques

You need follow no formal handling procedures for puppy training. Just be comfortable, relaxed, and consistent.

TRAINING

Getting Acquainted

First, spend a few days getting acquainted. Everything in your future relationship with the pup depends on rapport. Rapport depends on mutual understanding and respect. Each of you must understand and accept the place the other occupies in the relationship.

As long as you allow the pup enough time to sleep—and he will need to do a lot of that at first—you cannot spend too much time getting acquainted. However, if job commitments keep you away from home each day, you will have to wedge in your dog time around your work. A few minutes each morning and a longer period each evening will do nicely, especially when complemented with generous weekend allotments. During these times you will come to understand your pup—and, more importantly, the pup will come to understand you. Dogs read people better, faster, and more thoroughly than people do dogs. Given ample exposure to you, that pup will do most of the adjusting without you even realizing it.

Introduce the puppy to as many of the situations he will have to cope with throughout his life as possible. How to go up and down stairs. The sound of the doorbell. The TV. The washing machine. The dishwasher. The trashmen. Take the pup for walks around the neighborhood on the flex-lead. Let other people make up with him. An occasional trip to a shopping center will do wonders.

The Puppy's Name and the NO Command

The first word you want to teach the pup is his name. Not his long-winded registered name, but a short call-name you will use daily for the rest of his life. I usually make a call-name from part of a dog's registered name. Flick is registered as Orion's Flicker. Rocky is Eagleview Shamrock, and so on. Others choose names with no relationship to the dogs' registered names. It's your choice.

Two things are necessary in a call-name: It should be short, no more than two syllables; and it should not sound like any other word in the dog's vocabulary, especially the various command words you will teach him: NO, HUSH, KENNEL, RELEASE, SIT, HEEL, STAY, COME, BACK, OVER, FETCH.

You will use the dog's call-name to get his attention most of the time, so a short one will serve you better. "Sweet Penelope" might sound endearing as you fondle and pet the little puppy, but over the dog's entire life, you will find just plain "Penny" more comfortable. A person should seldom shout at his dog.

However, when you must shout—and it may save the dog's life some day—you'll find that a short name "shouts" better than a long one. One or two syllables, no more.

Call-names that sound like command words—Mack (BACK), Ray (STAY), Moe (NO), and so forth—will cause your dog to misunderstand you at times, especially at a distance. Sometimes you will get some strange responses, like having the dog take off when you want stop him. You holler *Mack* and he hears BACK, so off he goes.

Having selected a good call-name, start immediately teaching the youngster to respond to it. If you are a puppy cuddler (as I am), repeat the name as you carry the puppy around the house and yard. Over and over and over. Look at it this way: You have to say something while carrying him, so why not say his call-name? That way, he can learn something from your voice. Use that name when you put the food bowl down, when you go outside to let the pup out of his run, when you run away from him in play and he is chasing you.

Later you will occasionally use his name when you are displeased. Now, however, use it only under pleasant circumstances. If the pup comes to associate the sound of his name with rewards of various kinds—being held and petted, being fed, being let out of the run, chasing the boss around the yard, and so on—he will react positively to it. If he associates that sound with unpleasantness, he will react negatively and perhaps run away from you when you say his name, or at least ignore you. If you sometimes reward him and other times punish him after calling his name, he will become one bewildered youngster.

Initially, the only word the pup should associate with your displeasure should be NO. A normally inquisitive pup will get into enough mischief to learn quickly that NO means trouble. Use NO, without the pup's name, whenever you correct him.

Back up your NO's with whatever little force is necessary to gain compliance with your wishes. Pups of seven weeks to four or five months are easy to handle physically, so you won't need heavy-handedness. Simply forcing the pup to do or stop doing something normally suffices. On those occasions that call for stronger measures, you can convince the youngster of the wisdom of doing things your way with a light shaking coupled with a stern bawling out. Or a swat on the rump with a newspaper will do wonders. However, do not ever strike the pup in the face with your hand—*never*. If a spaniel becomes hand-shy, he will avoid taking a line to a bird from the hand he fears.

HUSH

Some puppies are naturally quiet; others are naturally noisy; most fall somewhere between. Regardless, if you are a city dweller, you must show consideration to your neighbors. You should train your dog to stop barking on command.

I prefer HUSH as the command word. Some prefer STOP-THAT-NOISE or SHUT-IT-UP, but the simple, one-syllable HUSH works as well and is easier to articulate when you are sleepy. Whatever you use, you must convince your pup that it means stop barking—*now*.

Sometimes in the middle of the night, by the time you dress and go out to correct the dog, he has stopped temporarily on his own. Then, as soon as you have snuggled back under the covers, he starts up again. I deal with this by opening a window and saying HUSH while he is still barking. Then I go out and shake his muzzle while repeating HUSH several times. Even if he stops barking before I get outside, he seems to understand the meaning of HUSH. After a few such corrections, most dogs stop barking when I open the window and command HUSH.

In summer, I sometimes squirt the offender with water from the hose, repeating HUSH as I do.

Don't start HUSH training as soon as your new puppy arrives. Look at things from his point of view: He has been removed from his mother and littermates, perhaps flown several hundred miles in an airplane, picked up by a total stranger, driven to a strange house, played with awhile, and then placed in an unfamiliar kennel run. No wonder that the poor thing howls a bit the first few nights.

Still, you must consider your neighbors. If you take the new pup around and introduce him, explaining that he may be a little noisy for a few nights, most people will be understanding. Then, if you get out of bed and reassure the pup whenever he becomes noisy in the night, he won't become totally obnoxious. When he begins to howl, let him out of his run, and allow him to follow you around the yard until he is sleepy again. Then, put him back and go back to bed. Don't pick him up. Don't pet him. Don't make a fuss over him. Just keep him walking until he is ready to sleep again, which won't take long. This rather impersonal approach prevents the pup from feeling that he is training you to come out and console him. After a few nights of this, when he is acclimated to his new environment, you can start HUSH training.

Most spaniels learn to stop barking on command easily. Flick, always so anxious to please, has never been a problem. Rocky wants to please, too, but he gets carried away sometimes. When I say HUSH from the window, he gets an "Oh, boy, I've really done it now" look and scurries into his doghouse.

Play-Retrieving

Many beginners create all manner of problems by starting play-retrieving as soon as they get the pup home. They cannot wait to experience the wonderful "retrieving instinct." Always a mistake, this can be a disaster if the dog is a bit soft and the owner too demanding.

The new puppy should not be asked to retrieve anything for a while. How long? Well, like everything else, it varies from pup to pup. Before starting, look for these two signs: the pup should have established a "lair"; and he should have formed an attachment to you.

Every pup establishes a lair, which is that one special place he considers his own, the place to which he retreats to sleep, meditate, or just get away from the tribulations of everyday life. For the outside dog, it will be the doghouse. For the inside dog, it will be where he sleeps.

Further, it is worse than pointless to try play-retrieving until the youngster feels that you are his special human, his buddy and his boss. Through early familiarization you become his buddy. Through NO and HUSH training, you become his boss.

The so-called retrieving instinct does not incline the dog to bring things to a person, as is commonly thought. No, it is an instinct to pick things up and tote them back to the lair. The trainer teaches proper delivery, initially by tricking the pup into it. The trainer places himself in the youngster's path and cons him into delivering as he goes by. Later, conditioning and the dog's feelings for the trainer make him (the trainer) a "secondary lair" while retrieving.

When your pup is ready, familiarize him with a puppy dummy. Hold him by the collar, and show him the dummy. This is something new, and many puppies are a bit apprehensive. Let him smell it and mouth it a bit. However, don't let him run off with the dummy. Control the pup with the collar and keep the dummy in your hand, even while he mouths it. This initial step is simply one of familiarization. Don't try yet to get the dog excited about the dummy by teasing with it. That could frighten him and set training back.

When he has no fear of the dummy, go near his lair. Release your grip on the collar and tease him with the dummy. Tap it on the ground, wave it in the air, talk excitedly, and so on. When the pup is frantic to get the dummy, toss it four or five feet. If all goes well, the pup will pounce on it, spin around, and head for his lair. Since you are in the way, he must go directly past you. As he does, grab his collar gently and stop him. *Do not take the dummy.* Just bring the pup to a stop beside you.

Pet and praise him for several minutes, all the time letting him keep the dummy. If you take it, he may run away from you next time. In the pup's mind, that dummy is canine property, fairly obtained, and you have no right to it. Respect that feeling. Just praise and pet him and make him glad he "chanced by you." After a few moments of this, see whether he is willing to surrender the dummy. If so, take it. If not, continue the praise and petting while allowing him to keep the dummy. Eventually he will let you take it.

Repeat this two or three times. Don't give even the most eager pup more than four retrieves per session.

Okay, that's how it goes if the pup reacts ideally. However, he may react in any of several less-than-ideal ways. He may not even go after the dummy. He may run out but not pick it up. He may go out, lie down, and chew on the dummy. He may pick the dummy up and run off.

If he doesn't chase after the dummy, you may not have done the preliminaries thoroughly enough. He may not feel comfortable with this new thing. You may have tossed it before the pup was adequately excited. Start over and see if that was the problem. Maybe he is too tired from playing with the kids or other dogs. You should confine him for an hour or so before each training session so that he will be adequately rested. Or maybe he doesn't feel well. However, if this reaction persists over several sessions, he may lack retrieving instinct. As soon as you suspect this—which should be as soon as there is no other explanation—you should take the pup to a competent professional trainer for an evaluation. Why waste a large segment of your future on a dog that has no interest in this very important part of his life's work?

All the same things apply to the pup that will not pick the dummy up. If he is well rested, healthy, and has been properly introduced to the dummy, but won't pick it up through several sessions, take him to a pro for an evaluation.

The pup that goes out, lies down, and starts chewing on the dummy will probably turn out to be a tough, independent cuss that will require a heavy hand throughout training. Solving the immediate problem is rather simple: Go take the dummy away from the pup; then put the flex-lead on and start again. If he does the same thing again, haul him unceremoniously back to you, *with or without the dummy*. This type of hooligan is not given to dropping dummies, or even letting them loose without coercion. However, if the dummy does fall out as you yank him back, keep on dragging. If you ease up, this little hardhead will learn to control you by dropping the dummy.

Also go to the flex-lead for the pup that runs away ("bolts") with the dummy. Like the chewer, this guy tends to be aloof and little affected by praise and petting, which makes it difficult to motivate him to return through anything but force and fear. Frankly, these negative motivators will play a big role in all training of such dogs. If you are too tenderhearted to apply copious force, you should consider starting over with a new pupil. If you decide to stick with what you have, there is one positive motivator that will help you through your immediate problem: food. Generally, I don't recommend bribing a spaniel with food for doing what all good spaniels should do. However, in this case I would make an exception. Use the flex-lead to force a proper return, and then "trade" the dummy for a piece of dog food. This encourages both the return and the release.

The anticipation of food may cause this pup to drop the dummy in front of you. Don't worry about this. It means he's coming around. Try eliminating the treats, and if things go well, you may be able to discontinue them altogether—which you should do as soon as possible.

Flick responded nicely to the basic lair procedure. Rocky didn't. He would start back in my direction, but seeing that I blocked his way, he would veer off. I solved the problem by working him in a long, narrow area where he couldn't veer off. He had to come quite close to me to get by. By petting him extravagantly, I won the battle. I encouraged him to jump up on me and hold the dummy over my shoulder while I petted him. He decided that was more fun than escaping.

If you must go to the flex-lead to get a decent return, stay with it until you have not the slightest doubt about your pup's return. If you try him without it too soon and too often, you may teach him to return when he is on the flex-lead and to run away when he is not. Then you will have a problem.

Continue doing these short (five- to ten-foot) retrieves directly in front of the pup's lair until the return is automatic—whether through habit or the flex-

I dealt with Rocky's reluctance to return by working him in the narrow space between the kennel runs and the house . . .

. . . and he returned like a little gentleman.
Theresa Spencer

Let your spaniel "find" his first bird (a dead pigeon) as this young Clumber is about to do. And don't rush him if he is a bit cautious. *Darrell Reeves*

lead. Then try short retrieves elsewhere in the backyard, with the flex-lead if you have had to use it in the initial steps. This is where the relationship between you and your youngster becomes especially important. So far, you have been making yourself a secondary lair. He ran to his original lair so many times and wound up beside you—with pleasant results—that his feelings for his lair have been transferred to you. To assist this conditioning process when you move away from the original lair, when the pup picks up the dummy, run away, clap your hands, and call him excitedly.

As he demonstrates more and more reliability in returning, move around to different places in the yard. Keep the retrieves short. If the dog shows any inclination to run the wrong way, go to the flex-lead immediately. This is a problem that will only get worse if ignored.

Your immediate goal is to get an absolutely reliable return anywhere in the backyard sans flex-lead. Until you have that, there is no point in leaving the backyard or lengthening the tosses. Five to ten feet is enough. A short success is better than a long failure.

Before moving out of the backyard, lengthen these retrieves as much as you can, given the size of your backyard. Use flex-lead if your pup hesitates to return at greater distances.

Three or four retrieves are plenty. You can have another session in an hour or so, but keep each session short.

The Commands for Retrieving and Returning

When your pup is retrieving acceptably in the backyard, you can facilitate his later training by using the commands you will use to send him and call him back. He is not yet ready to be line-steadied—forced to wait for your command before going out to retrieve—but you can introduce the command to retrieve as he breaks for these backyard retrieves. Association will simplify the steadying process later. Similarly, you can introduce the return whistle command now while he is returning automatically.

You can use *almost* any word as a command to retrieve—there is one exception—but most spaniel owners use the dog's call-name. That way, in brace work, each dog has his own command word. Neither dog is as apt to break when the other is sent to retrieve.

However, don't use FETCH. That is a specialized word in force-breaking. Even if you do not intend to force-break your spaniel—and most spanielites don't at this point—save that word in case you change your mind.

Whatever command you choose, start using it now as the pup runs after the dummy. It will mean nothing to him initially, but he will come to associate it with retrieving. Then later, when you steady him, he will realize that this word—not the flight of the dummy—releases him to retrieve.

Similarly, blow the COME-IN whistle as the pup returns to you. Most trainers use either a series of short toots (*twee-twee-twee-twee-twee*) or one long and two shorts: *tweeeeeeet-tweet-tweet*. Take your choice, but start using it now when he is returning automatically. That will simplify your later formal COME-IN training.

Introduction to Cover

Take your pup for romps in all kinds of cover from his earliest days. Let him get familiar with the feel and scent of the conditions under which he will do his life's work. Let him dig for field mice, chase songbirds, catch toads, and plow through every type of cover you can find. Let him romp up and down hills, through trees, across ditches, whatever. However, don't expect him to retrieve in cover yet.

Introduction to Birds

After your youngster returns to you reliably when retrieving in the backyard, and after he is comfortable romping in cover, let him "find" a dead pigeon there. As he romps ahead of you, drop a bird and keep walking. Later turn around and walk back toward it. Let the pup find it.

He may react in any of several ways. First, and most ideally, he may sniff it and grab it up and start running to you. If he does, grasp his collar and praise him, but let him hold the bird for a long time.

He may grab the pigeon and run off with it. If he does, run away from him, clapping your hands and talking excitedly. He will chase after you. After all, he's out in the country, and you are his secondary lair.

He may sniff the bird and show fear. If he does, say nothing, do nothing. Let him investigate on his own. If he doesn't pick the bird up during this first encounter, pick it up yourself, stuff it in your pocket, and act as if nothing happened. Don't hassle the pup over this "failure." Give him another chance the next time out, and the next, and the next, if necessary. If he continues to show fear for several trips, you might try something a little radical: Lay a dead pigeon beside his food bowl when you feed him. Stay out of sight, but observe how he reacts. When he eventually picks the bird up, let him carry it awhile, then step out of hiding and praise him. Go to him and "share" his discovery with him.

He may lie down and start chewing. If he does, snap the flex-lead on his collar and drag him roughly to you.

A word of encouragement: Most spaniels respond ideally to this initial bird contact, or come around soon.

Introduction to Gunfire

During these romps afield, your pup will occasionally flush and chase a songbird, or even a game bird. Great! Wait until he has chased several. Then, when he is some distance from you and highballing after the bird, fire your blank pistol. If he acts startled, ignore him, and keep walking. Let him flush and chase several more before shooting again.

He will probably not notice the first shot. If he ignores it, shoot every time he chases a bird.

Introduction to Water

While introducing your puppy to cover and terrain, you should also help him learn how to swim—assuming the weather and water are not too cold. I have often started spring and early summer litters swimming at four weeks of age. By the time they went to their new homes at seven weeks, every pup was a competent swimmer—no reluctance to enter, no beating the water with the front feet.

On the other hand, I once started a dog swimming after her third birthday. No problem. Sure, she took a little longer to smooth out her stroke and become comfortable in the water, but she went on to become an excellent water dog.

Are there any dogs that just can't adjust to water? The answer depends on what is meant by "adjust." I have never seen a normal, healthy spaniel that could not learn to swim. On the other hand, I have seen several that hated every minute of it, making it impossible for them to handle serious water work. If your pup doesn't come to enjoy water in a reasonably short time, he never will. If water work is important to you, you can save yourself a lot of frustration by starting over with another prospect. If you hunt only upland birds, don't worry about this reluctance to enter water.

You should never start a pup in water by tossing a dummy there for him to retrieve. Never. No matter how he loves retrieving. You would not expect the greatest field hockey player on earth to transfer his skills to ice hockey until he became comfortable on ice skates, would you? Ditto for the spaniel that retrieves on land but has never learned to swim.

The ideal place in which to introduce your dog to water is something like this: a lazy, firm-bottomed stream about twenty yards across with shallows on both sides and about eight or ten yards of hip-deep water in the middle. For very young pups, say those under twelve weeks, it should be even narrower.

Introduce him to water by leading him in. A stream is better than a lake. In a lake, you can only go out so far. If he refuses to follow, you will have to come back eventually. The dog wins. In a stream, you can walk farther away on the far shore, which will make the pup fear that you are leaving him behind.

The stream should be slow moving, of course, so the pup is not washed downstream as soon as his feet lose contact with the bottom. The bottom should offer good footing, too, or he may become frightened. Sinking down in mud to his elbows every step will not give him a good feeling about water.

You want shallows on both sides so the pup can ease in from either side. You will be going back and forth across the water in this work. Later, he will probably jump into the drink with a mighty splash, but initially he will enter cautiously.

Pluis Davern uses clipped-wing pigeons to introduce a young Sussex to retrieving from water. *Pluis Davern*

"Hey! This is fun!" *Pluis Davern*

"Boss, where are you? I've got something for you." *Pluis Davern*

Naturally, you want some swimming water in the middle. Eight or ten yards is plenty. Four or five would be better for the very young pup. He should get his feet back on the bottom quickly after swimming a few strokes.

If your area has such a stream, and it wanders through the property of several landowners, get permission from one of them to train on it and you're set.

Put on some old jeans and a pair of tennis shoes. *Never wear hip boots or waders when introducing pups to water.* They would prevent you from feeling the water temperature.

Walk around in the field adjacent to the stream and let your pup follow you. When you are good and warm—the weather should be pretty hot—wade into the stream and stand in the shallows. If the stream feels uncomfortably cold, get out and keep your pup from getting in. However, if the water is okay, encourage him to follow you in. When he does, praise him and walk up and down in the shallows. Continue to praise him as he follows you around. You might even sit down in the water and pet the dog awhile. Let him learn that following you in walking water is not much different from following you on land.

Through this initial phase, be sure that the pup doesn't get in deep enough to have to swim. Let him become familiar with the feel of water first. Most dogs enjoy it on the first trip, but not all. Adjust your training to the needs of your particular pup.

Next, wade across and encourage your pup to follow. If he has shown a little reluctance earlier, you should try to find a narrow place with no deep water to begin this. That way, he can follow you without swimming, a confidence builder. With most, however, this is not necessary. Just wade across the eight or ten yards of swimming water and encourage the pup to follow. He may balk at first, but if you stay on the other side and keep encouraging him, he will eventually follow.

When he gets to you, really make a fuss over him. Your pleasure in his accomplishment will do much to give the new swimmer a good attitude toward water. Then, wander around in the field on that side of the stream awhile before wading back across. This allows the youngster to warm up again.

Go back and forth several times each session, and praise the pup while he is in the water as well as after he reaches you.

Don't worry if he beats the water with his front feet, and above all don't dream up any clever techniques for curing this "problem." He will work through it in time with no help from you. I have heard of inexperienced (and insensitive) trainers tying weights on a pup's front end, wading along pushing down on his head and shoulders, and God only knows what else. The only thing such nonsense can do is make the pup hate the water. Dumb, dumb, dumb.

Once your puppy is swimming reasonably well back and forth across the stream, have him follow you as you wade in other places. The fact that you seem to enjoy water will affect his attitude. Eventually you can row a boat around for him to follow. Good exercise for both of you. Let him catch up and come aboard occasionally. That motivates the "chase" and makes the boat seem like a wonderful place.

Now, try some short water retrieves. If your pup enjoys water, even if he's not yet an Olympic swimmer, he can handle a few short water retrieves. However, remember both the words "few" and "short." Don't tire him out. Sometimes a water beater will first start swimming properly while returning with a dummy. He may beat the water all the way to the dummy, but level out and swim beautifully on the way back. I have seen this with several dogs. Most recently, it was Rocky.

The author steps off to start heeling "Flick." *Bob Finch*

12

Obedience

BACKGROUND

What Is It?

When a dog trainer speaks of obedience, he/she means a dog's conditioned responses to a series of commands. Different activities require different lists of commands. The list for spaniel training is: HUP, RELEASE, KENNEL, HEEL, STAY, COME-IN, and DOWN.

HUP is spanieleze for "sit." RELEASE frees the dog from control. KENNEL sends the dog into his kennel run, crate, and so forth. HEEL means walk beside the trainer. STAY means remain in position (usually sitting or lying down). COME-IN means return directly to the trainer (do not pass go, do not collect $200). DOWN means lie down.

Why Do It?

To be effective afield, a spaniel must be under control. To be enjoyable around home, a spaniel must be under control.

In the uplands, a spaniel must work close. The dog that punches out too far flushes birds out of the boss's gun range. The dog that chases a missed bird into the next county might flush other birds out of range. When trailing a running pheasant, the spaniel that goes out of control—refuses to stop on command—puts the bird in the air too far off for the huff-and-puffing hunter to shoot—is not under control. In the uplands, it is control, control, control.

In dove hunting on a pond, a spaniel must sit by the hunter. If several other people are hunting the same pond, the dog must concentrate on the boss's birds and ignore those downed by others. And he must wait until sent before making a retrieve. Around a dove pond, it is control, control, control.

In duck hunting, the dog must sit by the blind while the hunters talk fluent duck-talk to distant birds, while the birds circle overhead to check out the spread, while they settle in among the decoys, while they flare as the hunters come up shooting, and (with a little bit of luck) while several dead ducks *kerplop* into the water. Again, the dog must wait until sent before retrieving. In the duck blind, it is control, control, control.

Even around home, the spaniel must be under control to fit in with the family and neighborhood. Sure, at home we buddy around and play with our dogs. But we can only do that if, underneath all the frivolity, we have control. So even at home, it's control, control, control.

Obedience training establishes that control early in the dog's life and lays the foundation for the various types of control training we do for hunting. Each command has many uses in and of itself, but taken together, their most important contribution may well be the manner in which they establish control.

Prerequisites

You can start teaching HUP and RELEASE as soon as the pup knows his name and NO. When he understands HUP and RELEASE, you can introduce KENNEL. For HEEL, STAY, COME-IN, and DOWN, you should wait until the pup is five or six months old. These commands demand more seriousness and a longer attention span than the typical puppy under that age possesses.

Equipment

You need several additional pieces of equipment.

For heeling, you need a chain training collar. Learn to install it properly. It has been designed to allow you to make little rapid-fire jerk-and-release corrections while heeling. To be effective, these corrections should cause the collar to tighten quickly and release quickly. That way, the dog gets the message. If you put the collar on backward, it will neither tighten nor release quickly.

To install the collar correctly, mind your P's and Q's. Hold the looped collar in front of you with the ring that attaches to the lead at the lower left. If you slide the other ring up the chain a bit, you form the letter "P." If you hold it with the lead ring at the bottom on the right, it will form a "Q." If you heel your dog on your left side, the "P" configuration is correct. If you heel him on your right, the "Q" is correct.

One word of caution: *Do not allow your dog to wear a chain training collar when you are not with him.* He could catch it on something and hang.

You need a basic six-foot lead, in either leather or webbing. This is a handy all-round length, and the one preferred for obedience training. For Flick

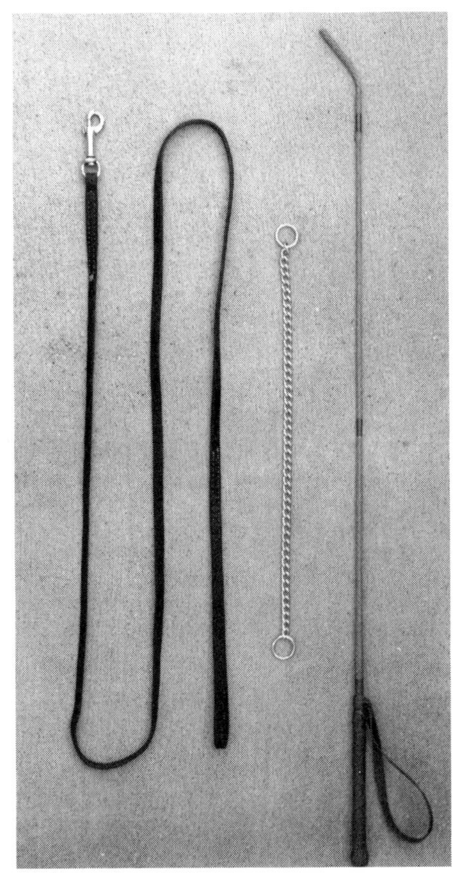

From left: 6' lead, chain training collar, riding crop.

Chain training collar in "P" configuration — for the dog that heels on the left.

Chain training collar in "Q" configuration — for the dog that heels on the right.

Chain training collar installed on "Rocky" — who heels on the left.

at 63 pounds, I use a leather lead, half an inch wide. For Rocky at 37 pounds, I use a three-eighths-inch leather lead.

When you heel your spaniel off-lead, you will need a short, light riding crop with which to remind him where he belongs when he strays.

Schedule

No one can do obedience training on a ''now and then'' schedule. Ideally, you should get in a couple of ten- to fifteen-minute sessions each day. Many working people cannot manage two sessions per day, so they have to make do with one. That's okay, too, as long as it's every day, not every once in a while.

Train when your dog is fresh, not after field work or a play period. Confine him in a kennel run or crate for about two hours before each session. That way, when you let him out for training, he will be jumping out of his skin to work. Training becomes a reward. He will prance through his drills, especially if you keep the sessions short.

How long should obedience training take? Well, in one sense, it is never completed. You will give your dog an occasional refresher throughout its active life to keep its responses sharp and immediate. However, the initial training doesn't take a lifetime. An experienced trainer with a smart five-month-old pup could probably complete the course in ten weeks or less. A green trainer with an average dog might take twenty weeks. Most teams fall somewhere between those extremes. However, since you do obedience training in parallel with quartering (chapter 13), it doesn't matter how long it takes. It isn't holding anything up.

Handling Techniques

I cover handling techniques, as necessary, in the training section for each command.

TRAINING

HUP and RELEASE

Dog training is full of seeming contradictions. For example, the very basis of all obedience training is freedom! The dog must understand when he *is not* on command before he can become reliable when he is on command. Without that understanding, he will take frequent liberties to determine his current status.

Thus, you need a specific release ''command.'' For too many years I have used *okay*, a singularly poor choice because I use it so often in ordinary conversation. I recommend that you choose something you don't use often, like RELEASE, FREE, SCHOOL'S OUT, or HAPPY TIME. Here I will use RELEASE.

HUP! . . . *Bob Finch*

. . . and RELEASE. *Bob Finch*

The release command does something else: *It allows you to praise and pet your dog without releasing him.* Praise and petting can be powerful motivators in training a dog—as long as the dog understands that they don't release him from control. Too frequently one hears such statements as "You can't pet a hunting dog and maintain control." That means the speaker doesn't use a formal release command.

Since RELEASE is so basic to all control training, it would be nice if you could teach it first. You can't, obviously, for until you teach some other command, you have nothing from which to release your dog. However, you can do the next best thing: You can teach it second, right after HUP.

To teach HUP, put a collar and six-foot lead on your dog. If he is a puppy, use the strap collar. If older, especially if difficult to control physically, use the chain collar.

Get your dog's attention and command HUP. Since he has no idea what that means, you must force compliance by pulling up on the lead and pushing his fanny to the ground. He is now sitting, even though involuntarily. While you continue to hold the lead taut, praise lavishly. If he tries to move—which he will—say NO! HUP! and push his fanny down again. Then, praise again. You are already teaching the youngster that praise doesn't mean release. Keep him sitting a few seconds, correcting every move and praising whenever he is sitting correctly. Repeat HUP often, too.

Now, say RELEASE and force the pup out of the sitting position. Play with him awhile. Then, repeat the sequence again: Command HUP, force the dog into position, praise, correct every movement, command RELEASE, force him out of position, and play again. If possible, do this about half a dozen times per session. The dog will quickly learn what HUP means, what RELEASE means, and he will at least suspect that praise doesn't mean freedom.

Don't try this off-lead yet, no matter how well your dog obeys. Later on, in your field work, you will need an immediate response to your HUP whistle signal when your spaniel is highballing the other way at some distance. If you insist on a quick response now, maintaining it later will be easier. If you remove the lead too soon, your pup will potter a few seconds before sitting—and you will learn to accept that—thereby forming a bad habit. Keep him on lead and insist that his posterior hit the ground immediately on HUP.

Extend HUP so your spaniel will do it when you blow a single sharp blast on your whistle. Called "stopping on the whistle" and "hupping on the whistle," this is the basis for steadying a spaniel after a flush. It is also the single most important command in blind retrieve training, for "if you can't stop 'em, you can't handle 'em."

Blow the whistle, immediately command HUP, enforce compliance if necessary, then praise. After a few times, your youngster will hup on either the voice or whistle command. Later on, in your post–field training romps, stop him on the whistle about once every five minutes. This will benefit you greatly when you get into steadying and blind retrieve work. Insist on immediate compliance every time you toot the stop whistle.

KENNEL

Next teach KENNEL, which means to go into the run, crate, doghouse, or even a boat. This introduces a type of control that makes the dog easy to live with, easy to hunt with, and easy to travel with. It requires only minimal control, for it involves just one simple act: Move into the place you indicate.

If you have a kennel run for your dog, use it to teach KENNEL. If not, use a crate—one with a wire door, so your dog can see you from inside. That is important, as you will see.

Put the collar and lead on your dog. Now, open the gate to the run (or crate) and command KENNEL. Again, your dog has no idea what you want, so guide him with the lead. As soon as he is in the run, close the gate. Now stand there and praise the pup. This extends the notion that praise doesn't mean release, for the gate blocks your dog's exit.

After a few moments, open the gate, say RELEASE, and encourage him to come out. Play, romp around, anything to make sure he feels no restraint.

Repeat the whole thing five or six times during each session. Command KENNEL, pull the dog in with the lead, shut the gate, praise awhile; then command RELEASE as you open the gate; play again to make sure he feels complete release. Before long, he will go in voluntarily when you command KENNEL. The praise you give when he is inside encourages this response. Once the youngster shows he understands KENNEL, you can use a light form of punishment for refusals and slow responses. Jerk the lead a little as you lead the laggard in. Whenever you punish, praise him after he is in the run. He should come to associate praise with compliance, even when forced.

After he obeys KENNEL readily, extend the meaning of RELEASE. Until now, the pup has come out when the gate opened, and he probably thinks the gate gives this freedom rather than RELEASE. Now you can teach him differently.

KENNEL and praise him normally. Open the gate slightly, but do not say RELEASE. He will try to come bouncing out, of course. Shut the gate in his face, commanding NO rather sharply. Then, be lavish with praise—this first time can be a bit of a shock to a sensitive youngster. Open the gate again and immediately command RELEASE. If he is reluctant to come out, encourage him to come to you—and then have a good play session.

Repeat this several times. When you open the gate and the youngster hesitates until he hears RELEASE, you are making your point. Gradually delay the time lapse between opening the gate and saying RELEASE. Naturally, until you are certain he will stay inside, don't open the gate too wide. If he escapes, put him back in the run and start over.

The only verbal correction you should give when he tries to escape is a sharp NO. Don't repeat the command KENNEL. You will become a better trainer if you minimize duplicate commands.

Above all, do not command STAY when shutting the gate in the pup's face. You will later teach STAY as a very strict "don't move" or "freeze" command. On KENNEL, you necessarily allow him to move around within the run. If you

Getting ready to put "Rocky" in dog box.
Bob Finch

KENNEL!
Bob Finch

Don't forget to praise for obedience.
Bob Finch

command STAY instead of NO to prevent an escape, you set yourself up for some serious training problems when you teach the more rigid meaning of STAY.

Once your pup understands RELEASE, extend it to everyday life. He should come to know that RELEASE frees him every time, not just when he is sitting or in the kennel run. When you take him for romps, always turn him loose with RELEASE. If you confine him to some area in the house when guests are visiting, let him out afterward with RELEASE. When you return from an on-lead walk, say RELEASE as you remove the lead. And so on.

Also extend KENNEL. Use it not only to get the dog to enter the run, but also a crate, a dog trailer, a car, and a boat.

HEEL

The dog that heels walks beside the handler, typically on the left side. When the handler stops, the dog hups beside him. This is a convenient skill for any civilized canine, regardless of breed.

I prefer waiting until the dog is five months old to start this. With a soft pup, six or seven months might be better.

Your goal is to train your dog so well that he heels reliably off lead. The slowest possible way to get there—absolutely the slowest—is to try off-lead work frequently before he is ready. Like all control training, this is a conditioning process, not a learning experience as we use the term in human education. You condition the dog to perform properly on lead until it becomes second nature. Even then he will need periodic refreshers when his off-lead responses become sloppy—which they will from time to time.

You condition your dog by rote drill. However, to do this successfully, you must adopt the attitude that you are teaching your dog to take full responsibility for knowing where you are and for sticking by your side continuously. That attitude will prevent you from making the most common beginner's mistake, namely "steering" the dog with the lead.

If you steer the dog through these heeling drills, he will never be properly conditioned. He will learn to follow the direction of the pressure on his neck. In human terms, you are remaining responsible for your dog's position and direction.

The chain training collar is one of the simplest but cleverest pieces of dog-training equipment ever invented. Properly installed, it tightens up *immediately* when you jerk on the lead, and releases *immediately* when you slack off. Tightened and loosened in a series of sharp jerks, these corrections don't drag the dog into position. They "induce" him to move voluntarily into the proper position. As soon as he returns to the proper position, the tugs stop and the lead goes slack. That conditions the dog to pay attention and stay where he belongs.

If the jerk-and-release technique were used alone, this training would be a negative process. The dog would come to heel in a hangdog manner. A lot of dogs are so trained—and show it!

You are more fortunate than most, however, for your pup already under-

Step off with your left foot when you start heeling. *Bob Finch*

Keep the lead loose while heeling — except to make jerk and release corrections. *Bob Finch*

stands that praise does not mean release. You can praise when he is doing things correctly without losing control. If you do that when your young charge is heeling correctly—and especially right after every correction—he will not only learn what you want more quickly, but will also enjoy heeling.

Now, some good news. Your dog—any dog—can only make six mistakes in heeling: lagging, forging, swinging wide, crowding, jumping up, and lying down. Each calls for a slight variation on the basic jerk-and-release-plus-praise technique:

Lagging: The dog is uncertain. Give fairly gentle tugs and talk encouragingly as you do. When he catches up to you, praise lavishly. Don't slow down or stop. If you do, you will soon find out that he is training you.

Forging: This is a bold, aggressive dog. Let the beast get ahead of you, then turn and go in the opposite direction. When he hits the end of the lead, apply a series of jerks. Don't slow down—in fact, you might go a little faster after you turn with this character.

Swinging Wide: The dog is expressing independence. Turn 90 degrees away from him and, when he hits the end of the lead, give a series of jerks. If he is hardheaded, speed up as you turn.

Crowding: The dog is sensitive and feels safer when touching you. Normally, no jerks are necessary. Just turn into the dog frequently, bumping him away as you do. If he is not too sensitive, give a series of fairly light jerks away from you—nothing too rough here, for the dog is trying to do things properly but is just being too cautious.

Jumping Up: Either the dog doesn't know that this is training, not playtime, or he is trying to con you into forgetting about training. Either way, give a series of sharp jerks down, say NO! HEEL! and keep on walking. Praise this dog calmly. Excited praise may incite another demonstration of playfulness.

Lying Down: This is a real problem. The dog is either frightened or trying a new method of training you. It is hard to tell which. If you are sure it is the latter, force the issue: Start walking, command HEEL, and jerk the dog along. If you are right, he will get up and play by your rules. If not, he will freeze on his belly. Stop then—don't drag the dog. He is frightened. Find out why and work him through it before continuing.

The way you walk can help or confuse your dog. He will key off your left leg (assuming you heel him on your left side, which I recommend). By moving that left leg consistently you help him maintain the proper position. Here are the handling techniques I recommend:

1. When starting to move from a stopped position, step off with your left foot as you command HEEL. Later, you will step off with your right foot for STAY.
2. When stopping, bring your left foot up to your right as the last step. Also, don't stop abruptly—slow down gradually.
3. Round your left and right turns to help your dog follow you.
4. When reversing direction, turn away from the dog; don't turn into him.

Okay, you now know how to walk and how to correct your dog. However, you don't do either automatically. A new trainer and an untrained dog can have unbelievable problems until the trainer gains some minimal level of competence. To avoid this poor start, don't bring the dog into the picture until you are comfortable with your part of the routine. Use a friend, spouse, or offspring instead. Put the chain collar on his/her right wrist and heel him/her until you are comfortable with your job. I have "played dog" for a number of beginning trainers.

Practice the basic foot patterns while heeling your surrogate canine. Have him/her simulate the six mistakes. Make the proper correction for each until it becomes instinctive. Practice those sharp little jerk-and-release corrections, and practice the immediate praise, too.

However, if any nondoggy person sees this seemingly insane process, you may end your training session running from someone with a butterfly net!

When you feel yourself ready, put the collar and lead on your dog, toot your whistle sharply to get him to hup, then command HEEL and step off at a moderate pace. He won't have any idea what HEEL means, of course, but will gradually learn to avoid the uncomfortable jerks by staying in place beside you. It is unfortunate that you can't sit down and explain—as you could to a child—exactly what you want. You must communicate through the lead and collar. You can minimize the negative and maximize the positive by giving your young spaniel as much praise as possible.

Stop frequently and toot the HUP whistle. This does two things: it gives the dog a command he understands in the midst of all this confusion, and it starts the "automatic" hup, in which he hups each time you stop.

The average spaniel will figure out what you want rather quickly. Then, vary your speed—normal, slow, normal, fast (run a bit)—just to convince him that he must always adapt to your speed. No sudden bursts, no sharp reductions of speed. Just the kind of changes of pace that could occur in a day's shoot.

After your dog heels nicely in the backyard, introduce distractions. Have family members come out and talk to you and to the dog, but insist on good heeling—all on lead, of course. When your spaniel has adjusted to that, have someone bring another dog (on lead) into the yard, and force your dog to heel in spite of the distraction.

Finally, take your dog to a shopping center. There are so many distractions in shopping centers that they make ideal final proving grounds for many obedience commands.

In your field training sessions, heel to and from the line, but keep your dog on lead for months. Even after you are confident that he will heel properly off lead, only try it now and then. Use the lead most of the time.

When you feel he can handle off-lead heeling, use a riding crop to tap him when he strays. If he shows you he's not yet ready, go back to the collar and lead. Ditto any time he gets sloppy.

STAY

STAY means "do not move," "freeze." You should *not* use it to bring your dog under control, but only to lengthen the period of control. You should teach your dog to STAY in a sitting position first, then later while lying down.

STAY has many uses. In blind retrieve training, you use it when you teach your dog to take hand signals. You position your dog, command STAY, walk some distance away, turn and give the appropriate hand signal. In dove and duck hunting you occasionally must station your dog some distance from the blind. If he doesn't understand STAY, the quality of your hunting deteriorates—as well as your relationships with your hunting partners. Around home, STAY has an important application. For example, when guests arrive, you should be able to delay an enthusiastic canine greeting until everyone is seated.

However, STAY is not a magic solution for all canine behavior problems. Most especially, you should never use it in an attempt to bring an unruly dog under control. If, for example, your dog is about to jump up on you, do not command STAY. Say NO, HUP. If your dog is about to make an "illegal" exit from his kennel, command NO! Reserve STAY for keeping the immobilized dog in place for a period of time.

Start teaching STAY as soon as your dog shows signs of understanding HEEL, surely within a week or so of starting HEEL.

STAY is, perhaps, too simple. You ask the dog to sit there and do nothing, which is no great accomplishment, really. Most spaniels learn this quickly, and thereby mislead inexperienced trainers about how far along they really are. You see, it is one thing to sit still in the backyard with no real distractions, but it is quite another matter to stay put in a hunting situation with birds flying, guns going off, and excited hunters moving and shouting. If you are to get the kind of response you want under any circumstances, you should introduce a variety of temptations for movement into the training. This takes time.

Start STAY training with your dog sitting at heel. Command STAY, and step around with your right foot so that you are standing facing the dog, and immediately in front of him. In heeling your dog has come to key off your left leg, but now you are blocking his path before that leg moves. Eventually, your dog will learn that the right foot lead means STAY and the left foot lead means HEEL.

After stepping around to block your dog, stand there, praising the pooch, and occasionally repeating the word STAY. If he attempts to move, command NO, reposition him, and repeat the STAY—then resume praising.

What constitutes a move that should be corrected? Personally, I feel you should allow normal head movements, but not any movement of the feet or rump. Not even slight shiftings. If you never allow them, your bright young spaniel never has to wonder how much is too much. I must admit that Flick has "nervous feet," but he doesn't move from the spot. I should probably correct him, but it hasn't created a problem—yet.

After a few moments, move back to the heel position. Praise again, then heel awhile. Try to STAY two or three times in each session.

After the dog obeys STAY under these ideal conditions, move a little farther away when you step around in front. Continue to step directly in front, right foot first, but then back up a few feet. If the dog moves, correct him. Actually, this is a good time for him to make mistakes, while you are close enough to make quick corrections.

Next, command STAY and step straight off with your right foot. Don't block your dog. Walk straight ahead to the end of the lead and turn to face him. If he remains in place, move a little to one side, and then to the other. Walk back and forth, back and forth. Then, return and praise.

Each time lengthen the distance, and widen the path you walk to either side. Keep the lead on, but drop it from your hand as you move farther away. Eventually you will be able to walk all over the backyard while your dog sits in place. The first few times you go behind him are critical. The animal will be strongly tempted to move around just to be able to see you better, so stay close for a few times. If he moves, you will be in a better position to make the correction.

When you can walk all over the backyard while your dog remains in place, eliminate the lead and tempt him to move by running instead of walking. If he moves, correct quickly and start over. When he can handle this, clap your hands, sing, talk loudly, whatever as you run around the yard. After a few corrections, a bright youngster will sit there like granite no matter what you do. But that is just the beginning.

Next, introduce all the standard backyard distractions: family members, other dogs (under control), and so forth. When your spaniel sits rock steady through all these, take him to a shopping center. After that, your dog has completed his basic training in STAY. It only remains for you to use the command frequently and insist on absolute obedience every time.

COME-IN

Next to HUP, this is your best tool for bringing your dog under control.

Teach COME-IN by both voice and whistle. Over the dog's life, you will use the whistle signal more often, especially afield, where the human voice can spook birds.

The COME-IN whistle can serve you well around home, too. At least twice a day I let my dogs out of their runs into the (fenced) backyard for a romp. Occasionally one of the gates is open by mistake and my dogs take off for an adventure. When they do, one of my neighbors calls and says that he just saw

Step off with your right foot for STAY. *Bob Finch*

Eventually you will be able to walk all over with your dog on STAY. *Bob Finch*

"Flick" does an enthusiastic COME-IN on the whistle. *Bob Finch*

To teach DOWN, grasp the dog's front legs and help him down. *Bob Finch*

The dog can't help obeying. *Bob Finch*

my herd heading south (north, east, or west). I grab a whistle lanyard, go out in the yard and start blowing the COME-IN call. In a few minutes, they come trotting back from wherever. That is so much easier than getting in the car and driving all over the neighborhood looking for them.

Continue to use whichever whistle signal you started out with in puppy play-retrieving (*twee-twee-twee-twee*, or *tweeeeet-tweet-tweet*). Your spaniel already suspects what it means.

For a verbal, some use COME or COME-IN. Some use HERE. Some even use HEEL. Take your pick, but be consistent.

Start teaching COME-IN as soon as your dog understands STAY. Leave the dog (on lead) in a STAY, walk away a few paces, command COME-IN (or whatever) and lightly pull him to you. At first, he may think COME-IN is just another distraction to tempt him to move from a STAY. Eventually he will understand that other commands can override STAY, but at first there may be some confusion and reluctance.

As he gains confidence, move farther away before you command COME-IN. Eventually you should be able to call the dog to you anywhere in the yard. One caution: If you call your dog to you every time you leave him in a STAY, you will damage his reliability on STAY. You should only call him to you about once in every four or five STAYS.

Next, bring in the whistle signal. Command COME-IN, and as he starts, blow the COME-IN whistle signal. And so on.

DOWN

DOWN means to lie down, to drop, normally from a sitting position. An optional command, one I have occasionally omitted for a dog's entire life, it nevertheless has its uses. Sometimes, in dove or duck hunting, your dog is less conspicuous lying down. Even around the house, you can usually keep your dog on a STAY command longer in the down position.

Start with your dog sitting on lead as you kneel in front of him. Command DOWN, grab both his front feet, and pull them straight toward you. He cannot avoid lying down. Praise just as if he had done something wonderful as soon as his belly hits the ground.

Place one hand on his withers to prevent him from rising. Continue kneeling. Repeat DOWN several times and praise often. After a few moments, step around beside him, command HEEL, and walk off.

Repeat this until he lies down without help when you command DOWN. Then, stand up beside him. If he tries to get up, force him back down, praising as soon as he is again in place. After he remains down with you standing, command STAY and move a short distance away. From that point, you just repeat the STAY training process with the dog in this new position.

Laura Reeves casts her Clumber off into his quartering pattern.

Darrell Reeves

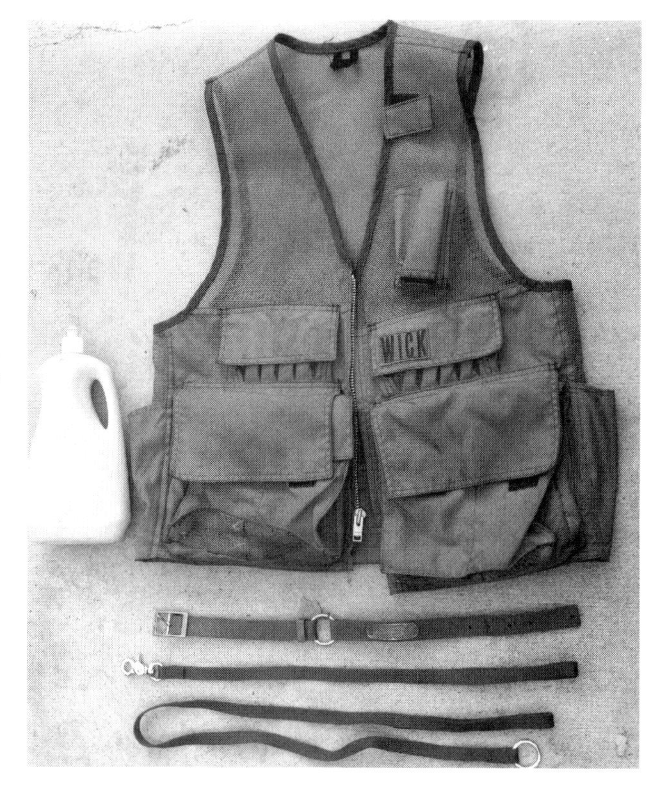

Training vest (with ventilated bird-pockets in front), water bottle, strap collar, and line-lead.

13

Quartering

BACKGROUND

What Is It?

A spaniel that quarters hunts in a ''windshield-wiper'' (or ''flat'') pattern back and forth in front of his handler. The dog stays well within gun range at all times, which means different things to different gunners. Some talented shotgunners carry full-choked weapons and encourage their spaniels to range out to thirty or thirty-five yards (which can make a typical shot forty to fifty yards). Those of us who are less talented with the scatter-gun prefer open-bored guns and spaniels that stay within fifteen or twenty yards.

Hunting into the wind, the quartering spaniel should run very flat, extending each cast about the same distance on either side of the gunner. Hunting with the wind, the dog should swing a little wider to give his nose a chance. In a crosswind, the dog should swing wider on the downwind side, making his pattern a ''banana'' curving from near the hunter to substantially downwind on the foreward cast. Each pattern allows the dog to wind all the birdy areas within gun range.

Why Do It?

Quail and pheasant hunting here in the Midwest sometimes does not lend itself to flat-pattern quartering. We often hunt along hedgerows, along the edges of grainfields and wooded areas. In such situations, all the good cover may be on one side of the hunter. I must admit that, while hunting such spots, I don't insist on flat-pattern quartering. Instead, I allow my spaniel to "seek objectives," as bird dog folks say, as long as he stays within range. I use three commands: RELEASE (verbal), which turns the dog loose to hunt as his nose and instincts direct; STOP (whistle), to keep him from getting too far ahead of me; and COME-IN (whistle), to keep him from swinging too wide to either side. This approach allows me to get the most out of my spaniel's nose and instincts while keeping him within open-bore shotgun range.

However, I teach flat-pattern quartering to every spaniel. Why? Well, first off, it's quite handy when hunting in many types of cover, even here in the Midwest.

Second, I run my spaniels in hunting tests, where flat-pattern quartering is required (whether anyone admits it or not).

Third, it so supports the rest of spaniel training that I can't think of a good reason to avoid it. I must teach the dog to hunt and seek game, so why not teach quartering simultaneously? Ditto for developing a bold flush, steadying to wing and shot, and so on.

Finally, it's too much fun to miss. Most spaniels have an instinct to quarter (some more than others, of course), so why not bring it out while training? It also extends the teamwork between handler and dog nicely, which helps in all other training.

Prerequisites

You can start quartering when your spaniel is quite young, as long as he is familiar with cover, retrieves dead birds to you reliably, and has been started into gunproofing.

If you have not exposed the youngster to all sorts of cover, do it before starting this training. Otherwise, he will be too engrossed in the many new scents to concentrate on quartering.

Retrieving is essential in teaching a spaniel to quarter, as you will see. The dog that doesn't yet deliver birds reliably will not make much progress.

Early in this quartering training, you will start shooting birds over your spaniel's flushes. If you haven't yet gunproofed him (per instructions in chapter 11, "Puppy Training"), go back and do it before you start quartering.

I prefer to have a pup sitting on the whistle reliably before starting it in quartering. Many trainers don't bother with this, but it does make controlling the dog so much easier. I also like to have him coming in on the whistle, for the same reason. But most of all I want to be able to stop him reliably, in case he hightails it too far out for my comfort. I depend on the stop-whistle to maintain my spaniel's range.

Equipment and Facilities

Your training grounds can be quite simple: a few acres of light to medium cover far enough from civilization to allow you to shoot a shotgun safely. To simplify this work, you should start out on relatively flat ground. Ideally, you should have several such places.

Also, you should train on grounds near a lake, stream, or pond, especially in warm weather. Quartering in the heat of summer can make a dog sick. In extreme cases, it can cause death. To avoid such a tragedy, keep your dog wet.

Carry a bottle of drinking water, too. Most spaniel trainers use small plastic detergent bottles with squirt tops. Rinse one out thoroughly and carry fresh water in it whenever working (or hunting) your spaniel. Dogs learn easily to drink from the squirted stream of water.

Wear a hunting or training vest in which to carry your squirt bottle and the birds your dog retrieves to you.

You need a shotgun and shells. You need pigeons in three configurations: dead, "clip-winged" (or "clips"), and flyers. Clips are live birds with the flight feathers removed from one wing only (to throw them out of balance so they cannot fly any distance).

After your spaniel is doing good work on pigeons, you will need game birds occasionally—as often as you can afford them, actually.

You can get by without assistants, but you will do better if you work with at least two other trainers. Then you can take turns handling your dog and shooting while the others handle theirs. In this chapter I describe training with and without assistants. I recommend the former whenever possible. Most of us have to train alone sometimes. Read both sections and switch back and forth as your circumstances dictate.

Schedule

This training is an extension of puppy field work. You should do it in parallel with obedience training (chapter 12) and single marked retrieve training (chapter 14). Within a month or so, your spaniel will have a decent pattern, but it doesn't end there. You can spend the rest of his life perfecting it. Just to keep him reasonably sharp and in shape, you should continue this training during the off-season for the entire active life of your spaniel. Besides, it's almost as much fun as hunting.

Handling Techniques

You need a special whistle signal to tell your spaniel to turn when he finishes his casts. Tradition dictates that this be a soft two-toot call, which I think of as a *pip-pip*. This signal differs from the single sharp blast that means stop. It also differs from the COME-IN signal (*twee-twee-twee-twee*, or *tweeeet-tweet-tweet*).

Your handling methods during this training change from one extreme to the other—rather suddenly—somewhere in the middle. Initially you "overact" significantly to condition your spaniel to respond to your directions by association. You *pip-pip* on the whistle every time he turns at the end of a cast. You wave your arm in the direction he is going as he runs past you on every cast. After that conditioning is well established, you back off and handle only when absolutely necessary.

Your goal is a trained spaniel that requires minimal direction from you, one that does the work right on his own. Anytime you handle your dog, you necessarily distract him from his job.

Yet you want to be able to handle him when necessary. When he doesn't complete a cast, you need the ability to turn him quickly and send him back to complete that cast. A quick *pip-pip*—at most a *pip-pip* plus an arm signal—should do it—every time. If he fails to investigate a particularly attractive piece of cover, you should be able to wave him into it easily and reliably.

You have only two choices in your approach to such training: force or association. Force requires long ropes and a lot of jerking around—or worse. As you may have guessed already, I'm against that approach.

Association is painless. You go through your handling routines—*pip-pip* on the whistle, arm signals this way and that—when your dog is doing what you want anyhow. He associates what he is doing with what you are doing. As Pavlov demonstrated with his bell and salivating dogs long ago, your dog will come to respond correctly to your handling techniques by association, by conditioning.

Another handling consideration: How fast should you walk as your spaniel quarters? That depends on his nose. You should never push him faster than his nose allows. If in doubt, slow down. The objective is to cover the ground completely, not to get to the "finish line" first.

Whenever your dog fails to complete a cast, stop and stand there while you insist that he cover the ground he missed. In general, walk slow enough and stop often enough to allow your dog cover the ground completely. On the other hand, don't potter along so slowly that he covers every inch several times.

TRAINING

Starting Out with Assistants

If you have the luxury of two assistants, you should start this training with a technique called "shaking."

Position one assistant about ten yards to your left, the other about ten yards to your right. Face directly into the wind. Each assistant should have a few dead pigeons in his vest.

Hup your dog in front of you, facing you. Hold his collar to keep him in place. Have one or the other assistant talk excitedly to your dog, call his name repeatedly, all the while shaking a dead pigeon near the ground. When the pup is going crazy to get the bird, wave an arm in that direction and release your grip on his collar.

If all goes well, your dog will race to the pigeon. Great. Just as the pup gets there, that assistant (let's call him assistant number 1) should raise the bird

"Shaking," step 1: Peggy Ruble handles "Luke" as Lin Boucher shakes a dead pigeon to induce him to run her way.

"Shaking," step 2: As "Luke" reaches Lin, she raises the pigeon out of his reach.

"Shaking," step 3: "Luke" runs toward pigeon Sheryl Finch shakes.

"Shaking," step 4: "Luke" almost reaches Sheryl's pigeon. Out of the picture, Lin throws her pigeon in.

"Shaking," step 5: "Luke" winds pigeon on ground when he returns to Lin.

"Shaking," step 6: "Luke" delivers pigeon to Peggy Ruble.

up out of reach and stop talking. The other assistant (number 2) should start talking excitedly to your pup and should shake a pigeon near the ground. As your pup turns to race to this other pigeon, *pip-pip* your whistle and give an arm signal toward assistant number 2.

If all goes well, your dog will run to the other pigeon. Just as he gets there, assistant number 2 should raise it up and stop talking. Immediately, assistant number 1 should start talking and shaking. *Pip-pip* on your whistle and wave your arm as your dog turns toward him.

As the pup races back toward assistant number 1, assistant number 2 should surreptitiously toss his pigeon on the ground about five feet directly in front of him. He should not allow the pup to see him do this. You want your dog to find the bird on the ground with his nose on his next cast that way. Assistant number 2 should also take out another dead pigeon to shake.

When the dog swings back to assistant number 2, he will wind the bird on the ground. He will pounce on it and retrieve it to you. That's why you waited until he learned to deliver to you reliably. This should never become a catch-me-if-you-can game.

Continue this shaking technique for two or three retrieves, but quit before your pup tires. After a session or two, you and your assistants can start walking forward. That way, the dog is actually quartering ahead of you, not just running back and forth in one area. However, you should set the pace, and your assistants should stay even with you. While walking, your assistants should toss their pigeons far enough ahead so the dog doesn't pass them upwind.

But what if all doesn't go well? What if your pup doesn't race from one "shook pigeon" to the other? Rocky didn't at first. He looked at the talkative assistant as if to say, "What's your problem?"

I had the assistant toss the pigeon about five feet ahead while Rocky was looking at him. Rocky ran over to make the retrieve. After a few of these, he got into the shaking game with abandon.

To encourage the pup to run straight back and forth, you should walk in a zigzag pattern yourself. Move with your arm signals. For a few sessions, you may cover almost as much ground as the dog. Later, you can back off and walk straight ahead while directing spaniel traffic with whistle and arm signals.

To maintain the pup's interest, you should let him find a bird every second or third cast. Later you can have him quarter longer and longer between retrieved birds. But not at first.

Starting Out without Assistants

With no assistants, you have to teach quartering almost by example. Stuff a few dead pigeons in your game bag and toss them in behind your dog (when he is not looking, of course). Preplant one bird to start on.

Work into the wind. With your spaniel sitting in front, facing you, wave your arm toward the first bird and start walking in that direction. Continue until he finds the bird. Let him retrieve it to you. Then wave your arm in the opposite

Laura Reeves demonstrates how to train without assistants. She has sent her Clumber off and then tosses a bird behind him (nice and high for the photographer).
Darrell Reeves

The Clumber finds the bird. *Darrel Reeves*

The Clumber delivers to Laura.
Darrell Reeves

direction. Walk that way a few yards. Then get your dog's attention, turn and as he turns with you, *pip-pip* on your whistle. After he passes you, toss in a bird behind him. Don't let him see you do this. Then turn and work him to that bird. And so on.

After a few sessions, your dog will get the idea and bounce off happily in the direction you indicate. Let him find a bird on his initial cast until you are convinced that he understands the game. Then work him longer and cast him back and forth a few times between birds. *Pip-pip* the whistle as you turn each time and give him an appropriate arm signal for each cast.

Clipped-Wing Pigeons

If you are training with assistants, you can discontinue shaking when your dog has learned to run to or past each assistant on his casts. The assistants should then walk along quietly on either side of you. They can also spread out a little more each session until they reach the full twenty to twenty-five yards. Continue directing your spaniel with whistle and arm signals. Every few casts, have one or the other assistant toss a dead bird in when the dog is going toward the other assistant. Your dog should never see an assistant tossing a bird in.

Whether you have assistants or not, as your dog becomes proficient at this basic quartering game, start using clipped-wing pigeons instead of dead birds. When the dog dives in to retrieve the bird, it will flap its wings and try to fly away. However, it won't be able to fly, so the dog will catch it.

This encourages a bold or "hard" flush, which is highly regarded in this country. The dog that never catches a bird comes to believe he cannot catch them, so he pauses when he scents a bird. Some even start pointing. The more birds a dog catches, especially those trying to escape, the harder his flush.

Flick once started going soft on pheasant flushes even though he was hard enough on pigeons. I realized I hadn't been giving him enough clipped-wing pheasants in training. I gave him a few just before a hunting test and he performed beautifully. In fact, one of the judges commented later that Flick had a real kamikaze flush.

Shoot a .22 blank pistol as the dog chases a clip. The dog is so focused on the bird that the sound will not disturb him.

When you are convinced the youngster can handle the sound of the gun this way, start giving him a few live flyers. For this, assistants are really nice. They not only dizzy and "roll in" the flyers, they also shoot them while you handle your dog. You can do it all, but you should try to work with assistants if at all possible.

As you quarter your spaniel, you or your assistants should roll in dizzied pigeons behind your dog—when he is not looking. Your dog should not see the bird being rolled in. If he does, he will turn his attention to you and your assistants instead of working the cover as he should.

A properly dizzied pigeon will sit tight long enough for the pup to flush it. Too little dizzying and it flies away too early. Too much and it doesn't fly at all,

"Rocky" flushes a clipped-wing pigeon to flight . . .

. . . but "Rocky" catches up.

The pigeon reverses its field, but "Rocky" is ready.

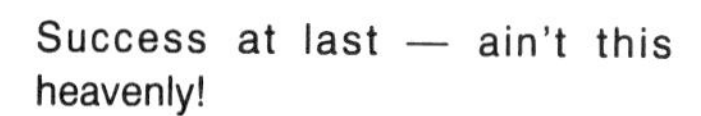

Success at last — ain't this heavenly!

but lets the pup catch it on the ground. You and your assistants will learn how much dizzying to do with experience.

When everything goes right and the dog flushes the flyer, let him chase it well out of gun range, then fire a shotgun in the air. Don't try to kill the bird. Do this a few times to make sure the sound doesn't disturb your pup. Then start shooting them for him. Ride each bird out as far as possible. That allows the chasing pup to get farther from the sound. You should also shoot only high birds, for your dog won't be far behind.

When the bird falls, the dog will be almost on top of it. Getting the bird in its mouth right after the shot will strengthen the notion in the dog's mind that gunfire is a good thing.

If all goes well, start mixing clips with flyers. The clips keep the dog's flush hard. The flyers simulate real-life hunting. If he softens up on flush after several flyers, give him a few clips. When he's flushing boldly, give him flyers. I usually try to give the dog two of each in each session.

Keep your sessions short. After three or four birds give your dog a rest and act as an assistant for one of your training buddies. In hot weather, keep your dog wet, in a well-ventilated crate, and well supplied with drinking water.

Planted Birds

Since you or your assistants are rolling in all the birds, your spaniel finds all the birds close in. He has no reason to range out far. He is running a very close pattern. He may even swing behind you sometimes. You need to move his pattern out in front of you a little. To do that, you use planted birds, which he will smell at a distance (since you are still going into the wind all the time).

Load three or four live pigeons (clips and flyers mixed) in your vest. Have your dog where he cannot watch you. Walk down the centerline of the course. Dizzy and toss the first pigeon fifteen or twenty yards to one side. Walk another fifty or sixty yards, dizzy and toss another pigeon off in the opposite direction. And so on. You walk down the centerline and toss pigeons some distance to the right and left to keep your dog from learning to trail you to the birds.

With planted birds on the course, your spaniel will hit scent from some distance. He will race in and flush birds farther from you than he has in the past. Enough of this and he will run his quartering pattern farther out, as you wish. Too much of it and he will reach out (''punch out'' in spanielese) too far, flush birds out of gun range.

Thus, your training becomes a balancing act. When your dog stays too close, you work him on more planted birds. When he punches out too far, you work him on rolled-in birds.

Anytime he gets out of gun range, even if he has a snootful of bird scent, you should stop him with the whistle. You need that level of control when hunting. Catch up and release him. He will soon understand that being stopped like that is only a temporary interruption, not an end to his pursuit of the bird. If he punches out too far out when not trailing a bird, call him back with the

COME-IN whistle. Occasionally toss a bird right in front of you before you do this, so he will find it as he comes to you. That encourages a prompt COME-IN. If your dog refuses the COME-IN whistle, use the STOP whistle as a court of last resort. Stop him and make him wait until you catch up. Absolute obedience to the STOP whistle is essential to controlling your spaniel's range. Never accept a refusal. And train on it often.

Game Birds

After your spaniel is handling flyer pigeons well—flushing boldly, chasing happily, retrieving nicely—you should introduce game birds into the program. But you should back up a step or two to do so. Never ask your youngster to flush a live bird until he has retrieved similar dead ones often enough to show you he likes them.

If possible, go from pigeons to the next larger bird, and then the next larger, and so on. Have your dog retrieve a dead chukar a few times. Then have him flush live chukars while quartering. Next, try hen pheasants. If all goes well, move up to rooster pheasants.

Many spaniels will move comfortably from pigeons to rooster pheasants. However, some are a bit more cautious and need the gradual buildup through chukars and hen pheasants. If you know dogs well enough to tell the difference, go with your instincts. If not, play it safe and start with chukars.

You can make clips out of each game bird species. In addition to pulling flight feathers from a pheasant, tie a short string between the bird's legs. Just enough to hobble it a bit, not enough to immobilize it.

In planting a chukar or pheasant, you can either dizzy it or "put it to sleep." Most prefer the latter, especially with pheasants. Tuck the bird's head under one wing, lay the bird down on that wing, and stretch the legs out until the bird relaxes. Then leave quietly.

Wind

So far you have done all your quartering into the wind. Now that your dog has a good pattern that way, you should run him with the wind and in quartering winds at least some of the time.

He will learn how to use the wind most effectively under all circumstances. But you must learn to let him do this. He will swing a bit wide going with the wind, and within reason you should let him. He will banana front and back in a crosswind, and again, within reason you should let him. As long as he is working the wind effectively and putting birds up within gun range, let him do it as nature indicates. Only if he gets too far ahead or behind you should you use your whistle and arm signals to direct him.

To keep his basic pattern appropriately flat, do most of his training work into the wind. Anytime he gets ragged because of different wind directions, go back to into-the-wind quartering to straighten him out.

Terrain and Cover

Terrain variations can destroy your young spaniel's pattern. He will tend to stop uphill casts too short and extend downhill casts too far. Or if the land drops off sharply on one side of the course, he will end his casts short of the drop-off.

Run him in every terrain situation you can find. To help him run a good pattern, walk this way and that yourself, use your whistle and arm signals to direct him more—*and let him find birds where you want him to go*. Plant birds way up the hill, or down past the drop-off, and keep working him in the proper direction until he finds them. Once he figures out where the birds are, he'll go there happily.

Ditto for cover variations. Plant the birds in every cover situation you can find, and work him through them until he finds the birds.

Author signals Sheryl Finch to throw a single marked water retrieve for "Rocky". *Bob Finch*

14

The Single Marked Retrieve

BACKGROUND

What Is It?

In a ''marked'' retrieve, the dog sees the bird fall and ''marks'' its location. The term ''marked'' distinguishes this retrieve from the ''blind'' retrieve, in which the dog does not see the fall but is directed to the bird by the handler.

Spaniels do two kinds of marked retrieves: nonslip and quartering. In a nonslip retrieve, the dog starts sitting at heel. These happen mostly in dove and duck hunting. In a quartering mark, the dog hups after flushing a bird some distance from the handler.

Marked retrieves may be ''single'' or ''multiple.'' In a single marked retrieve (also a ''single mark'' or a ''single''), only one bird falls for the dog to retrieve. In a multiple mark (''double,'' ''triple,'' ''quad,'' ''quint,'' and so on) two or more birds fall before the dog is sent to retrieve any of them.

Why Do It?

Why train specifically for nonslip, marked retrieves? During training for quartering, a spaniel gets many retrieves. The dog flushes a bird; one of your training buddies shoots; the bird falls (well, most of the time); your spaniel retrieves it. Marked retrieve? Hey, if the dog didn't mark it, how did he find it? Case closed, eh?

Wrong. Initially, your spaniel was in hot pursuit when the bird fell. He was almost on top of it. That is marking with a small "m." Later, after being steadied, he will flush and hup. Then his retrieves will be much longer, much more difficult. Marking with a capital "M." If you don't do some specific training for longer marks, young Tangle-Coat will miss a surprising number of shot birds.

Terrain changes, cover variations, and unusual winds can make seemingly simple falls quite difficult. For example, if a bird falls beyond a deep ditch, as your dog goes through the ditch, he loses eye contact with the spot in which the bird fell. When he arrives on the other side, everything looks different. Ditto for falls across creeks, on the other side of heavy cover patches, and over groves of trees. Anything that makes the dog lose eye contact with the spot he has marked will confuse the inexperienced spaniel.

If you want to see a really confused dog, shoot a bird so it falls on the far side of a second creek. You know, in a place where a winding creek doubles back on itself so that the dog must cross it twice to get to the bird. Dogs not specifically trained for such situations will almost invariably hunt the ground between the two bodies of water instead of crossing the second.

These situations won't happen in quartering training often enough for your spaniel to figure them out on his own. But they will happen often enough in actual hunting to make it worth your while to train him specifically for them, using the nonslip approach.

Two more compelling reasons for doing this training: The line-steadying in nonslip retrieving prepares the dog for the more difficult steadying to wing and shot; and the honoring here prepares him for the more difficult honoring in brace work.

Prerequisites

This training is an extension of your backyard play-retrieving (chapter 11). You should do it in parallel with your quartering work (chapter 13).

Equipment and Facilities

The additional equipment you need for this includes several retrieving dummies, a dummy launcher, a couple of launcher dummies, and a "belt cord." A belt cord is a short (three-foot) piece of stout cord with a loop on one end. You attach the loop to your belt and slip the other end through the dog's collar. You double that end back on itself and grasp it in your left hand to control your dog. Until you release your grip, your spaniel cannot leave your side. That is how you use it for line-steadying.

Initially, you need a large field (like a park) with closely clipped grass. I call this "bare ground." It allows you to build your dog's confidence during the

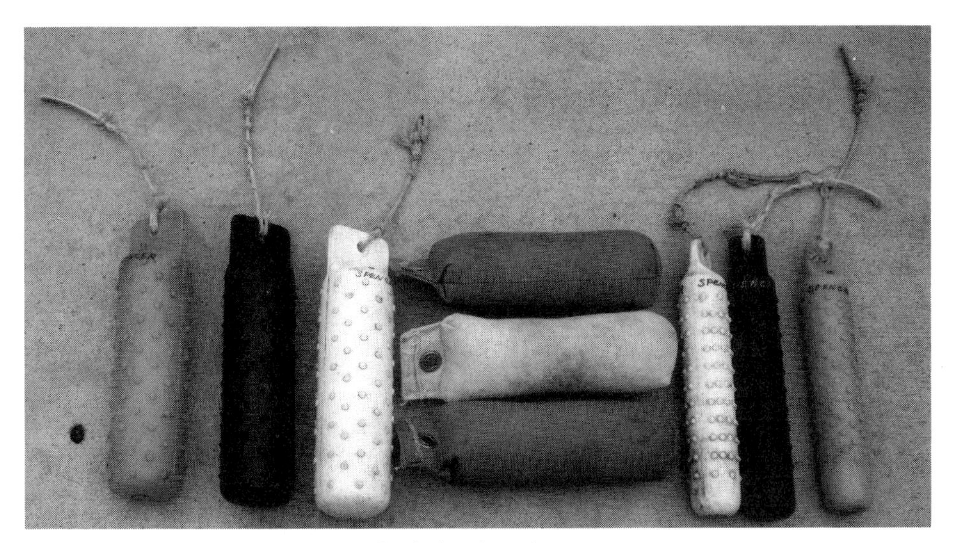

Retrieving dummies.

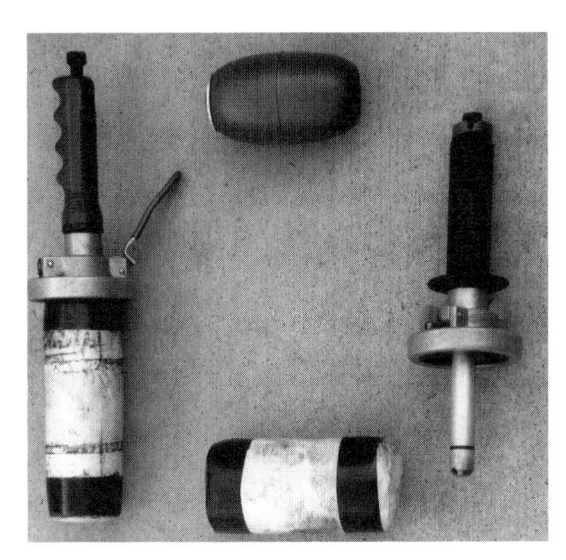

Dummy launchers and extra dummies.

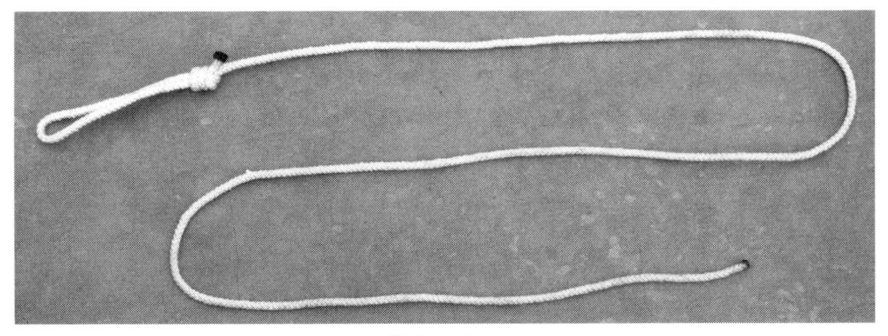

Belt cord.

early stages of this training. The area should be large enough for one-hundred-yard retrieves.

Schedule

If you do this in parallel with quartering, your spaniel should be reasonably proficient at nonslip retrieving when you start steadying him to wing and shot while quartering. You should continue nonslip retrieve training all through his active life. It will keep his marking sharp and allow you to work on any specific type of fall he may have trouble with.

Handling Techniques

Follow the KISS system (Keep It Simple, Stupid). Heel your pup on lead to the "line" (starting point). Face the clearly visible thrower. Signal for the throw only when your dog is sitting at heel concentrating on the thrower. Use the belt cord until you have completed line-steadying.

TRAINING

Two Techniques

There are two techniques for nonslip retrieve training: you can locate an assistant at some distance from you and have him throw birds or dummies while you handle your dog, or you can fire dummies from a .22 blank-powered dummy launcher.

The advantages of having an assistant throw for you are: It facilitates line-steadying; you get accurate placement of falls, which is especially important when you rerun a mark (which you should most of the time); you can use birds as well as dummies; and your assistant can help your dog out when it cannot find a particular fall. The disadvantage is that the falls don't look much like those a spaniel normally runs into while quartering.

The advantages of the dummy launcher are: The flight of the dummy simulates that of a flushed bird quite nicely, and you can train alone when you don't have an assistant. The disadvantages are: Operating the launcher keeps you too busy to line-steady your dog; you can't get accurate placement of falls, especially for reruns of troublesome marks; and you can't use birds.

I recommend that you use the assistant for all initial training and the dummy launcher for polishing. With the assistant, teach your dog about ditches, patches of cover, groves of trees, crossing two creeks, and so on. Then use the launcher to keep your dog sharp. Steady with an assistant. Then extend steadiness with the launcher.

Introducing an Assistant

Introduce the assistant to your spaniel in your backyard. You should use only short retrieves and white dummies. Hup your pup at heel facing the assistant. Naturally, young Tangle-Coat doesn't know what that "other guy" is doing out there, so he may ignore him. When you signal for the throw, the assistant should holler "Hey! Hey! Hey!" to get the dog's attention before throwing the dummy.

He should toss the dummy in a nice high arc so that it falls about fifteen or twenty yards from him (the assistant). He should not throw the dummy straight at or straight away from the dog and handler. Either will encourage the dog to run to the assistant instead of to the dummy.

Let your pup break to retrieve, but give the command to retrieve as he does. When he picks up the dummy, blow the COME-IN whistle and encourage him to return.

Your pup may try to deliver the dummy to your assistant. Some pups learn the correct procedure—always bringing the dummy to the handler—easily. For these, you only need blow the COME-IN whistle, run away, and clap your hands during his first few returns. Other pups grasp this concept slowly. For such a dog, start out placing your assistant in an inaccessible spot, such as in a pickup bed or on the other side of a fence.

Lengthening Falls on Bare Ground

Next, extend the distance your dog retrieves, out to about one hundred yards. Bare ground facilitates this because the dog will find the dummy every time. Even then, trick your dog into not noticing that the falls get longer and longer. Position your assistant in one place and have him make every throw the same. Then establish three "lines" (positions from which you start a retrieve), the first about twenty yards from the helper, the second about thirty-five yards, and the third about fifty yards.

The assistant should have at least six white dummies. That way he will only need to replenish his supply between dogs, which saves a lot of time. He should carry the dummies in his vest, not toss them on the ground at his feet.

Heel your youngster on the belt cord to the line at twenty yards. When the pup "locks in," signal for the throw. The assistant should toss a dummy and fire a shot. As your dog breaks, give your command to retrieve. With a white dummy on bare ground, he should run right to it. As he does, you should run back to the next line (thirty-five yards). When he brings the dummy to you, he will not even notice that his next retrieve is almost twice as long as the one he has just completed.

Signal for another throw from the thirty-five-yard line. As your pup sails after it, run back to the fifty-yard line. When he brings the dummy to you, have him do a couple or three retrieves from there.

In one lesson, you have stretched your dog out from backyard distances to fifty yards. In the next session, set the closest line up at thirty-five yards, the middle one at fifty, and the far one at seventy. In each session the lengths should be increased until one hundred yards is no problem to the dog. All through this process, let the dog break.

Line-Steadying

Your young spaniel has learned to do retrieves out to one hundred yards on bare ground. Before you move him into cover, you should line-steady him, that is, train him to sit at heel until sent to retrieve.

Why on bare ground? To eliminate all problems not directly associated with the line-steadying process. If you were to line-steady in cover, your dog would fail to find the dummy too often. A dog that is struggling to break just cannot mark a fall. On bare ground with white dummies, he will complete every retrieve, no matter how tangled you and he get as he struggles to break and you struggle to restrain him.

Your basic line-steadying tool is the belt cord. The secret of using it effectively lies in leaving it slack as the pup sits beside you. A slack belt cord doesn't let him feel your control until he tries to break. Then it snubs him quickly. The dog comes to believe that some mysterious force prevents him from breaking. Similarly, since the dog doesn't feel the slack cord loosen as you give the command to retrieve, he comes to feel that your command removes the mysterious force.

If you pull the cord up tight, the dog can feel physical restraint before he attempts to break. He can also feel it slacken when you send him to retrieve. He learns to remain steady as long as he can feel the restraint, and to break when it disappears. That is definitely *not* what you want. You should teach the dog that only your command releases him.

Until now, you have given the command to retrieve as your dog broke. You did this so he would associate that command with the act of leaving to retrieve. Now you make that association stronger by teaching the dog that he cannot leave until he hears that command.

Set up a simple bare ground retrieve of about forty yards, using a white dummy. Rig up the belt cord. Signal for the throw, and brace yourself. As the dog breaks, jerk him rudely back into position, saying NO! HEEL! From now on, you will use these words (followed the optional expletives of your choice) as a verbal correction for breaking.

The first few retrieves can be hectic. The dog may stand up and paw the air. He may flip over on his back. He may tangle the belt cord around your legs. No matter what happens—even if you wind up on the ground with him—get him back sitting at heel before giving him the command to retrieve.

After a few sessions, when he shows that he has begun to grasp this strange new idea, you can pause longer and longer before releasing him. Don't get ridiculous about this. Four or five seconds is plenty. Actually, it is more important that you vary the pause than that you lengthen it significantly. If you establish a predictable rhythm, he will start jumping the gun on you.

Proper use of belt cord in line-steadying. *Bob Finch*

Line-steadying with an assistant. *Bob Finch*

Some people give a signal with their left hand along with the command to retrieve. I view this as superfluous, even distracting, in a single.

You can tell when your pup is locked in and ready only if you look at him before you send him. Watch the fall until it hits the ground, but then turn your complete attention to your dog. This is much like the "keep your head down" maxim in golf.

Vary the length of the retrieves during this process, from very short to one hundred yards. The short ones offer the greatest temptation to break. The longer ones build his confidence. When he was allowed to break, he may have covered twenty or twenty-five yards while the dummy was in the air, so his one-hundred-yard retrieves were really only seventy-five or eighty yards. Now, they are a full one hundred yards.

Honoring

Once your spaniel is reasonably steady, have him honor while another dog retrieves every chance you get. Use the belt cord, and correct him quietly when he breaks (lest you disturb the other dog as it goes to retrieve). This nonslip honoring, being so much simpler, is an excellent preparatory step for the later honoring in brace work.

Moving into Cover

After your spaniel is line-steady and handling bare ground retrieves out to one hundred yards, you can move into cover.

On bare ground, your only real concern has been distance. That is only one dimension in cover work, where you must also be concerned about terrain variations, cover variations, and wind direction. Actually, distance is the least important factor in cover.

However, keep the distances short while introducing the other factors. Give your dog plenty of short retrieves in all sorts of cover and terrain, and add distance gradually. In cover he may fail to find dummy or bird. If he fails too often, especially at first, he may become discouraged and lose interest in retrieving. Trial and success can teach him more and faster than trial and error.

Use two techniques to minimize failures: reruns and "salting."

Rerun your dog on every mark he doesn't "step on" or "pin" (do perfectly). This not only builds his confidence, but it also develops his marking ability. The first time he runs a test, he learns where the dummy is (even if he has been helped); in the rerun he sees the fall from the line again while knowing exactly where it is. He fine-tunes his marking much as a marksman sights in a rifle.

"Salting"—scattering several dummies in the area of the intended fall before you run your dog—can also be helpful at first. If the pup gets to the area, he will find one of those dummies. Occasionally a dog picks up two dummies,

Honoring. Mike's English Cocker retrieves while Chad's English Springer honors.

"Salting."

Rocky hits the water big. *Bob Finch*

or drops one and picks up another. A little of this is nothing serious, but it should not be encouraged, so discontinue salting as soon as possible.

Never salt with pigeons. If the dog picks up two pigeons, he may mash one, which could be the first step in your spaniel developing a hard mouth—a serious fault.

Even with salting, your dog will sometimes fail to find the dummy. When that happens, you have only two choices: You can signal the assistant to help your dog out; or you can walk out there and help him yourself. I prefer the former, for I have had two dogs that decided that they shouldn't even leave the line without me after I helped them a few times. That is a nasty problem to deal with, and should be avoided. I have never had a problem with a dog that has been helped exclusively by the assistant.

Give your dog every opportunity to find the dummy on his own. As long as he is hunting aggressively, even if he is some distance from the area of the fall, leave him alone. Spaniels tend to hunt a large area when having difficulty with a fall. Often such a dog will work things out for himself, which will do much for his confidence.

However, when he shows you that he can't find it, either by returning toward you or by wandering off uninterestedly, you should signal the assistant to help him out. The assistant should walk toward the dummy and holler "Hey! Hey! Hey!" to attract the dog back into the proper area. If possible, the assistant should not pick the dummy up but should simply walk close to it and holler to bring the dog closer. That way the dog finds the dummy on the ground. If this doesn't work, the assistant should pick the dummy up, show it to the dog, and drop it again where it was.

As your youngster works through these problems, gradually lengthen his retrieves and incorporate various cover, terrain, and wind hazards. Wind can be tricky. Downwind retrieves are to be preferred because they force the dog to drive deeper to scent the bird. Crosswinds away from the assistant make most tests easier, for the dog only need swing a little wide to use his nose. Crosswinds into the assistant complicate things because they tempt the dog to run behind the helper where scent from the dummies in his vest can confuse him. Upwind retrieves are too easy.

Retrieving in Water

Water work should lag behind land work throughout your training program. Why? Three reasons: Water is a more difficult medium; you cannot easily correct mistakes there; and your pup should develop a good attitude toward water from the start, so he should be very successful there.

His initial water retrieves should follow closely after his introduction to swimming (chapter 11). As soon as he shows that he enjoys swimming, you can start tossing puppy dummies a few feet in the drink for him. Keep them short. Keep them fun. Keep him successful.

By the time he is well into his bare ground marking drill work, before you line-steady him, he should be doing short water retrieves that you throw for him.

Don't lengthen his retrieves as rapidly in the water as you have on land. If you rush him along faster than he is ready to go, he will eventually refuse to enter the water. When that happens, you have two choices, both bad: You can accept his decision not to retrieve, and let a "no-go" habit start; or you can force him in some manner, and start a bad attitude toward water. Any refusal at this point is a losing proposition, so don't press him any faster than he seems willing to go. Very important.

Another thing that will help prevent refusals is plenty of praise from you when the dog reaches the dummy. Let him know you are pleased, and he will want to repeat the performance.

At first, your dog's delivery will probably not be too good. He will stop as soon as he is out of the water, drop the dummy, and shake the water out of his coat. You can deal with this in two ways: Start running the other way as soon as he gets to the shore, and shout encouragement to him to follow you; or meet him at the edge of the water and take the dummy before he can drop it. Above all, don't show any disapproval of his delivery, no matter how bad. He must think water is more fun than anything, so any displeasure from you is counterproductive.

However, you should be concerned about another delivery problem, if it occurs. Some dogs return near shore and stop to play with the dummy instead of bringing it on in to you. This can become a nasty problem in a hurry.

To deal with it, first completely cure any return problem on land before asking the dog to retrieve in water. Then, if he refuses to leave the water, put the flex-lead on him and force him to come to you, with or without the dummy. Do this until he has no thought of playing games with you. If you eliminate the flex-lead too soon, the dog will learn that he has to return when it is on and can do as he damned well pleases when it is not.

If your dog is still beating the water with his front feet as he swims, keep his retrieves short. Frequently a pup beats the water on the way to the dummy and then swims properly on the return. Once he starts this, it is only a short time until he will swim properly all the time. After he is over the water beating, you may safely start toughening his water marks up a bit. There are two dimensions to this process: length and cover.

It is safer to work on length first, and save cover until after the dog is very comfortable with fairly long water retrieves, say seventy-five yards, and has been line-steadied. Always use large white dummies as you lengthen his water retrieves. Their visibility will prevent him from giving up partway there, another form of refusal.

What should you do if your dog does refuse? Normally, with a young spaniel, you should admit you overtaxed him, back up a few steps, and try to prevent another refusal. If your thrower is young and athletic, have him swim out, holler to get the youngster's attention, and toss the dummy up again—and again and again until the pup gets to it.

Set up all water marks so your pup will not be tempted to run the bank, going or coming.

During this lengthening process in water you will probably start line-steadying on land. Since you can't allow him to break in water while insisting that he be line-steady on land, interrupt the lengthening process in water, go back to short water retrieves, and do the line-steadying on both land and water simultaneously. Once this is completed, you can resume lengthening your dog's marks in water.

When your dog is retrieving in open water out to about seventy-five yards and loving it, you should start introducing cover work in water.

There are three different cover situations: cover in the water where the dummy falls; cover in the water between the line and the fall; and falls on land (in cover) across water.

The last is the easiest to set up, but the least beneficial to the dog. You see, if the dog becomes convinced that the dummy is *always* on land, he will run the bank. Most of your water marks should fall in the water rather than across it on land. An occasional land-water-land retrieve is fine, but don't overdo it.

Throw as many marks in cover in water as possible. However, initially make sure that your assistant can help your dog out if he fails to find the dummy. This means sloshing around in the pond, something everyone in your training group must be willing to do.

Cover between the line and the mark is more difficult, so should be added only after the dog is comfortable with retrieves in which the only cover is around the fall. Don't rush things. Remember: success, success, success. Every failure in this early water work is a disaster.

Shorten up when you start tossing water marks in cover. Let your dog develop confidence in his ability to do the work before making it difficult. Since a dog swims so much slower than he runs, he must remember each water mark much longer than a land mark of equal distance.

If you work your dog in stump-infested water, check for underwater stumps where your dog will enter. If he leaps in, he could seriously injure himself on such a stump.

Some dogs take naturally to water with cover in it, while others are a bit spooky. I have had one or two that acted like the lake was full of ghosts if there were stumps, brush, and other visible obstructions between the line and the mark. Interrupt retrieving and wade around with such a dog until he is more comfortable there.

Introducing Decoys

If you plan to hunt ducks with your spaniel, this is the time to teach him to leave decoys alone. You certainly don't want to send him after a strong cripple someday only to have him stop short and bring you a decoy, do you?

Start on land. The backyard's okay. Scatter several decoys around. Then put your dog on lead and heel him around through them. Every time he tries to sniff a decoy, jerk up on the lead and say NO! After a few corrections, he will ignore the decoys. Then, set up a simple retrieve. Toss a dummy off to one side of the decoy spread and send him for it. If he veers toward the decoys, holler NO! If he persists, go shake him up, and start again.

After he can handle retrieves off to the side, make things a bit tougher—toss the dummy beyond the decoys, so he has to run right through them. Correct him if he even sniffs one as he goes through. Next, toss the dummy right in the middle of the decoys.

When he can handle this bare ground work, move into *shallow* water. Heel him through the decoys, just as you did in the backyard. Then, toss a dummy off to one side—and so on.

Why not start out in water? You want to correct your dog in water as infrequently as possible, so you do the initial work, when he is most apt to need correction, on land. Take him to sea only when you know he will not need a correction.

After your dog is decoyproofed, use them in his water marks frequently. Let them become old hat to him, things that are always there and can be ignored. Place them close to the line at first, then farther out, and finally near the fall itself.

One caution: Never use pigeons in the water, especially pigeons that have been frozen and thawed several times. They are delicate, and your spaniel could get a mouthful of fresh meat. I have seen several normally soft-mouthed dogs eat wet pigeons in water.

Training with a Dummy Launcher

This is a polishing rather than a teaching tool. Therefore you should wait until your spaniel is through all the above training with the assistant before starting it. Or you can use it in parallel, but lagging behind, work with an assistant. I would recommend that you wait at least until you have line-steadied your dog.

Even then, start out by having your assistant fire the launcher while you tend to your dog. If you do the shooting, your spaniel will quickly learn how easily he can break—or at least creep—while you are occupied firing the launcher.

After your assistant has fired it for you long enough for you to convince young Tangle-Coat that he must remain steady for this new retrieving game too, you can start firing the launcher yourself. You can then simulate all manner of the tricky falls and make them more like the falls he will see in actual hunting.

Reruns are difficult because you cannot hit the same spot twice with the dummy launcher. However, if you save the launcher for polishing only, you should be able to get close enough. Your spaniel should hunt a big enough area to find your slightly errant shots after a short hunt.

Mike Tillotson shoots the launcher for "Molly," his English Cocker.

"Molly" delivers the launcher dummy.

HUNT-DEAD

Your dog won't see every bird you knock down, especially when he flushes a covey and you hit two or three (quit kidding) on the rise. Maybe you knock down a dove while your dog is busy retrieving another one. Or maybe a buddy hit a bird while out of sight. Whatever the reason, you have a pretty good idea where the bird is, but your dog didn't see it.

The easy way to pick up such birds is to heel your spaniel to the spot, tell him a bird came down around there, and watch him hunt busily until he finds it. That is called a hunt-dead. Teaching it is so easy that no upland hunter should leave it out of his spaniel's repertoire.

Start out in the backyard. Before getting your dog out of his run, toss a dummy or dead bird down in plain sight. Get your dog and heel him near the dummy or bird. As soon as he sees it, release him and say HUNT-DEAD (HUNT-EM-OUT, SEEK DEAD, or whatever you prefer). He will dive in eagerly and retrieve it.

After a few of these on bare ground, move into light cover. When he shows you he understands this new game, start him from farther away. Then move into heavier cover. And so on until he handles these hunt-deads anywhere. Your hunting buddies will be impressed. Don't tell them how easy this is to teach.

Trailing

You can teach your dog to trail running birds by extending the hunt-dead. Before planting the dead bird, drag it a short distance through the cover. Lead your dog up to the start of the trail and command HUNT-DEAD. He will pick up the scent and trail it to the bird. You can extend this as far as you care to. I know one professional trainer who does this after dark. He turns a clipped-wing bird loose in cover, waits five minutes, and brings his dog to the starting point. He says HUNT-DEAD, and off the dog goes into the darkness. In a short time, the dog comes back with the outraged bird in his mouth. I was really impressed when I saw—well, no, witnessed—this demonstration the first time.

Toss the dummy away from the dog. To get all the training elements in these pictures — dog, handler, dummy in air — close enough to be seen, I had to set them up rather than shoot them in actual training. I felt the improvement in visibility was worth it. *Bob Finch*

Walk out and pick up the dummy yourself about half the time. *Bob Finch*

Let your dog retrieve the other half. *Bob Finch*

15

Steadying to Wing and Shot

BACKGROUND

What Is It?

A steady spaniel flushes his bird, hups as it flies away, and remains sitting until sent to retrieve, or—if the shooters miss—until recast into a quartering pattern.

Why Do It?

Many hunters do not steady their spaniels. Some even claim the chasing dog recovers more cripples than the steady one. They say the dog is closer to the fall, so it gets to the running bird sooner. Maybe so. But the break-and-chase model spaniel has some drawbacks, too. If the bird flies low (as many quail do), the hunter may not be able to shoot because of the close proximity of the chasing dog. Regardless of the bird's flight path, if it gets away unharmed, the dog in an uncontrolled chase will disturb a lot of cover out of gun range and delay the hunt unnecessarily. Hen pheasants are a constant problem for the hunter with an unsteady spaniel.

The chasing dog will not mark difficult falls as well as the steady dog. Bouncing eyes just don't see things properly.

Some hunters compromise. They steady their spaniels to wing and shot but allow them to "break to fall," that is, break to retrieve if the bird is hit. That eliminates the uncontrolled chasing of flyaways and allows the dog to mark almost as well as the steady dog. These trainers steady their spaniels normally (to wing, shot, and fall), then encourage liberties when a bird folds aloft. All the encouragement most dogs need is consistently quick commands to retrieve. I call such dogs "semisteady."

A semisteady dog cannot do brace work because he would interfere with the other dog's retrieves. Bad form. Could even lead to a scrap over a bird. It is also much harder to keep such a dog steady to wing and shot.

The (completely) steady spaniel is a joy. He does his job as merrily as the breaker, but under complete control. He's never in the way when you want to shoot. He marks the falls as well as his genes and training allow. He never holds up the hunt, or flushes a bird out of range during an uncontrolled chase.

The steady spaniel is also a source of pride to his owner, an ego trip if you will. Most of his hunting buddies have never trained a dog to do anything. They regard the most basic training as some sort of voodoo magic, beyond the abilities of all but a gifted few. When they see a steady spaniel operate—quarter swish-swish-swish, flush boldly, maybe even leap high as the bird escapes, hup nicely in place (!), and then retrieve on command—well, by God, the guy who trained that dog has to be some kind of genius. They will believe this even if, maybe especially if, the owner demurs quietly, disclaiming any special talent, saying something like, "Aw, shucks, guys, I didn't do much training. This dog's the genius." Ah, it's fun to be modest when your audience refuses to agree with you.

The truth is, steadying a spaniel is not all that difficult. It takes some good basic techniques, some time, and some patience. But it doesn't take a canine magician. Steadying is a conditioning process. That means many repetitions of a conditioned response under a variety of circumstances over an extended period of time. That means a *gradual* increase in the level of temptation to break. It means maximizing trial and success, minimizing trial and error.

Prerequisites

Your spaniel should have developed a good quartering pattern. He should quarter nicely in any combination of cover, terrain, and wind conditions.

He should have a solid flush. That indicates that he loves birds, which is a necessary prerequisite for steadying. Granted, some dogs flush harder than others, but before you steady your dog, he should put his birds in the air confidently, showing no fear, no hesitancy. If he flash-points, he should do it boldly, with eagerness, not in a manner that indicates doubt or fear.

He should stop *reliably* on the whistle. If you can't stop 'em, you can't steady 'em. If you have followed the program described in the puppy training and obedience chapters, you have so conditioned your spaniel to hup on the whistle that it never occurs to him that he could do otherwise. Flick was so conditioned to turn to face me before hupping on the whistle that he turned his back on the bird the first time I tooted him to stop after a flush. He sat there facing me, glancing anxiously back and forth between me and the escaping bird behind him. He quickly figured out that he didn't have to face me when a bird was in the air, but he continued hupping quite reliably.

Your spaniel should be line-steady in his nonslip retrieving work. If he won't stick around when sitting at heel, how will you get him to do so when he is twenty-five yards away?

Given these prerequisites, each spaniel's temperament dictates when he is ready for steadying. Very tough dogs need more control earlier than very soft dogs. Fortunately, very tough dogs can handle the prerequisite training earlier than very soft dogs. If yours is a hard-case spaniel, he might be ready for steadying at nine or ten months old. If yours is super soft, he might not be ready until he is eighteen to twenty months. Most spaniels fall somewhere in that range.

Equipment

You need no additional equipment for this training. If you have homing pigeons, you can use them here, but they are not necessary.

Schedule

The initial steadying shouldn't take longer than three or four weeks. However, once you start steadying, you never finish. If you ease off a bit, your dog will start breaking again. Only constant vigilance keeps a spaniel steady. In the opinion of many experienced spaniel owners, the rewards are more than worth the effort.

Handling Techniques

You need no additional handling techniques for this training.

TRAINING

Preliminary work

If you have been giving your dog frequent romps after training sessions, you have a perfect setup for the preliminary work with a retrieving dummy.

Tuck a small white plastic dummy in your training vest. Why a dummy rather than a bird? To start at the low end of the temptation scale. Birds are for later. Why white? So both you and your dog can find it easily wherever you happen to toss it. Why hide it in your vest? Well, if your dog's like mine, he won't really romp if you carry a dummy where he can see it. He will hang around you, expecting a retrieve.

Let your dog out of his crate and release him for a romp. Let him roll for a few minutes. Then, when he is some distance from you, attract his attention, and toss the dummy high in the air. Throw it in the opposite direction from the dog. That way you can intervene if he refuses your stop whistle.

As he starts to run after the dummy, blow the stop whistle. If you have done the preliminaries correctly, he should stop. If he does, stand in place and praise him for obeying. Very important in the initial stages of all training. If he doesn't stop, *do not blow the whistle again*. Instead, block his path, grab his collar, and take him back to where he should have stopped. Hup him there and toot the whistle again as you do. Now, back up until you are where you were when you blew the whistle the first time. Toot it again. Praise the dog. He's doing it right now, even if you forced him. He needs the praise, the reassurance, after a correction.

If he ran some distance before stopping, walk calmly to him, grasp his collar, and return him to the spot on which he should have stopped. Hup him there, tooting the whistle as you do. Do not scold or otherwise punish this dog. On the other hand, don't praise him until he is where he belongs. He did it right, but not fast enough. He must learn—and the sooner the better—that the stop whistle means "here and now," not "at your earliest convenience." Once he is in the proper place, return to where you were when you blew the whistle, toot it again, and praise him.

Whether he stopped on his own or with your assistance, walk out and pick up the dummy yourself. You might walk backward so you can watch your dog. If he breaks, grab him, reinstall his fanny where it belongs, and start toward the dummy again.

After you have retrieved the dummy, put it back in your vest, return to your original position, praise your dog again, and release him for more romping.

When he seems to have forgotten the incident (which means when he stops looking to you for another throw), repeat the drill. This time, if he stops, send him to retrieve the dummy.

Do this only three or four times per session. Let him retrieve about half the time. If you let him retrieve all the time, he will stop-and-go on you. To keep him solidly steady, keep him guessing as to whether he will retrieve the dummy.

After a few sessions, when you are confident that your spaniel will stop *every time*, toss the dummy off to one side instead of straight away from him. And so on, until you can toss it right directly over his head and depend on him stopping. Take your time. You win nothing for crossing the finish line first. But you lose a lot by pushing your dog too fast. If he starts breaking, you have to go back and start over.

During this process, your dog may begin to hup as soon as he sees the dummy in the air, before you blow the whistle. Great! Just what you want. Continue blowing the whistle, but be encouraged that he is making the correct association between the flying object and hupping in place.

Next, do the same drill with a dead bird. Start out throwing behind you, then off to the side, finally directly over your dog's head. Again, take it slow.

Next, toss the dummy off to the side, rather than straight away. *Bob Finch*

Then, toss it right over the dog's head. *Bob Finch*

When your spaniel is rock-steady with dummies, try a dead pigeon. Straight away first, then off to the side, and finally right over his head, as in this picture. *Bob Finch*

Stopping to shoot. *Bob Finch*

Next, use a clip-winged pigeon. Start by tossing it behind you, and so on. Don't try to toss it over the dog's head, for pigeons being such unpredictable critters, it might land on your hupping dog's head. That you don't need.

All through this work, let your dog retrieve about half the time. And mix up the sequence. Don't, for example, have him retrieve the second throw each day, but not the first. If you do, he will learn to anticipate what you will do on each bird.

If you plan to use your spaniel in brace work, you should also condition him to hup when he hears a gunshot, or "hup to shot." That way, when his bracemate flushes a bird he doesn't see, he will hup when the guns sound. You can begin conditioning him to hup to shot as soon as he is stopping reliably on the whistle with the dummy. Occasionally fire a shot before you blow the whistle. Maybe once every three times. That will transfer the conditioning to the gunshot with no corrections whatsoever. Painless training.

Flyaways

If you have never steadied a spaniel before, you are probably amazed at how easy it has been so far. Even if you have done it before with a more forceful method, you are probably amazed at how much control you now have over your dog, and how little punishment you have meted out. This is the way steadying should be.

Next, introduce your new control into your spaniel's quartering work. Start out with flyaways. That way, if he chases uncontrollably, he won't get to retrieve the bird. If you have some homing pigeons, use them. They will get you through this phase a lot cheaper than common pigeons (commies), which fly away never to return.

Mix in plenty of clips with your flyaways. If you work your dog on four birds per session, make two of them clips, the other two flyaways, and in random sequence. The clips keep your dog's flush solid, and keep his motivation up. The flyaways are your training birds.

Mix planted birds with rolled-in birds, to keep your dog's pattern good through this work. Remember: planted birds to stretch him out, and rolled-in birds to flatten him out.

Start out working into the wind. That makes your dog's pattern easier to maintain. It also makes finding the birds easier. As in all quartering work, two assistants make this training easier. They can roll birds in. If you don't have assistants, you can do it all yourself.

When your dog flushes his first flyaway, let him chase a reasonable distance, say until he shows signs of realizing he won't catch the bird. Then blow the STOP whistle. He should stop and hup automatically—at least if you have completed all the above steps thoroughly. If he doesn't, run out there and make him do it. Then, go back to the preliminary work until he has it down better.

If he stops properly and hups, praise him and blow the COME-IN whistle.

When he reaches you, give him a drink of water and resume quartering. Let him catch a clip or two before encountering his next flyaway.

Gradually stop him closer and closer to the flush on these flyaways, until you are able to stop him quite close to the flush. If you do it properly, it all happens so gradually he almost steadies himself.

One important point: Never try to stop him right at the flush; always let him drive through the bird and a bit beyond before blowing the whistle. If you toot too soon, you will soften his flush. You may even start him pointing.

All through this process, sometimes fire the gun as the bird flies away, but always after you have successfully stopped the dog. Remember, you have taught him to hup on the sound of a gunshot and you don't want to mess that up. But shooting after he has hupped will help with the next step, in which you will start shooting birds over him.

Shot Flyers

By now, your dog should be hupping near the flush. He may even be hupping automatically, that is, before you toot the whistle. Great, but toot it anyway, just to reassure him that the rules still apply. Personally, I'm the belt-and-suspender type who prefers to blow the whistle for every flush for the dog's entire active life. Others gradually dispense with it. Either way, it's too early to skip it yet.

I ruined Flick's first shot at a qualifying score in the master level of AKC hunting tests by not blowing the STOP whistle after he had hupped automatically. Since I usually toot the whistle regardless, he took my silence as permission to break to fall, which he did. I stopped him before he reached the bird, but that wasn't good enough in the master level. I never made that mistake again, believe me.

You can now give your spaniel his first shot flyer. You should have two assistants for this work. One will do, but two are so much better. Let them do the shooting while you concentrate on your dog. If you simply cannot find an assistant, you will have to do everything yourself: plant birds, roll birds in, handle your dog, shoot the commies, and miss the homers. You may feel like a one-man band with a broken arm. But you have to do what you have to do.

You (or your assistants) should not shoot the first bird until after your dog has hupped. That takes a cool hand with the shotgun. But it's really important, as you can see. If the dog breaks, he can't be allowed to get the bird. Thus no hup, no shot.

If all goes well, as it should if you've done all the preliminaries, your dog will flush and hup. The gunners will shoot the bird, and it will fall a reasonable distance from the dog.

Things get pretty tense here. The dog may be quivering to go. If he does go, you won't be able to stop him before he gets the bird. Then it's too late, really. Sure, you can take the bird from him (without a correction), reposition him where he should have remained, walk out and toss the bird up again, and block him if he breaks. That helps, but it's so much better if he doesn't break at all. That's why you took all the time you did on the preliminaries.

With him sitting there, probably quivering, toot the STOP whistle vigorously again. Then walk toward the bird. As you pass the dog, turn around to face him and walk backward to the bird. Toot the STOP whistle again every few seconds. Even praise him quietly for sitting there.

Pick up the bird and return to your dog's side. Toss the bird a short distance and send your dog to retrieve it. Do it again. He deserves the extra reward.

Pick up shot birds this way several times, until your dog expects you to retrieve them. When you are sure that he will remain steady while you make the retrieve, give him a pleasant surprise: send him to make a retrieve of a shot bird. Whoopie! That is what both of you have been working toward all this time.

After that, let him retrieve about half of them. You retrieve the other half to keep him from anticipating. If you want to teach him to break to retrieve (after being steady to wing and shot), have him retrieve all of them. It won't take him long to figure out that you send him every time the bird falls. From there it's a short hop to breaking when the bird falls. (I don't recommend this, but if you want to do it, this is how.)

Even when you send him to retrieve, vary the time you wait (after the fall) before giving the command. If you unconsciously form the habit of waiting for a two-count every time, your dog will pick up that timing. He will tend to break after a two-count even when you don't give the command. Dogs read us so much better than we read them. Maybe that's why we work to support them while all they do is hunt and chase girls.

Wild Flushes

You want your spaniel to hup when a bird flushes wild, too. That's pretty easy for the steady dog. Some teach it before completing the steadying process, as part of the steadying process.

Start by having an assistant toss a bird up as your dog makes a cast in his direction. If necessary, you can toss the bird yourself. As soon as the dog sees it, toot the STOP whistle. If the dog obeys, shoot the bird, and let him retrieve it. Let him retrieve about half of these, too.

You can get true wild flushes by planting pigeons that have been lightly dizzied. Quarter downwind to these birds to let them know you're coming. If necessary, you can toss a handful of gravel at the bird as you approach, or shoot a marble from a slingshot in the bird's general direction.

Game Birds

Once you have steadied your spaniel, extend the training to game birds. You just can't run him on game birds too often. Your financial situation will dictate your personal limit here. Chukars and pheasants are the most popular game birds, although bird breeders can also provide quail if you want them.

One important point: Let your dog catch game birds, too. Give him a few clips. If you don't, he will soften up on flush when he smells a game bird, even if he flushes boldly on pigeons.

"Flick" has just flushed a pigeon in training. He has stopped and is in the process of hupping.

The essence of bracework is honoring. Here "Flick" honors as another of Pat Bramwell's Springers goes out . . .

. . . and returns with a shot bird.

Five people and two dogs lined up for some bracework. From the left: Mike Tillotson, Kevin Stillwell (with dog), Chad Betts, Rita Betts (with dog) and Gary Long.

16

Brace Work

BACKGROUND

What Is It?

In a brace, two handlers work two spaniels on separate but parallel beats (or courses). Each dog covers his own ground. Neither "poaches" on the other's territory. Having two dogs cover the same ground is a waste of "dog power."

The essence of brace work is honoring. When either dog flushes a bird and hups, the other dog also hups (either to wing or shot). The dog that flushed the bird retrieves it on command while the bracemate remains in place, "honoring" the retrieve.

True brace work does not include several variations (aberrations?) I see every fall. Like one hunter working two dogs simultaneously. Some people do this and seem to enjoy it. I would feel overwhelmed as a handler. One dog is my handling limit. Besides, the two dogs typically cover the same ground, more or less at the same time.

Nor does it include two people working two different "functional" types of dogs together, like a pointing dog and a flushing dog. Typically, the pointing dog locates the birds first because of its greater range. The spaniel never gets much work. If the birds don't hold for a point, no one gets any action. If the birds hold, the spaniel will flush them out from under the pointing dog's nose. That doesn't help the pointing dog's training a bit. A few such instances and he will start diving in to flush the birds when he senses the spaniel approaching.

A spaniel and a retriever can work together as a brace, because they are the same ''functional type.'' They both flush their birds. (The recent interest in ''pointing Labs'' creates an exception here.)

Why Do It?

Under most circumstances, one dog at a time is my enjoyment limit. Even when I take two dogs hunting, I alternate them, so I can watch and enjoy everything each dog does. When I hunt with another dog owner (dogged hunter?), I prefer to alternate our dogs. We hunt one and rest the other(s). We always have a fresh dog on the ground. As I grow older, my dogs more often need a fresh old man hunter than I need a fresh spaniel. But it wasn't always that way, and it's probably not that way for you—yet.

However, I do make exceptions to my one-dog-at-a-time rule. Some huntable areas almost demand brace work. Like along a hedgerow, creek bottom, or any location with an extended obstacle that makes it difficult for one dog to work all the likely cover. With two steady flushing dogs, I prefer to hunt such an area in a brace, with one dog/handler team on each side of the obstacle. If two steady dogs are not available, one dog can work up one side and down the other.

Brace work is required in spaniel Field Trials, so if you plan to compete in them, you must train your dog this way.

Prerequisites

Your dog should have a solid quartering pattern and should respond to your directions (whistle and arm signal) before you attempt brace work. Only then can you keep him on his own beat and prevent him from socializing or poaching on the other dog's course. The dog should be under *quiet* control, too, for your bracemate's dog would be confused if you did a lot of yelling, whistling, and running this way and that to handle your dog.

Since the essence of brace work is honoring, your dog must be reliably steady to wing, shot, and fall. Attempting brace work with a dog not completely steadied is unfair to the other dog. Your dog should have learned to honor in nonslip retrieving.

Equipment

The most important ''equipment'' for brace work, of course, is another dog and handler team. You should really have three gunners, too. One should walk the centerline between the two beats. The other two should act as flankers on the extreme edges of the course.

When you introduce your spaniel to brace work, you should get an experienced dog for its bracemate. If both dogs are new to the game, and anything goes wrong, both could be set back several steps in their steadying work. If you absolutely cannot find an experienced dog, do the best you can with what you have, but expect more problems.

Bracing dogs of similar speed makes sense. Otherwise, trying to keep them approximately together on the course may be a big problem. Consciously or unconsciously, one handler will push his dog along too fast and the other will rein his in to an unnaturally slow pace.

You should have some way of marking the centerline, so each handler knows when his dog is poaching. Most trainers use long fiberglass sticks, which are sold in bicycle shops.

Schedule

This, like so many forms of advanced training, is an ongoing job for the life of the dog. However, if you have completed all the prerequisites, and if you train several times a week, you should have your spaniel running braces and honoring in two or three weeks. He will make mistakes after that, but the rough work will be done.

Handling Techniques

Brace work requires no handling techniques beyond what you have learned while quartering. However, in all your handling, be considerate of the other dog. Don't distract him or confuse him with noisy handling.

TRAINING

Getting Started

First, stake out the centerline of your course. Set it up so you can run into the wind, which facilitates keeping each dog on his own course. Make it long enough so each dog can get at least two and maybe three birds.

You can either plant the birds or have the two outside gunners roll them in. Don't have the center gunner roll in birds, for those would be too close to the centerline for an inexperienced dog. If you plant your birds, plant them on the outside edges of the two courses, not in the center. Later you can plant them anywhere on the courses, but not yet.

If you have homing pigeons, you might consider using them for the first few sessions. Flyaways are a good way to start. Neither dog gets to retrieve, so both learn to relax a bit after a flush. If either dog breaks, the handler can bring him under control without any danger of him getting to a shot bird first. Most of all, flyaways prevent a dogfight over the bird if the honoring dog breaks after the other dog has been sent to retrieve.

To spice things up for the dogs, and to keep them flushing boldly, mix in clips with the flyaways. Each dog gets to retrieve the clips and neither gets to retrieve the flyers. If you give each dog three birds, make one a clip and two flyers, in random order.

All five people should line up at the starting line: gunner, handler, gunner, handler, gunner. The handlers should set the pace for the gunners. In Field Trials, if one handler moves faster than the other, the center gunner stays with the faster handler. However, in hunting, when both handlers carry guns, that would be unsafe. So in training, keep the line straight. If one handler's dog moves too fast for the other, he should occasionally stop the dog and wait.

On the first few flushes—by your dog and by his bracemate—your dog will be more tempted to break than ever. Perhaps because this is a new situation. Perhaps because your dog feels the pressure of competition for the birds with his bracemate. Perhaps because you are more tense than you have ever been (and you will be, trust me). Maybe all of the above. But don't be surprised if he breaks. That's why the birds should be flyaways.

Flick broke on the first bird his first bracemate flushed. When that happened, he had been solidly steady for several weeks. I was caught flatfooted because I didn't expect it. And I did exactly the wrong thing. I hollered "Flick!" That, of course, is his command to retrieve, so instead of stopping, he really kicked it in gear.

If your dog breaks, stop him with your whistle, not your vocal chords. Not only does that work better, but it also disturbs the other dog less. In fact, in all of your handling, be considerate of your bracemate's dog. Mostly that means be as quiet as you can.

If your dog breaks but stops promptly on the whistle, let him sit there a few seconds and watch the bird fly away. Then, recall him with the COME-IN whistle and prepare to restart his quartering when your bracemate is also ready.

If he breaks and ignores the whistle, or runs a long way before stopping, hustle your stumps out there, grab his collar, and drag him somewhat roughly back to where he should have stopped. Sit him down firmly, tooting the STOP whistle as you do. Then return to your place in the line, praise him, let him sit there a few seconds, recall him, and be ready to proceed.

After a few sessions with flyaways, you should be able to mix in a few shot flyers. Don't abandon flyaways for a while. Don't let either dog retrieve the first couple of shot birds. The handlers should do it. This is an insurance step you shouldn't skip.

While you are doing this brace work, you should begin every session with some water retrieves that include honoring in the line-steady position. That prepares your spaniel for the more difficult honoring during brace work. The work in water will also take the edge off your dog's energy level, making brace work steadiness a tad easier for him to endure.

With all that preparation, the rest should go smoothly. Control any breaks with your whistle. If you have to run your dog down now, maybe he really wasn't ready for honoring yet. Go back a few squares.

Here's a tip for the first time your dog successfully honors while his bracemate retrieves: After the other dog delivers the bird, take a dead pigeon from your vest, attract your dog's attention, throw the bird off to the side opposite your bracemate's course, and send your dog to retrieve it. If you do that occasionally throughout his training, he will come to focus his attention more on you and less on what his bracemate is doing during the bracemate's retrieve. Don't do it every time, but often enough to relax him a bit.

And So On

After you get that first solid honor from your dog, you should celebrate. Champagne may be a bit much, but a round of beers for your training buddies at the local pub after the session is definitely in order. Give your dog a treat, too. You have both accomplished something rare in the world of spaniel training.

From that magical point on, it's just work, work, work. Brace your dog as often as you can, with as many different bracemates as possible, in as many types of cover and terrain as possible. Change your courses to run in every conceivable wind direction. The most difficult wind condition is a crosswind blowing from your bracemate's course to yours. Don't do it that way if the wind is so strong that it will pull your dog a substantial distance into the other course. Be reasonable, and respect your dog's nose. He will go where it leads him. It's your job to set up the courses so they don't get him in serious trouble.

Continue to mix things up: clips, flyaways, shot flyers you retrieve, shot flyers your dog retrieves, planted birds, rolled-in birds, and so on. Keeping your spaniel steady to wing, shot, kill, and honor means keeping him guessing.

Only after you have run him a lot on pigeons under all these conditions should you use game birds. Here again, expect a break. You might let the first few fly away. I know, it's tough to let those high-dollar birds sail to the horizon, but it's for your dog's good.

A brace of Tawney Crawford's English Cockers. *Bill Crawford*

We force-break primarily to get reliable delivery to hand, especially in water work.

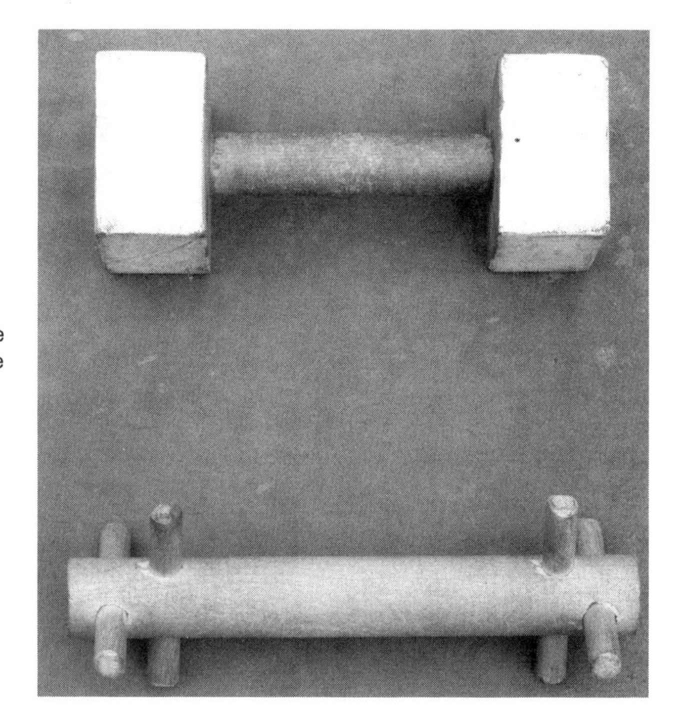

Below, the author's homemade "buck"; above, an obedience trial dumbbell.

17

Force-Breaking—Gently

BACKGROUND

What Is It?

A dictionary definition of force-breaking might read like this:

> A structured procedure by which you train a dog to pick up, to hold, to carry a bird on the command FETCH and to release it on the command GIVE.

In the slow and gradual six-step process I describe, the youngster starts with a passive role, then moves into a somewhat active role, and finally takes full responsibility for the job. Step 1 (accept, hold, and release) requires no force (as the term is used in this training). Nor does step 2 (carry). You introduce force (mild discomfort to induce compliance) in step 3 (reach) and continue it in step 4 (pick up). Step 5 (jump) is an optional happy-'em-up process, and step 6 transfers the skills learned in force-breaking to field work.

A bird-dog trainer, David Sanborn, first developed force-breaking back in the 1880s to teach basic retrieving to bird dogs that lacked natural retrieving instinct, as many do.

The very name, force-breaking, reveals the technique's bird-dog origins. Bird-dog trainers have always used "break" and "breaking" to mean formal training. They call obedience training "yard breaking." They call steadying to wing and shot (which is their major big deal) simply "breaking." They often call a steady dog a "broke dog." You'll hear them say "whoa breaking," and so on. Small wonder that David Sanborn called his structured approach to retrieving "force-breaking."

Years ago I had a pointer, Jigger, that would hunt until he dropped, and point birds joyously all day, but would not retrieve. He might shake a shot bird to make sure it was dead, but after that he would take off, searching for new birds to point. His retrieving instinct was a big zero. Even force-breaking didn't make him a retrieving wonder, but it helped a little.

Pointers and setters are typically high-strung and sensitive. Moreover, they must show "class" (animation, enjoyment) while working. Thus, Mr. Sanborn developed a force-breaking technique that is gentle.

Retriever trainers were very slow to adopt force-breaking. James Lamb Free, in his 1949 classic, *Training Your Retriever*, came out strongly against it. He argued that a retriever should not have to be forced to do what it was bred to do. (Sound familiar?)

Sometime in the early 1950s, retriever trainers discovered that force-breaking had fringe benefits which helped even dogs with natural retrieving instincts: reliable delivery to hand, smooth between-birds handling in multiple marks, and a framework for curing hardmouth and stickiness. Since then most retriever trainers have routinely force-broken all of their dogs.

Retriever pros face a unique problem. They must force-break quickly. When a pro gets a dog for training, he knows that within a month the owner will check on progress. If he doesn't see significant improvement, he will take the dog back. That is a simple fact of life for all professional dog trainers, regardless of breed(s).

For the bird-dog trainer, that improvement must be in finding and pointing birds. The owner won't care much about retrieving at first. Thus, the bird-dog trainer is under no pressure to force-break rapidly. Not so for the retriever pro. When the owner shows up at the end of the first month, the retriever had better show significant progress in retrieving. The pro knows that progress beyond simple puppy stuff comes only after force-breaking. Thus he must force-break in about one week to give himself three weeks to do field work before the owner returns.

Thus, retriever pros invented Hell Week force-breaking. It is quick and very rough—on both dog and trainer. Every pro I have discussed this with hates it, but it is an economic fact of life. Retriever pros are not insensitive Neanderthals. They work for impatient clients.

Why Do It?

Most serious spaniel trainers of my acquaintance do not force-break their dogs. Most of them all but foam at the mouth at the mention of the term. They offer two arguments against it. First, life is too short to waste on a spaniel that has to be force-trained to do something it should do naturally, namely retrieve. Second, force-breaking is a heavy-handed, negative procedure that takes too much out of a dog.

I certainly wouldn't waste my time working with a spaniel that lacked natural retrieving instinct. I don't recommend that you do either. Even so, I force-break every dog I train, including spaniels and retrievers, both of which love to retrieve almost from birth. I do this to gain the above-mentioned fringe benefits.

But I don't use the heavy-handed Hell Week. I use the slower, more gentle Sanborn procedure, which won't take anything out of a normal spaniel.

If you have reservations about force-breaking, at least read this chapter before deciding what is best for your spaniel. You have three options: You can skip force-breaking; you can do only the very gentle preforce steps; or you can do the complete job.

If you use your spaniel almost exclusively on land, where delivery to hand seldom becomes a major problem, you can get by without force-breaking. Even so, I recommend that you do the preforce steps (hold and carry) to maintain good delivery to hand through the dog's life.

The more you use your spaniel in water, the more you will gain from the fringe benefits of force-breaking. When a dog lands, his coat is full of water. Nature demands that he drop the bird and shake. Many dogs refuse to pick the bird up again. They seem to say, "Hey, I got it this far. If you want it, walk over and get it." That often requires that you slog through knee-deep mud. Further, the more water retrieving your dog does, the more apt he is to start mashing birds later in life. Wet birds lose feathers, and if the skin splits, the dog has a tasty morsel of meat in his mouth as he swims back to you. That fresh meat tempts the dog much longer than it would on land, too, because the dog swims so much slower than he runs. Every successful technique for curing hardmouth has its roots in force-breaking. Ditto for stickiness, in which the dog refuses to release the bird on command.

If you plan to teach your dog to do multiple marked retrieves, you will benefit from the reliable delivery to hand force-breaking teaches. The non-force-broken dog may drop the first bird a few feet from you to race off after the other fall. The dog will drop the first bird farther and farther away, until he stops returning between birds.

Prerequisites

Your spaniel should understand the following obedience commands: SIT, STAY, HEEL, COME-IN. I prefer to wait until the pup convinces me he is a good prospect—likes cover, likes birds, retrieves naturally, has pleasing style, enjoys being trained, and is a dog I enjoy.

How old should the dog be? Like most, I force-break retrievers early, at abut seven to nine months. But I wait longer for spaniels. It is not essential to their primary function (quartering). Besides, I prefer to wait until a spaniel is more mature. I did Flick when he was about sixteen months. I will probably wait until the very soft Rocky is two years. In general, I recommend waiting with spaniels until they are fifteen to twenty-four months old.

Equipment

The only additional equipment you need is some sort of wooden force-breaking "buck." I make my own, using one-and-one-quarter-inch dowel for the crosspiece, and half-inch dowel for the legs. The illustrated buck is nine inches long with one-inch legs, a nice size for spaniels. If you don't want to make your own buck, you can do nicely with an Obedience Trial dumbbell of appropriate size. I have force-broken many dogs with them.

The legs on the buck (or solid block ends on the dumbbell) do two things. First, they hold the buck up off the ground when the dog picks it up in step four. Second, they prevent him from allowing the buck to "accidentally" slip out of the side of his mouth as he holds it in step one. If he wants to get rid of it, he has to spit it out.

Schedule

If you do two sessions per day, you should complete this training in three to five weeks. Flick took fifty-four sessions—four a day for fourteen days. I have never completed force-breaking in less than two weeks. I spent two and a half months on one Chesapeake and three months on one Pointer. With each dog, I just keep throwing strikes until I get that final out. (Clearly, the Chessy and the Pointer got to me for a few hits and runs.)

Handling Techniques

Remember two things through this training: short sessions and plenty of praise.

Your sessions should not run over five minutes each. Back in the mid-1970s, I filmed (on Super-8 sound film) the force-breaking of Tina, a Golden Retriever. Each session took one fifty-foot roll of film (three minutes, twenty seconds). If possible, do two or three sessions each day. However, if that is not possible, you can succeed with one session a day, although it will take you longer.

Praise speeds this training. I have shown the film mentioned above to beginning trainers so often that my family has long refused to watch it again, claiming it is devoid of plot, setting, and character, or something like that. They especially despise the sound track. I can clear the house of all offspring by simply announcing that I am going to show the film. It works even better than my old Glenn Miller records.

My kids call it the "Good Girl" movie because I say that so often for the entire thirty-three minutes of film. My wife tried to count the "good girls" and gave up well past two hundred.

Yeah, all these "good girls" drive my kids out of the house—but let me tell you, Tina never tired of them.

One other thing: Don't become discouraged. At some point with every dog

I have force-broken, I have doubted whether I was making any progress. With some dogs, that has happened more than once. However, I have found that if I just persevere, every dog comes around. You will surely hit such a snag with your dog, so be forewarned that it's coming, that it's normal, and that you can get past it if you just stick with the program.

In steps three and four of force-breaking, the dog goes through a "period of resentment" which, if transferred to field work, would cause him to refuse to retrieve, or "blink." To prevent this, take the following precautions.

First, and perhaps most important, use an object for force-breaking that the pup will not connect with field work. That's the purpose of the wooden buck. With it, the dog never suspects this training has anything to do with birds or dummies. After the force-breaking process, the dog's resentment disappears. In fact, he will come to enjoy it. Then you can transfer his new skills to dummies and birds without risk of blinking.

Second, until force-breaking is complete, don't use the commands FETCH and GIVE during field work.

Third, force-break in the backyard, not in the field. Dogs are very "place conscious."

If you violate any of these simple rules and allow your dog to make the connection too soon, he will start blinking birds and dummies in the field. If that happens, discontinue field work until you complete force-breaking, when your dog's resentment will vanish.

TRAINING

Step 1: Accept and Hold the Buck (Preforce)

You must maintain physical control over your spaniel during force-breaking. Some pros have rather fancy (and expensive) facilities for this. The average amateur, who only force-breaks once every few years, can do nicely with his chain training collar and six-foot lead.

With your dog sitting at heel, wearing his chain collar with the lead attached, kneel beside him, throw the lead over your shoulders, and step on the end of it with your right foot. That gives you complete physical control without requiring the use of either hand. Further, the discomfort that gradually comes over you in this position will remind you to keep your sessions short.

Show the buck to your spaniel. Let him smell it, but don't let him mouth it or play with it. It's not a toy. Before proceeding, let your dog become completely bored with the buck.

Once your pup shows boredom, open his mouth with your left hand, say FETCH, and insert the buck with your right. Some use HOLD for this, reserving FETCH for reaching and picking up the buck. I use FETCH for everything and have never had a problem.

Keep your right hand under his jaw to prevent him from spitting out the buck. Keep the buck in his mouth for a few seconds, all the time praising him quietly. Then say GIVE, remove the buck, and praise calmly. Some use OUT, LEAVE IT, or DROP instead of GIVE.

Control his various efforts to avoid this training. If he turns away from the buck, bring his muzzle back around with your left hand. If he tries to spit it out, prevent it with your right hand under his chin. If he tries to get up and run off, control him with the lead.

The rest of step 1 is fairly easy. Just repeat the FETCH-GIVE process several times each session. He will gradually learn to hold the buck voluntarily. Then, withdraw your right hand and wait a little longer before you say GIVE and take the buck. If he drops it, say NO! and reinsert the buck with a firm FETCH! Then, of course, praise him.

When your dog holds the buck unassisted for a short time, stand up (keep your foot on the lead). If he drops the buck, correct him. Once he holds it while you stand up, step away from his side (hold the end of the lead in your hand). When you can walk to the end of the lead, walk all the way around him.

After he holds the buck through this without correction, introduce distractions. Clap your hands or have a member of your family come into your training area unexpectedly. These should give you a few opportunities to teach the dog that he is not allowed to drop the buck until you say GIVE no matter what.

Step 2: Carry the Buck (Preforce)

Next, teach him to carry the buck, first at heel and then when you call him to you.

Have him hold the buck, as in step 1. Then stand up, command HEEL, and start walking. He will probably spit the buck out before taking his first step. Wonderful! That gives you a chance to correct him. If he hangs on and heels properly, continue walking and praising until he does drop it, which probably won't take long. While you walk, praise him as long as he holds the buck. If he drops it, say NO!, stop, reinsert it with FETCH! and resume heeling and praising.

Initially, Flick had no problem with this. But after a few stops, he started spitting the buck out before moving when I said HEEL. For a while, I didn't think he would ever come around, but he did.

Your spaniel will gradually realize that he not only *can* but he also *must* carry the buck at heel. Two cautions: First, don't bump the buck out of his mouth while heeling; second, don't be too picky about how well he heels.

Next, have him carry the buck while coming to you. Leave him in a HUP-STAY, walk to the end of the lead, and call him to you. If he drops the buck, rush at him and make the usual correction.

In each session, have him heel with the buck for a while, and call him to you two or three times. Also in each session, continue the step 1 work: FETCH, GIVE, FETCH, GIVE, FETCH, GIVE. By the time he is carrying reliably, he should frequently open his own mouth automatically on FETCH.

STEP 1

First, let your dog become comfortable with the buck. *Bob Finch*

FETCH! *Bob Finch*

GIVE! *Bob Finch*

Carry at heel. *Bob Finch*

Carry while coming in. *Bob Finch*

The next step is the beginning of force. If you plan to do only the preforce steps, you're through right now. Your spaniel will hang on when you say FETCH (or HOLD) and release when you say GIVE. That will get you through most delivery problems on land. For water work, however, you need the rest of the procedure. Read on.

Step 3: Opening and Reaching (Force)

Through step 2, you have opened your dog's mouth and inserted the buck. His role has been passive: holding, carrying, and releasing on command. Now you teach him to take a more active role. First, he must open his own mouth when you say FETCH. Then he will have to reach for the buck.

To teach him these new accomplishments you must apply "force"—mild physical discomfort—whenever he fails to comply. Trainers have developed four types of force:

The Lip Pinch: Grasp the dog's muzzle and press his lip against his canine tooth hard enough to induce mild pain as you open his mouth.

Advantages: This is a natural extension of the previous training. You can adjust the pain level to the needs of the individual dog easily. You maintain control over the dog's muzzle.
Disadvantage: Your hand blocks the dog's view of the buck momentarily.

The Ear Pinch: Pinch the little flap on the back of the dog's ear, which will induce enough pain to make the dog open his mouth. Some trainers pinch the earflap against the ring on the collar for greater effect.

Advantages: The dog has good visibility of the buck. It takes little strength to create enough pain to get the attention of the hardest-headed dog on earth.
Disadvantages: It gives poor control over the dog's muzzle. It doesn't allow you to adjust the pain level to the individual needs of the dog. After a number of pinches, it hurts a lot no matter how lightly you pinch.

The Paw Squeeze: Squeeze one of the dog's front paws. That will open any canine mouth that hasn't been wired shut, believe me.

Advantages: The dog has good visibility of the buck. You can easily adjust the pain level to the tolerance of the individual dog.
Disadvantage: It gives almost no control over the dog's muzzle.

The Choke: Position the chain training collar high on the dog's neck, right behind his ears, and jerk the lead up sharply, which will open his mouth.

Advantage: It gives the dog good visibility of the buck.
Disadvantages: It doesn't give good control over the dog's muzzle. It is difficult to adjust the amount of force to the individual requirements of each dog.

Take your pick. They all work. When I say "apply force," use whichever method you prefer.

Force-method 1: Lip pinch. *Bob Finch*

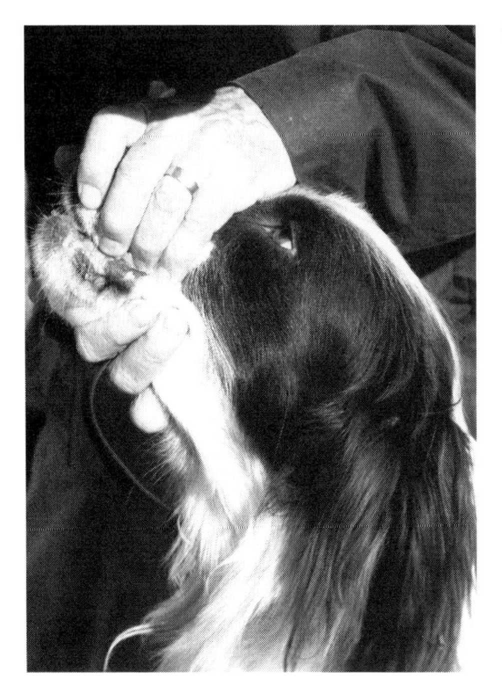

Force-method 2: Ear pinch. *Bob Finch*

Force-method 3: Paw squeeze. *Bob Finch*

Force-method 4: Choke. *Bob Finch*

This force will put your spaniel into his necessary "period of resentment." However, with the buildup of steps 1 and 2, you shouldn't have to apply force often, so this period won't last long.

Kneel beside your dog. Toss the lead over your shoulders and secure the end of it under your right foot.

Place the buck in front of his muzzle, almost touching it, and say FETCH. If he opens his own mouth, insert the buck and praise. If he doesn't open, apply force and insert the buck—*then praise lavishly.*

Repeat this over and over through several sessions, until he opens automatically on FETCH.

When you can get through an entire five-minute session without force, move on to reaching. Try this little shortcut: Heel your dog around without the buck; then put it in front of his mouth—continue moving as you do—and say FETCH. His own motion will cause him to reach. Praise as soon as he has the buck in his mouth. Do this several times until he is comfortable with this new exercise.

With that background in reaching while heeling, have him reach while sitting beside you. Place the buck an inch or so in front of his mouth and say FETCH. He will probably open but not reach. Fine. Push his head forward with your left hand so that his mouth goes around the buck. Continue this until he reaches before you push his head forward. Intersperse this drill with plenty of reaching while heeling.

After he reaches with reasonable regularity—enough to show that he understands what you expect—apply force whenever he refuses to reach (even though he may have opened voluntarily).

Lengthen the distance he must reach—*gradually*. Lengthen down, to either side, and slightly above his head. It shouldn't take long to get him to reach almost to the ground in front of him. Anytime he refuses, apply force.

He will try a new ploy: He will look away from the buck. If you hold the buck on the left side of his head, for example, he will look to his right. He's saying, "Hey, I can't see it, so I don't have to reach for it, right?" Wrong! Hold the buck in place and say FETCH. If he refuses, apply force and make him go to the buck. He must take responsibility for grabbing the buck on FETCH, no matter where it is.

After he learns the joy of avoiding force by acting quickly, he may not wait for you to say FETCH. He may open and reach as soon as he sees the buck. While that indicates that he is hearing the gospel you are preaching, you shouldn't allow it. Say NO and restrain him. He must open and reach only on the command FETCH, not whenever he sees the buck.

Throughout step 3, continue the step 2 training—having your spaniel carry the buck at heel and while being called to you. Do this every session.

When he reaches almost to the floor—reliably, which means almost every time—he is ready to move on to step 4.

Step 4: Picking Up (Force)

Next, teach your youngster to pick the buck up off the ground. Although this is a natural extension of the reaching in step 3, many dogs balk here. Until now, you have held the buck in your hand every time you commanded FETCH. Now, you lay it down first. This subtle difference confuses many dogs.

Misty (Weimaraner), the first dog I ever force-broke, balked for a month. If I held the buck on the ground, she picked it up. If I took my hand off it, she refused. Since I was inexperienced, and overly soft with her, I wasted too much time working her through this problem. Today, I would apply more force and solve the problem in two or three days at most.

To ease your spaniel into picking up the buck off the ground, start it while heeling. Heel your dog and periodically have him reach for the buck as he walks, just as you did in step 3. Then, "accidentally" drop it as you say FETCH. If you are deft enough, he should pick it up before he realizes that something is different.

After he has done this several times, ease him into picking it up while sitting at heel. Have him reach a few inches straight in front of him. Then hold the buck farther and farther away until he has to stand up and move forward to get it, even though you are still holding it off the floor. Have him return to heel with it. When he moves away and back to heel comfortably, place the buck on the floor far enough in front of him so that he has to get up to pick it up. Because of the preparatory work you have done, he should move out, pick it up, and return to heel. If he refuses, apply force, and repeat the pickup while heeling and getting up to reach.

The very essence of force-breaking is picking up and returning to heel. Whenever your dog accidentally drops a bird, a simple FETCH should induce him to pick it up and deliver to your hand.

Place the buck on the ground directly in front of him a few feet, then off to each side, then behind him. Of course, praise every success as well as correct every failure.

Step 5: Jumping (Postforce)

Once your dog consistently gets up, goes out a few feet, picks the buck up off the floor, and returns to heel, his resentment will rapidly disappear. In fact, he should show signs of enjoying this new game. Especially if you have praised every success.

Step 5 is pure fun-and-games, intended to sweeten him up and remove the last trace of resentment. You have convinced him that he must comply with the commands FETCH and GIVE. Now, you should lighten things up a bit to help him enjoy complying.

Start out while heeling. As you move along, hold the buck a few inches above the dog's head and command FETCH. He will reach up for it. Great. Praise him lavishly, even excitedly here, for you want to pump him up. Do this several

Step 3: "Flick" starts to reach while heeling. *Bob Finch*

Step 4: "Flick" picks up from the ground while heeling. *Bob Finch*

Step 5: Jumping up — happy time! *Bob Finch*

Step 6: "Flick" goes out to pick up dead bird. *Bob Finch*

Step 6: "Flick" returns to heel, carrying a bird. That's delivery to hand. *Bob Finch*

times, higher and higher, until his front feet leave the ground as he rises for the buck.

Next, try it while he is sitting at heel. Shorten up, too, to just a few inches above his head. Let him learn gradually that he can succeed at this new aspect of the game. Eventually he will jump as high as you want from a sitting position when you hold the buck over his head and command FETCH. I never hold it higher than my shoulders (and I am short). I want to sweeten the dog up, not set a new high-jump record.

Once your dog will jump a reasonable height, your force-breaking with the buck is completed. You used the buck to channel your dog's resentment away from dummies and birds and to thereby allow you to continue field work during the force-breaking process. Now you no longer need the buck as a decoy. You are now ready for step 6, in which you transfer force-breaking to dummies and birds and begin to use it in field work.

Step 6: Dummies and Birds (Postforce)

In transfering FETCH and GIVE to dummies and birds, take the following precautions to avoid getting into a battle of wills with your dog.

1. Don't introduce any dummy or bird that your dog has not previously retrieved. You are extending FETCH and GIVE to retrieving objects with which your dog is familiar—not advancing his work to things he has never handled before.
2. Increase the size of the dummies and birds gradually. Start out with the small plastic and canvas dummies, then bring in the large plastic and canvas dummies. Next, a dead pigeon. Then, a dead hen pheasant. After that, a dead rooster pheasant.
3. With each new object, start in step 1 and go through step 5.
4. Remember to praise lavishly for all successes.

Once you have introduced all these dummies and birds into the force-breaking routine with your dog, you should begin using FETCH and GIVE in the field. If he drops a bird or dummy, make him pick it up with FETCH. If you think he is about to drop one, say FETCH to make him hold it. Anytime he refuses to comply with FETCH or GIVE—which should be seldom—apply force as convincingly as necessary.

In a multiple mark, the dog may need a "helping hand" to remember the memory bird(s).
Bob Finch

18

The Multiple Marked Retrieve

BACKGROUND

What Is It?

A multiple marked retrieve consists of two or more marked falls. The dog first watches all birds down, and then retrieves them one at a time. We call a multiple mark involving two birds a "double," one with three birds a "triple," and so on.

In a double, the dog watches the two birds fall. He must remember the one he will retrieve last while he is retrieving the other. Thus, a double tests not only marking but also memory. Dogs naturally pick up the last bird down first. Thus, we call the first bird down (the last one retrieved) the "memory bird." We call the second bird down the "diversion," because it diverts the dog's attention from the other bird.

Doubles also introduce a new problem: switching. A dog switches when he gives up on one bird and tries to retrieve the other. Why is this such a big no-no? First, it shows a lack of perseverance. Second, a dog that switches disturbs a lot of cover unnecessarily between the areas of the falls. Finally, a switching dog normally does not successfully complete the double. Frequently, he doesn't retrieve either bird.

A triple has two memory birds (the first two down). A quad has three, and so on.

Why Do It?

Most waterfowlers, even lousy shots like me, now and again knock down two birds from an incoming flock. When that happens, it's really nice to have a dog along that can pick up both birds as a double. I would recommend this training to all spaniel owners who hunt waterfowl extensively.

Doubles also happen in the uplands, especially on covey birds like quail. Triples occur more in waterfowling than in the uplands. I have only witnessed one true triple on a covey rise.

Many feel that triples require a lot of training time relative to their actual usefulness afield. They prefer to do a triple as a double and a blind in water, a double and a hunt-dead on land.

However, those who run their spaniels in the UKC and NAHRA hunting tests for retrievers must train on both doubles and triples.

Prerequisites

Before starting doubles, your spaniel should be quartering well, be steady to wing and shot, be doing good work on single marked retrieves. I prefer to force-break mine first, too, because that smooths out the between-birds handling. The dog doesn't drop the bird and take off for the other one. But force-breaking is not absolutely essential.

If you plan to train your spaniel for blind retrieves, you can do multiple marks in parallel with that training.

Equipment

You need no additional equipment for this training.

Schedule

You should complete the bare-ground work for doubles in a couple of weeks. After you move into cover, your progress will slow down considerably. However, if you train regularly, within a couple of months, you should have brought your dog along well enough for ordinary hunting conditions. You can spend the rest of your dog's life perfecting multiple marks.

Handling Techniques

For this training, start out in basic nonslip mode: standing with your dog sitting at heel, with assistants placed in the field to throw for you. Later, you can go to the dummy launcher, to make the falls more like upland hunting situations.

Your job as handler is to help your dog do his job. The dog must mark and remember the falls, but you can help him in several inconspicuous ways.

Respect your spaniel's desire to retrieve doubles in the natural sequence (or biblical sequence: "The last shall be first and the first shall be last"). Later, you can "select" the opposite sequence for him, but not yet.

You can use your own body movements at the line to help your dog. Start off facing the memory-bird thrower. After that bird is down, turn to face the diversion-bird thrower, using the belt cord to encourage your dog to shift around with you. He will learn to shift with you automatically.

After the birds are down, watch your dog, not the location of either fall. How else can you know whether your dog is properly locked in on the bird at hand? If you send him when he is looking the wrong way, he will wander off like a drunken sailor and never complete the retrieve.

Should you use your left hand to give a line to the fall? The diversion bird is fresh in your dog's mind, so why distract him that way? Simply give him the command to retrieve. Ditto for the memory bird if he locks in on it and seems confident. If not, use your hand to help him. Even then, don't use a bowler's arm sweep. Don't even flick your fingers. Just place your hand along side his head, let him lock in, and send him. That helps him without distracting him.

As your dog returns to you with the diversion bird, turn to face the memory bird. That way, when he sits at heel to deliver (as he should for a double), he faces his next retrieve. Take the bird, place it behind your opposite hip (so it won't distract your dog), let him lock in on the memory bird, and send him. If you have force-broken your spaniel, this between-birds transition will be smooth. No difficulty getting him to come in to the heel position and hup. No dropping and picking up the bird. No jumping at it as you take it. In short, no hassle between birds.

TRAINING

Bare Ground Work

Because doubles are so much more difficult than singles, you should go back to bare ground to introduce them. Set up your dog's initial doubles so that he will easily find both dummies and so he cannot switch. That way he learns to do it right, and he receives praise, not corrections. To make sure he finds both dummies, use highly visible, big white ones. To prevent him from switching, use a barrier (fence, building, even a row of cars) between the falls.

A tennis-court fence does nicely. Stand at the corner and toss one fall down each side. Later, when your dog understands that he is to retrieve them one at a time, you can go onto the tennis court itself and use the net as the barrier. The net isn't as impenetrable as the outside fence, but it still discourages switching. Another good barrier is one of those old-time school yard fences, made of eight- or ten-foot high chain link with frequent openings for traffic. You can set the line up at an opening and toss one fall on either side.

Initially toss both dummies yourself, but bring in a couple of assistants as soon as possible. You need to be free to concentrate on handling.

Stay with the barrier until your dog is comfortable with doubles and until you are comfortable with your handling techniques. Then, move away from the barrier for more advanced bare ground work.

Make the initial doubles without a barrier widespread, at least 120 degrees apart. You are still conditioning your dog to do them correctly, not tempting him to switch—yet.

Set up your tests downwind. Into-the-wind tests invite the dog to quarter to the bird. A crosswind is okay, as long as it does not blow scent from the memory bird to the dog as he goes to retrieve the diversion. If it does that, it will encourage him to switch, obviously, and in correcting him for the switch, you will be telling him to ignore his nose—which "ain't too bright" for a trainer.

When your dog can handle bare ground doubles to a hundred yards with the falls 120 degrees apart, rerun every test with dark dummies. If he has a problem with the memory bird, back up and use a dark dummy for the diversion and a white one for the memory bird for a while. If that causes him no problems—and it shouldn't—then rerun with both dark dummies.

Then start using dark dummies on the first run of each test. Still keep the 120-degree angle between the falls. Vary the length of the falls. You would be surprised how poorly a dog does on short retrieves if he doesn't get them often.

Your dog probably won't attempt to switch in any of this bare ground work. However, if he does, remember two things: He must not succeed, which means that the thrower must pick up the dummy before the dog gets to it; and you must correct your dog in the area to which he switches—to take advantage of his "place consciousness" relative to punishment.

Say nothing as your dog switches. Instead, run out there, catch him, and punish him in the area to which he switched. If he has left that area, run him down and drag him back. Don't call him to you. Don't stop him with the whistle. Don't heel him back.

How severely you correct him depends on his temperament, but he will quickly tell you how much is too much, as I will explain.

After correcting him, heel him to the correct dummy. Command FETCH, then HUP and STAY. Walk back to the line and whistle him in. Then praise him. He has done it right, even though you helped him plenty, so praise him.

Then, rerun the entire test. If he switches again, you didn't correct him vigorously enough. If he refuses to return to the area in which you corrected him to make a normal retrieve, you overdid it. If he does the test properly, you corrected him about right. This is one of the few places in training in which the dog tells you immediately whether your correction was proper or not.

Cover

Make your dog's initial doubles in cover very short and very wide: thirty yards long with 120 degrees between the falls. Keep the hazards simple, too.

After the birds are down, watch your dog, not the falls. If your dog is looking the wrong way when you send him, he will go the wrong way. Here I am watching the last fall while "Flick" is looking at the first.

Bob Finch

Here I am watching "Flick," as I should be, so I can . . .

Bob Finch

. . . pat my leg to bring him around before I send him.

Bob Finch

As your dog returns with the diversion bird, turn to face the memory bird.

Bob Finch

Reasonably level terrain, light to moderate cover, downwind falls. Trial and success in the beginning gives the dog a good attitude toward each new phase of his training.

Use the following three techniques to insure success: salting, rehearsing, and rerunning.

"Salting" has already been explained in chapter 14. A temporary measure, it is useful in the beginning phases of doubles.

"Rehearsing" is a technique to assist the dog to remember the memory bird. You run him on the memory bird as a single before running the double. After picking this fall up as a single, your dog will be more likely to remember it as the memory bird of the double. This, too, is a temporary measure which should be discontinued after the dog has shown the ability to remember two falls.

"Rerunning" is your greatest training tool for marking and memory. The dog remembers the falls better the second time. He "calibrates" his marking when he gets another look at the falls after he knows exactly where they are.

Gradually stretch the distances of the falls to one hundred yards or so, always keeping them widespread. Vary the throwing sequence and directions, and vary the length of the falls. But don't change them in one test between runs. That would only confuse your dog.

When he shows competence and confidence on these wide hundred-yard doubles, tempt him to switch. Shorten up to thirty yards, so you won't have to run so far to correct him. Then bring the throwers closer together, so that the angle between the falls (birds, not throwers) is about 90 degrees. Have both throw "in" (toward each other). This encourages switching, because the throwers are not "blocking" the path from one fall to the other.

Run this test without salting and without rehearsal. By now a thirty-yard double should be easy. If your dog tries to switch, correct him as explained above, rerun him until he doesn't switch, praise him, and put him up. If he doesn't try to switch, praise him, rerun him, praise him, and put him up. Then, toughen the next test.

Intersperse switching tests with confidence builders from now until you have him pretty well switchproofed. Switchproofing takes time.

The remainder of double marked retrieve training on land consists of introducing all sorts of variations into the tests: cover, terrain, wind, placement, and sequence of the falls. Start using your dummy launcher when your spaniel shows he is comfortable with doubles with visible throwers.

Honoring

You should have your spaniel honor another dog's retrieves in doubles, too. The second bird will tempt him to break, so keep him on the belt cord until he has demonstrated he doesn't need it.

Water double (memory bird at extreme right end of picture). *Bob Finch*

Water double. Heading for the memory bird. *Bob Finch*

Water double. Success! *Bob Finch*

Water

Let water work lag considerably behind land work in double marks, especially when you are switchproofing. You can't correct your dog effectively for a water switch. So avoid the situation until you are sure he won't switch, until you have cured him completely on land.

Selecting

Eventually you will run into a hunting situation in which you want to pick up the memory bird first. Maybe it's a lively cripple for a memory bird when the diversion is stone-dead and in plain sight. When you change the natural sequence of the retrieves, you are said to "select." Don't try it until you have trained for it.

Start out selecting on reruns only. Your dog knows where both birds are, so retrieving them in reverse sequence should be no problem. When your dog is comfortable with this new game, set up a very simple double and select the first time. And so on. However, don't do it so often that your dog gets confused. Maybe one double in five to ten is about right for most dogs. Mostly, let him retrieve in the natural sequence.

Triples

If you decide to extend multiple mark training to triples, go back to bare ground, and repeat all the above steps with the third fall.

Since a triple has two memory birds, the retrieving sequence is not so simple. The dog indicates which memory bird he wants first as he returns with the diversion bird. He will glance, sometimes several times, at one or the other of the remaining falls. That's the one he wants, and the smart handler sends him for that one next.

Quads? Quints? Aw, come on, now.

19

The Blind Retrieve: Preliminary Training

BACKGROUND

What Is It?

A blind retrieve is one in which the dog does not see the bird fall. The handler, who knows where the bird is, directs the dog to it with whistle and arm signals. The dog is running "blind." In England, these are called "unseens."

The blind retrieve has three parts: lining, stopping, and casting. Initially, the handler "lines" his dog toward the bird. If the dog drifts off-line, the handler "stops" him with a whistle signal and "casts" him in the appropriate direction with an arm signal.

We teach the blind retrieve by drilling on the three pieces (lining, stopping, and casting). Later, we assemble them into a whole. The preliminary lining, stopping, and casting drills bear little resemblance to the real blind retrieve. It's something like the difference between football practice and football games.

A football practice seldom looks much like a football game. Instead, one sees drills: calisthenics, wind sprints, running through tires, pushing sleds, hitting, blocking and tackling dummies, footwork drills, weight training, and on and on. The uninformed might say, "But that's nothing like football! Why don't they scrimmage all the time?" The more knowledgeable understand that successful football plays are developed by assembling a large collection of small skills, each of which has been separately perfected. Further, when plays break down during a game, the coaches look at the individual skills to find the problem.

Blind retrieve training begins as a set of drills to teach lining, stopping, and casting separately. In lining drills, called "pattern blinds," the trainer conditions the dog by rote repetition to leave on command and run or swim in a straight line. In stopping drills he conditions the dog to stop, turn, and hup facing him (the trainer) in expectation of an arm signal. In casting drills, he uses "baseball" techniques to teach the dog to respond correctly to arm signals.

This chapter describes these preliminary drills. Chapter 20 describes the techniques used in assembling them into real blind retrieves.

Why Do It?

When your dog fails to see a fall in waterfowling (as often happens), your only hope for picking the bird up is the blind retrieve. The more water work you expect from your spaniel, the more you need the blind retrieve.

Blind retrieves happen in the uplands, too, although less often. If your dog fails to see a bird that falls across a creek, or in a pond, you can't heel him to it and pick the bird up with a hunt-dead. You need a true blind retrieve.

Prerequisites

A certain amount of conflict exists between quartering and lining. In quartering you want your dog to run "real crooked." In the blind retrieve, you want him to run "real straight." For spaniels, quartering takes precedence, so delay blind retrieve training until your dog has a solid quartering pattern. Do the preliminary drills covered in this chapter in parallel with the multiple marked retrieving covered in chapter 18.

Equipment and Facilities

You need more dummies now than you have for any previous training. A minimum of eighteen is good—thirty-six would be better. In these drills, the more dummies you put out, the fewer times you have to interrupt training to "restock your shelves."

You need three traffic cones, the bigger the better. These cones are bright orange. To be visible to your dog, they should be white. You can paint them, but paint doesn't stick too well to slick plastic. I have white fabric sleeves for mine, and when they get dirty, I toss them in the washing machine. If you can't make these sleeves yourself, you probably know someone who can.

You need some way to mark the location of a blind retrieve so that it is visible to you but not to your dog. Some use little strips of surveyor's tape. I prefer wooden stakes with long nails in one end and make my own from one- to one-and-a-half-inch dowels. I drill a hole for the nail, pound it in, and then grind the head off so I can stick that end of the nail in the ground. I also drill a hole

The water blind retrieve, showpiece of AKC hunting tests for spaniels.
Bob Finch

Traffic cones, either painted white or covered with white sleeves.

Marking stakes.

in the other end, so I can stack these stakes for better visibility in high cover. I make them in various lengths, from about twelve inches to about thirty inches. These stakes are also useful for marking the line, elevating the cone, and staking out a "baseball" diamond in casting drills.

Schedule

You can do the drills for lining, stopping, and casting in parallel. Even so, this is slow conditioning work. In one sense you never complete this training, for you will continue drilling your spaniel on blind retrieves for the rest of his life. However, you should be able to start him into the transitional drills (chapter 20) within a couple of months.

Handling Techniques

The blind retrieve is interactive. You know where the bird is but can't get there. Your dog can get there, but doesn't know where "there" is. Picking up such a bird requires teamwork. Your handling techniques are extremely important.

You must tell your dog that you plan to send him after a bird he hasn't seen fall, rather than a mark. I do this by saying DEAD BIRD. Others use BLIND. The exact term matters little, of course, as long as the dog understands it.

You must tell your dog when he is lined up properly for the blind. When you say DEAD BIRD, he searches for the right "picture" in front of him. Each time he gets the wrong one, you tell him NO. When he gets the right picture, you place your left hand along his head and say LINE.

You must tell him when to leave. I use BACK for this in blind retrieves. Since I use the dog's call-name to send him on marks, BACK further distinguishes blinds from marks.

The blind retrieve sequence I recommend, then, is DEAD BIRD . . . LINE . . . BACK, each given at the appropriate time relative to the dog's situation. Use NO in place of LINE when the dog has the wrong picture. You normally say DEAD BIRD once. You say NO as often as necessary. You normally say LINE only once, followed quickly by BACK.

You must blow the whistle properly to get your dog to stop, turn, hup, and look at you for arm signals. The dog may be quite some distance away, and the wind may be blowing, so you must blow your whistle hard.

You must give clear, consistent arm signals. There are four basic casts: OVER to the left; OVER to the right; straight BACK; and COME-IN.

Give an OVER by extending the appropriate arm at shoulder level, with the thumb down (to prevent the arm from flying up above shoulder level). As you pump your arm and say OVER, take a few steps in the proper direction. If you shout OVER (a "hard" OVER), your dog will go back rather than over. Honest. Sometimes this little quirk comes in handy, but more often it is a problem. Say OVER gently (a "soft" OVER).

Giving clear signals: OVER! *Bob Finch*

BACK! *Bob Finch*

COME-IN! *Bob Finch*

Give the BACK cast by extending either arm straight up so your hand is as high as possible. Many handlers lock their elbows and swing their arms out in front of them and then on up as high as they can reach. Change arms when a BACK cast follows an OVER—give a right-arm BACK after a left-arm OVER, and vice versa. If you give both with the same arm, your dog may well continue the OVER.

Give the COME-IN cast with the whistle, plus a little body English. Crouch and extend one arm down as you blow the COME-IN whistle.

TRAINING

"Pictures"

In a blind retrieve the dog doesn't—as people thought for many years—"take a line." No, he runs to a preselected spot. Think about it: If you were asked to walk one hundred steps in a certain direction, you would pick a distant object—tree, building, cliff, etc.—and walk toward it. You could never succeed if you looked at your shoes and tried to walk straight, could you?

A dog does the same thing. He runs to a preselected spot, or "picture." After he has run a number of pattern blinds and real blinds, he selects a spot in the indicated direction that his experience tells him should hold the bird. He sits at the line and leafs through his mental "picture album" of past blind retrieves until he finds one that resembles what lies before him.

If his picture is absolutely accurate, he will run right to the bird, or "line the blind." If it is off a bit, the handler must stop and redirect him. The farther off he is, the more work the handler has to do.

Pattern Blinds

Lining drills consist of "pattern blinds," which are simulated blind retrieves. The dog knows where the bird or dummy is, although he has not seen it fall. The pattern blinds I recommend (cone blind and floating blind) encourage the dog to use pictures.

The *cone blind* surpasses all other pattern blinds not only for introducing the dogs to lining, but also for rapidly building his picture album in terrain, cover, and wind variations on land and in water. In this technique, you teach your dog that the dummy will always be by the highly visible white traffic cone, that he only need run (or swim) straight to the cone, no matter where it is, and he will find the dummy.

I didn't invent this technique. I learned of it from Margaret Patton of Tishomingo, Oklahoma. She told me that she picked it up from a pro down in Texas, who may have learned it from someone else, and so on.

After you have conditioned your dog to run to the cone on DEAD BIRD . . . LINE . . . BACK, you can set up pattern blinds anywhere, land or water, and line

INTRODUCING CONE PATTERN BLINDS

DEAD BIRD! *Bob Finch*

LINE! *Bob Finch*

BACK! *Bob Finch*

Success! *Bob Finch*

your dog to it successfully the first time. After he has run it once or twice with the cone in place, you remove the cone and rerun him a couple more times, to condition him to run to a picture without the cone.

The *floating blind*, in which you toss a large white dummy in open water before bringing your dog to the line, can only be used in quiet water. However, it does offer great visibility to the dog and encourages him to work with pictures.

Your Training Program for Lining

Start on bare ground. Set a white cone out about one hundred yards from your intended starting point, or line. Ideally, the cone should be straight downwind and strongly frontlighted. If both are not possible, favor good lighting over "proper" wind.

Now, grab a half a dozen white dummies and let your dog out of his crate. Heel him from line to the cone and stop. With him sitting at heel, toss a dummy near the cone, saying DEAD BIRD as you do. Toss another dummy near the cone, saying DEAD BIRD. And so on, until all six dummies are down. Saying DEAD BIRD helps your dog associate that expression with dummies at the cone. Gradually he will come to expect a blind retrieve when he hears DEAD BIRD.

Now, heel your dog back toward the starting point. Stop about twenty-five yards from the cone, turn to face it, and say DEAD BIRD . . . LINE . . . BACK with your dog looking at the cone. He will race to the cone and pick up a dummy.

As he goes to the cone, run back another twenty or twenty-five yards toward the line. When he delivers the first dummy, you can send him again from a greater distance, without him noticing the difference.

Repeat this until you can send him from a hundred yards. This may take time. Fine. A short success is better than a long failure. If he is a little wobbly at some length, shorten up immediately.

Don't overwork your dog in any one session. While you stand still at the line, he runs back and forth between you and the cone, up to two hundred yards round-trip. If you exhaust him too often, you may permanently damage his attitude toward blind retrieves.

After a few sessions, your spaniel will recognize the significance of the cone. Then you no longer need to heel him to and from the cone before running him.

Once he can handle single cone pattern blinds out to one hundred yards in several different places, teach him that there can be two cones in sight, each with dummies, and that it is your option, not his, which one he is to go to. This teaches him not only to take the line you select, but also what NO means when he has the wrong picture.

Put out two cones with dummies, each one hundred yards from the line, with an angle of about 90 degrees between them. The sun should light the two cones equally. Hup him facing, say, the left one, and say NO softly. Now, reheel him so he faces the right cone. Go through your blind retrieve sequence, sending

INTRODUCING TWO CONES

NO him off one cone. *Bob Finch*

Line him to the other cone. *Bob Finch*

Success! *Bob Finch*

REMOVING ONE CONE

NO him off remaining cone. *Bob Finch*

Line him to dummies with no cone. *Bob Finch*

MOVING INTO COVER

First, with cone in place. *Bob Finch*

Then, without the cone. *Bob Finch*

him on BACK. At that wide angle, he should have no problem going to the cone you selected.

When he returns, hup him facing the same (right) cone. Tell him NO softly. Reheel him to face the left cone. Go through your blind retrieve sequence, sending him on BACK. Again, he should have no problem.

You have started teaching him that even though there are two cones out there, each with dummies, he should go to the one you select. Later, when he gets the wrong picture on a real blind retrieve, you will be able to NO him off it easily. He may remain convinced that there is a bird where he had it pictured. However, he will understand that you want a different bird, so he will look for a new picture.

After several such sessions in different locations, start bringing the cones closer together—60 degrees . . . 45 degrees . . . 30 degrees. No closer than that, please.

If he veers off and goes to the wrong cone, correct him much as you do for switching in a multiple mark. Say nothing, but run out and punish him near the cone he has gone to in error. Then, heel him to the correct cone, have him pick up a dummy. Hup him facing the line. Return to the line and call him to you. Praise him when he arrives.

When he can handle two cones at an angle of thirty degrees consistently, start using three cones. Begin with forty-five-degree angles between adjacent cones. NO him off two cones and send him to the third. Vary the cones you send him to each time. Then, move them closer together, but not closer than thirty degrees.

While you are teaching your spaniel to handle multiple cones, you should also begin accustoming him to the process by which you will later "wean" him from the cones. Set up a single cone pattern blind with three white dummies and two dark ones. Run him on it twice with the cone in place, and then confine him while you remove the cone, but not the dummies. In all likelihood, he will have picked up two white dummies, leaving two darks and one white. If not, when you remove the cone, put out new dummies so there are two darks and one white. Now, get your dog out again and rerun him with the cone gone. The one white dummy will be a visual aid, and he will undoubtedly pick it up rather than a dark one. Next, rerun him twice more, with only dark dummies out there. You are encouraging him to use pictures even when the cone is not in sight.

After he can handle these reruns without the cone and also multiple cones, you can mix the two.

Next comes a really major step, and a critical one in giving you the ability to NO him off a picture later on in real blinds. Set up two cones at 45 degrees with dark dummies. Run him on each of them twice. Then, rerun him with only one cone removed. NO him off the visible cone and send him to the other dummies (without a cone). This could take some time, and some corrections, but it is an important step in training your dog to find a picture along the line you give him. Repeat this drill in most training sessions. Through it you will gain absolute control over the line your dog takes. You will also, in later real blind retrieves, be able to NO your dog off any white patch (milk carton, plastic bag, etc.) he may see.

At this point, you are ready to move into cover on land and to begin water lines at the same time.

In cover, set up any type pattern blind you want, as long as the cone is visible. Keep them frontlighted or strongly sidelighted. In tall cover, elevate the cones on stakes of appropriate length. Anytime you question the visibility of the cone, squat down and look at it from your dog's point of view.

Start cone pattern blinds in water quite simply. Here again, a short success is better than a long failure. Since corrections are nearly impossible in water, avoid them. Do your correcting on land.

Place the dummies in the water rather than on the opposite shore, just as you do with your water marks, and for the same reason: Dogs that always find the birds on land tend to run the bank. With the cones, you have two ways to keep the dummies in the water. First, you can put the cone on shore with the dummies in the water in front of it. Second, you can stake the cone up out in the water and drop the dummies in front of it. The latter is better, but more difficult, and impossible in wind.

Run all your water pattern blinds so there is no real temptation to run the bank. Let your dog "square" into the water, and put the dummies where there are no nearby shores parallel to your dog's path.

Do all the things in water that you did on bare ground: Single, double, and triple cones—but keep the angles at least 45 degrees in water; rerun without the cones; rerun with one of two cones removed; and so forth. Finally, move into cover in water and continue the same basic drills.

Also use a few floating blinds from time to time. They are especially useful in the beginning of these water patterns, and periodically thereafter, to convince your dog that the blind can be a long way from shore. Do most of your lining work with cones, but an occasional floating blind is beneficial—and easier to set up.

Your Training Program for Stopping

Your dog has learned to sit on either HUP or the single whistle blast. Stopping on the whistle is the single most important part of blind retrieve training. If you can't stop your dog, you will not pick up many blinds with him. He can't "line" them all.

Take your dog for a romp at the end of every training session. Stop him with the whistle about once every five minutes. If you are training more than one dog, you can work them simultaneously during these recreational romps—after each is reliable on his own.

Never make your dog regret obeying the STOP whistle. For example, don't stop him with the whistle when you want to punish him. He will never understand why you are correcting him. He will think it is for the last thing he did, which

MOVING TO WATER

First, with cone in place. *Bob Finch*

Then, without the cone. *Bob Finch*

FLOATING BLIND:

DEAD BIRD . . . LINE. *Bob Finch*

Bingo! *Bob Finch*

unfortunately was to obey the whistle. Next time you toot it, he will be inclined to ignore it. Wouldn't you? Instead, run him down, no matter how long it takes.

Your Training Program for Casting

James Lamb Free, in his 1949 classic, *Training Your Retriever*, described a casting drill, using an imaginary baseball diamond. You place your dog on the pitcher's mound. You stand at home plate. You put dummies at first, second, and third bases. Then, you give your dog arm signals to send him to each of the bases. A left-hand OVER directs him to third base. A right-hand OVER directs him to first base. A BACK (either hand) sends him to second base. A COME-IN whistle directs him to pick up a bunt between the mound and home plate.

"Cone baseball," a combination of cones and Free's baseball, improves on basic baseball because it offers the visual aid of white cones at each "base."

Start on bare ground. Mark out a small baseball diamond with the pitcher's mound only ten yards from the bases. At first, put only one cone out, say, at third base. Now heel your dog to the pitcher's mound and have him sit facing home plate. Leaving him in a HUP-STAY, walk over to third base and drop several big white dummies there, making sure your dog sees them. Now, walk to home, turn to face your dog, and give him a left-hand OVER. Having seen you place dummies there, he should run to third base. Repeat this a few times to cement it in. On the reruns, there is no need to walk to third base. He knows where the dummies are. Simply heel your dog to the pitcher's mound, return to home plate, and cast him.

Once your dog understands the left-hand OVER, repeat the process with the cone at first base. Then, at second base. Still, keep the casts short, about ten yards, so you can run your dog several times per session without tiring him. Next, teach him to "pick up a bunt" between the mound and the plate—with the COME-IN whistle. (I don't bother putting out a cone for the bunt.)

After he has learned to run to the cone no matter which base it occupies, try him with two cones in place, but with dummies at only one of them. That way, if he makes a mistake, he won't find a dummy. Repeat this with the two cones at different bases—first and third, first and second, second and third. When he does this without any mistakes, repeat it with dummies at both cones.

Finally, put cones and dummies at all three bases and go through the same drills until he completely understands what is expected of him.

Lengthen the casts out fairly rapidly. Twenty-five yards each. Then, fifty yards for the BACK, thirty-five for the OVERS, and twenty for the COME-IN—and so on until he will do seventy-five-yard BACKS, fifty-yard OVERS, and fifty-yard COME-INS. That is plenty long enough. Naturally, you can't run him as often on these long casts without rest as you did on the shorter ones.

Change locations often. Most city dwellers live within a short drive of several parks and school yards suitable for this work.

After he can handle all four casts at the maximum distances you have selected, start conditioning him to take your casts without the cones. Set the

CONE-CASTING DRILL

Left-hand OVER. *Bob Finch*

Right-hand OVER. *Bob Finch*

BACK. *Bob Finch*

COME-IN. *Bob Finch*

cones up and cast him to each one at least once. Then rerun him without the cones.

Next, set up three cones and run him on each cast at least once. Then rerun him after picking up only one cone. Cast him to the dummies without a cone. Do this with each cone position over several training sessions. It will condition him to take your cast, even when there are cones somewhere else and no cone where you are sending him.

Run the same casting drills in cover that you have been running on bare ground. Start out short, but lengthen him out to your maximum distances quickly. He understands the work already.

In cover, be sure your dog can see all the cones from his position on the pitcher's mound. If that means that one or more of them must be propped up on stakes, fine. If the lighting isn't right for one cone, heel him to it so he can see it before you start.

Set up your casting drills in every imaginable combination of cover, terrain, and wind conditions. Uphill, downhill, through swampy areas, through trees, with the wind, into the wind, crosswind, through light cover, through heavy cover, through mixed patches of cover, and on and on.

After your dog can handle these drills in all the cover situations you want to use, he is ready for water casting. The ideal place for water casting is at the tip of a peninsula, with water on three sides.

Moving On

After you have done dozens, perhaps hundreds, of lining and casting drills in all the cover, terrain, and wind variations available to you, your spaniel should be ready for the transition to real blind retrieves, which is covered in chapter 20.

However, plan to continue these lining, stopping, and casting drills the rest of your spaniel's active life. They are not a phase you take him through. They are a way of life for both of you, so don't rush through them the first time, and don't hesitate to return to them whenever he gets a bit sloppy (which he will, believe me).

20

The Blind Retrieve: The Real Thing

BACKGROUND

What Is It?

Blind retrieves come in two varieties: ''cold'' and ''mixed.'' In a cold blind, one or more blinds are run by themselves, without any marked retrieves. In a ''mixed'' blind, one or more blinds are run in combination with one or more marked retrieves. Typically, the dog picks up the mark(s) first.

Mixed blinds are more difficult than cold blinds. The marks offer ''suction'' to the dog, in that after retrieving the marks, he will be tempted to return (''suck back'') to the marks when sent after a blind.

Why Do It?

This chapter extends the drills explained in chapter 19 to real blind retrieves. As indicated in the previous chapter, blind retrieves come up in both waterfowl and upland game hunting.

AKC spaniel hunting tests include a water blind retrieve in the master level. UKC and NAHRA hunting tests for retrievers, in which spaniels may run, include blind retrieves in the intermediate and highest levels.

Prerequisites

Your spaniel should have completed the preliminary blind retrieve drill work covered in chapter 19.

Equipment

You need no additional equipment for this training.

Schedule

If you train regularly, you should have your spaniel running real cold blinds on land within a month, in water in another month. After that, progress will be slow and steady for the rest of your spaniel's active life.

Handling Techniques

To handle your dog on a real blind retrieve, you should understand the "fairway" concept. Just like every hole on a golf course, every blind retrieve has a fairway. Why? Because a blind retrieve is a test of control, not a "random run."

To determine the fairway for a blind retrieve, stand at the line and extend your right (or left) arm toward the bird with your fist up. Position your second knuckle on the bird. Now raise your thumb and little fingers. The area between those raised digits marks a very tight fairway for that particular blind. Practically speaking, let your fairway be one and a half to two times that width. That's comfortable for most spaniels. You can train for such a fairway without having to use excessive force.

Whenever your dog strays from that fairway, blow the whistle and handle him back into it. If you allow him to run wild and handle him only when he reaches the approximate distance of the bird, you surrender control to the dog.

You need to understand that there are times when your dog will run a better blind if you give him a false line, that is, aim him a bit to the right or left of the true line to the bird. For example, in a strong crosswind, line your dog a little into the wind, because he will drift naturally with it as he runs. Similarly, if the line to the bird runs along the side of a hill, angle him slightly uphill, because he will drift naturally downhill. How far into the wind or up the hill? Depends on your dog. You are responsible for knowing how much he drifts.

Your spaniel has idiosyncrasies you should understand. For example, you should know how far he continues to run after you blow the STOP whistle. That allows you to toot the whistle so he stops where you want him to, or close to it. To be aware of this, you must study your dog in training.

You should also know which way he turns when you cast him BACK. He may always turn to your right. He may always turn to your left. He may turn left with a left-arm BACK and right with a right-arm BACK. That is ideal, but not

DEAD BIRD! *Bob Finch*

worth training specifically for. Instead, watch your dog in training until you know which way he turns naturally, and take advantage of that knowledge.

If your dog always turns to your right on a BACK, you should compensate by stopping him differently on left and right OVERS. On a right OVER, you should stop him a bit early, because he will move farther to the right as he turns. On a left OVER, you should stop him late, because he will move back to the right as he turns. If he always turns to your left, you should reverse these handling procedures.

TRAINING

Transitional Drills

You use two transitional drills, one for land and one for water, to ease your spaniel into real blinds.

The *dummy-string blind* assures your dog success on his early land blinds. In light cover, string out a couple of dozen dummies in a twenty-yard straight line. Mark each end of the string with an orange stake, so you will know where the dummies are from a distance.

Start no more than twenty yards from the string, facing perpendicular to it. Go through your blind retrieve sequence. If he runs twenty yards (which he should by now), he will find a dummy on his initial line. Even if he wobbles off-line a bit, he will still stumble into a dummy. As he runs, run back several yards so you can rerun him from the greater distance, and so on out to about one hundred yards.

The *thrown blind* is the transitional drill for water. In it, you hide an assistant somewhere near where the blind is to be. After you send your dog—with no dummy in place—you signal to your assistant, and he throws a dummy so that it lands where you want it. Your dog leaves and goes whatever distance you feel he can handle on his own. When he starts to waiver, you signal for the throw. To the dog, the flying dummy is manna from heaven.

Although excellent for water, this drill is not satisfactory on land. In water, the dummy remains visible after it is thrown. On land, it may be hidden by cover or terrain, making your dog hunt for it like a mark. If he forms the habit of hunting on blinds, he will be very difficult to handle.

Your Training Program for Cold Blinds

This is about the only training for which you don't return to bare ground. You can't, for the dog would see the dummies from the line.

Start land blinds first, using the dummy-string technique in light cover. Start out at about twenty yards and extend to one hundred or so in the first session. Change locations for your next session. Start at about forty yards and lengthen out to one hundred yards. Each session you should go to a new location and start from farther back. As you start farther and farther away, lengthen your dummy string, lest your dog miss it altogether.

It is more important for him to run one hundred yards and find a dummy than it is for him to run a precise line at this point in his training. You are trying to convince him that if he runs far enough, he can find a dummy. Once he really believes that, you can work on straighter lines.

Start thrown blinds in water as soon as he can do a hundred-yard dummy-string blind on land. Have the dummy thrown in open water, never in cover, where your dog would have to hunt for it.

Keep your assistant completely hidden from your dog's view through this training. If the dog sees the thrower at any time—from the line, on the way out, when the dummy is thrown, or when the dog returns—he will associate him with the thrower in marked retrieves. That will complicate your training program when you get to mixed blinds and marks.

Initially, signal for the throw right after you send your dog. On the rerun, wait until he gets to the water's edge. On the next rerun wait until after he swims a short distance. And so on until he will swim all the way before it is necessary to call for the throw. Of course, rest him whenever he needs it. He swims a long way out and back every time you send him.

In your second session, don't call for the throw the first time until your dog is at the water's edge. In your third session, wait until after he swims a short distance, and so on. This will build his confidence that the dummy will always fly eventually if he just swims far enough.

After that, change locations often for these thrown water blinds, and delay signaling for each throw as long as your dog is swimming purposefully in the right direction.

When he will run hundred-yard dummy-string blinds on land, and is well started in his water thrown blinds, he is ready for more advanced work on land.

Run him on a real blind with all the dummies in one place rather than strung out. Mark the dummies' location with something you can see that your dog can't (orange stake or piece of surveyor's tape). Make this a very easy blind, no more than seventy-five yards long, straight downwind, in light cover, perhaps even downhill a little.

Even with all those simplifying features, he may not hold his original line well enough to find the dummies without help. Great. That's just what you want. Handle him.

No matter how poor his initial line is, let him run for at least forty yards before stopping him with the whistle. In training, you shouldn't hassle your dog right after he leaves your side, lest he think he erred in leaving, which could cause him to "no-go" next time.

After you stop him, make sure he locates you before you give him a cast. When you have his attention, give him the appropriate cast—typically an OVER one way or the other—exactly as you have been giving it in casting drills. Don't let your own excitement affect your movements or rhythm.

If he takes your cast, great. If he fails to take it, stop him again, let him

STRING OF DUMMIES BLIND

Dummies are in line between two stakes. *Bob Finch*

LINE. *Bob Finch*

sit and look at you a few seconds to clear his head of extraneous ideas, then give him the cast again, very clearly. He will surely take it if you have done the basics thoroughly enough in the casting drills. When he gets back to the correct line, stop him again and give him a BACK cast (with the arm opposite that with which you gave him the OVER).

On a simple blind like this, you should be able to put him on the dummies with a couple or three handles. When he brings you the dummy, praise him as if no other dog had ever done anything so wonderful in the history of the world.

Then, rerun him two or three times. You always rerun blinds, just as you always rerun marks—but for different reasons. In marks, you are trying to sharpen his marking. In blinds, you are encouraging pictures. After he has run the blind and knows where it is, he sits at the line again and formulates a picture of it. Lining the blind on the rerun reinforces the picture. Reruns build pictures, just as pattern blinds do.

The rest is obvious: Continue running real land blinds that are well within your dog's capabilities, toughening them up only as he shows he can handle more advanced work. Continue with the thrown blinds in water until you are sure—judging from his land work—that he will respond to handling in water well enough to risk a real blind there.

The extension into multiple cold blinds, in which you plant two or more blinds in different locations and handle your dog to each in turn, is obvious. Start short and wide, NO the dog off the first one before sending him for the second, and correct him as in switching if he returns to the wrong area. Multiple cold blinds constitute an intermediate step between single cold blinds and mixed blinds.

Of course, you should continue the normal lining, stopping, and casting drills. In each training session, run him on a real blind first, with appropriate reruns. Then, go to another area and give him a new cone pattern blind, preferably multispoked, first with cones and then without them. This will give him more pictures for his "album." Rest him, and then run him on a cone baseball drill. If you don't have time for both lining and casting, alternate the two in your sessions. After each session, go for a walk and stop him about once every five minutes.

Problems in Cold Blinds

You might run into any of three major problems in real blinds: poor initial line, no-go, and popping.

Poor Initial Line (PIL): At some point, your dog will think he has a better idea than you have. You will sit him facing the blind, but he will look in some other direction. When this happens, reheel him facing the direction he is interested in and say NO, just as you have been doing when selecting a cone. He should understand that you are vetoing his idea. Reheel him to face the blind again. If he looks the wrong way, send him. He will go the wrong way, of course. Let him go for forty yards. Then, hustle out and correct him firmly. Bring him back and start over.

He will not want to return to the area in which you corrected him. When you rerun him he will be more inclined to listen to your NO and take the line you give him. Sit him facing where you just chastised him and say NO. Reheel him to face the blind and go through your blind retrieve sequence. He will probably take your line this time. In fact, he may even overcorrect and take a line too far on the other side of the line you gave him. If he does this, let him run forty yards and handle him to the blind. He was trying to obey. In fact, he was trying too hard.

No-go means your dog remains at your side when you command BACK. Determine why he refused before trying to correct the problem. If you have rushed him into real blinds, he may be so uncertain of what you expect that he freezes at your side. Or, if you have punished him too severely for PIL, he may have decided it is safer by your side.

If you have rushed him too much, the solution is obvious: Back off awhile, and do the basics more thoroughly. If you have overcorrected him, the solution is also obvious: Go back a few spaces, start again, and when he makes a mistake, go a little easier on him.

Popping is stopping to ask for directions when you haven't blown the whistle. Every dog does this occasionally. If your dog pops often, you may have rushed him into real blinds before drilling in the basics adequately. Popping can become a nasty habit in which the dog won't go more than a few yards on his own without stopping and asking for help.

When your dog pops occasionally, ignore him. Wait him out. Look the other way. Do anything except give him the arm signal he wants. If he is tough enough, you might even run toward him as if you are going to punish him. The important thing is to avoid giving him that arm signal.

If he pops often, go back to cone pattern blinds to build up his confidence. The cones encourage him to use pictures, and a picture encourages him to run to a certain spot on a blind, rather than ask for help. Thus pictures, and the cone pattern blinds that encourage them, are preventatives and cures for popping.

Mixed Marks and Blinds

While you are working your dog on real cold blinds, you should also do the preliminary conditioning for mixed marks and blinds. Do this in conjunction with your regular cone pattern blinds.

Set up a hundred-yard pattern blind and run him with the cones in place once or twice. Then, set up a simple fifty-yard single mark at a 45- to 60-degree angle away from the line to your cone blind. Run him on the mark. When he returns, sit him facing the mark and tell him NO—this is very important—and then reheel him and sit him facing one of the cones. Go through your blind retrieve sequence and send him for the blind. Since he has already run it, and since the cone is still there, he should have no difficulty with it.

STRING OF DUMMIES BLIND

BACK! *Bob Finch*

Success! *Bob Finch*

Sheryl Finch tosses the mark. *Bob Finch*

Flick heads for the mark. *Bob Finch*

Author NOs Flick off area of mark. *Bob Finch*

DEAD BIRD . . . LINE. *Bob Finch*

BACK! *Bob Finch*

Success! *Bob Finch*

Rerun the entire test without the cone. Since he has run the test at least twice, he should have no trouble with it. When he can handle a single mark and blind, add a second mark, then a second blind. Take your time and let your dog succeed as much as possible.

However, at some point in this training, your dog will suck back to the mark. Correct him much as you do for switching. Punish him in the area to which he sucked back. Then, heel him back to the line and run him on the blind again. After he runs it successfully twice, rerun the entire test, mark and blind. As in the correction for switching, your dog's reaction on the rerun will tell you whether you are correcting properly.

After you have run him on mixed tests incorporating many cone pattern blinds, use the transitional techniques (string of dummies, and thrown blinds) to introduce real mixed blinds. After he has shown he can handle these, go ahead and start real mixed blinds—just as you did real cold blinds.

21

Keeping Your Spaniel Trained

YOU MAY have heard this old joke, maybe even about your own alma mater. If not, feel free to nail some of your buddies with it at an opportune moment.

"Why doesn't the boss let graduates from (fill in the blank) college take coffee breaks?"

"I don't know. Why?"

"Because it would take too long to retrain them."

Dogs are like that. If you don't keep their training up with regular sessions, more or less year-round for their entire active lives, they forget what you have taught them. That shouldn't surprise anyone. Think what happens to a good shotgun shooter when he lays off for several months. Ditto for scratch golfers. And this natural tendency to atrophy is not limited to physical skills. How would you like to retake the final exam from, say, your high school geometry class? We live in a use-it-or-lose-it world, and so do our dogs.

What's more, if you don't make sure your spaniel uses his training correctly while hunting, he will lose it even while using it. He will make mistakes every fall. He will get away with some of them, too, because you will be concentrating on hunting so much you won't see his errors until they get a bit out of hand. For example, just an instant before you send him, he will break to retrieve a running rooster pheasant. Just an instant, mind you. And you will be so happy to see him romping in carrying the bird that you will forget his break. Next time he will go a bit sooner, and you may notice it subconsciously but not worry about it.

Eventually he will flush and chase a low-flying bird, preventing you from getting a shot. You'll notice that mistake.

At that point, you will have a decision to make. Should you stop shooting for a few flushes to concentrate on resteadying your dog, or should you ignore the problem until after hunting season? There is no pat answer that will work for everyone. You have to answer this one for yourself, based on your own situation. If you fix the problem immediately, it will be relatively easy and quite effective. If you wait, the fix will be more difficult and less permanent. On the other hand, if your work schedule for this particular fall allows you only a few hunting trips, you may prefer to enjoy your limited hunting now and fix your dog's problems next spring. Or, if this is the last year you plan to hunt with your aging spaniel, what the hell, let him have fun. Why hassle the old-timer about problems?

Regardless of how you deal with problems that develop during hunting, you should work your spaniel regularly during the off-season months to keep him sharp. If you started when he was a puppy and worked regularly through all the training in this book, your dog is now somewhere between two and three years old. He has another five to ten years of active life ahead of him, during which he will either get a little better or a lot worse each year. It's your choice.

To help him improve, work him regularly. At least a couple of times a week year-round, weather permitting. Work him on everything you have taught him, but not in every session. Keep your sessions short. The secret of good maintenance training is this: Underwork the dog frequently rather than overwork him now and then.

When your dog makes a mistake in your maintenance sessions—as he will—don't be surprised. Don't react emotionally. None of this "How dare you do that *to me*!" stuff. Your dog isn't doing anything *to you*. He's just making a mistake. Remain calm and take appropriate, constructive action. This usually means giving a relatively mild (nonemotional) correction, followed by going back a step or two for reconditioning.

The typical neophyte trainer feels humiliated when he has to repeat preliminary procedures with his first "fully trained dog" (whatever that means). He acts like a kid who has been put back a grade in grammar school. Wrong attitude. Dog training is a conditioning process. That means repetitions and more repetitions of the correct responses. That in turn means reiterations and more reiterations through a series of progressive training steps over a long period of time. That's no disgrace. That's just dog training.

These frequent, short training sessions all year long have some significant fringe benefits. First, they strengthen and improve the rapport between you and your dog. He will come to understand you better and better, and vice versa (although you will never read him like he reads you). Second, they keep your spaniel in good working condition. A flushing spaniel is a canine athlete. He has speed, agility, coordination, and unbelievable endurance. But to be the best athlete he can be, he must be in shape. Frequent short training sessions help. And finally, these frequent training sessions keep your wing shooting as sharp

"Flick" flushes a rooster pheasant during hunting, but will he remain steady under these conditions?

as it can be. (For me, that's not very sharp, but at least it's as good as I can hope for.)

However, we live in a busy, busy world. So many things to do. So little time. You might, almost unwittingly, let other activities crowd maintenance training out of your life. Motivation—yours, not your dog's—can be a problem after you have been all through the training program once. Procrastination, the "I'll train tomorrow" syndrome, can set in.

To overcome this, you should establish new goals for yourself and your spaniel. Think about running him in some of the off-season games spaniel people play with their dogs: Field Trials, hunting tests, Working Certificate tests. Each of these will give you a new reason to get out and train regularly. Each will also introduce you to fellow spaniel fanciers, some of whom will become lifelong friends. Section 3 explains these games.

Bill and Peggy Ruble with a pair of their hard-hunting Welshies.

SECTION III

Enjoying Your Spaniel

OVERVIEW

Training a spaniel is fun in and of itself. You get out in the country. You watch your dog, and the dogs of your training buddies, progress from session to session. You shoot birds for your buddies' dogs. (In some groups the shooting becomes quite competitive.) You stand around and talk before and after each session.

However, you didn't undertake spaniel training for its own enjoyment. No, that's a fringe benefit. You probably started training because you wanted to develop a good all-round hunting dog for your kind of hunting. That's why most of us get into dog training.

Chapter 22 gives you several suggestions on how to hunt more successfully with your spaniel. Trouble is, hunting seasons don't last long. Three, maybe four months from early fall through winter. That leaves eight or nine months with not much for your trained spaniel to do. Not too surprisingly, you are not the first to encounter this problem. And not too surprisingly, those who have been here ahead of you have developed several solutions for you: Field Trials, hunting tests, and Working Certificate tests. I call them "dog games," not derisively, but just to keep their importance in perspective.

Chapter 23 explains the oldest of these games: competitive Field Trials. They have been around since 1924, are well established and steeped in tradition. Limited to English Springer Spaniels, Field Trials have a most challenging performance standard. Field Trial dogs get the job done with more pizzazz than any other kind of spaniel. Even Field Trial washouts make spectacular hunting dogs.

Chapter 24 explains the very new, noncompetitive game called "hunting tests." These were initiated for spaniels in 1988 as part of the overall expansion of the AKC noncompetitive testing program, the fastest-growing program in AKC history. They are open to all breeds AKC classifies as spaniels: English Springers, Welsh Springers, English Cockers, American Cockers, Fields, Sussex, and Clumbers. Being noncompetitive, they are less demanding than Field Trials in terms of time and money commitments. Having three levels of testing and titles, they are less all-or-nothing than Field Trials. Being new, they address more completely than trials all aspects of spaniel use in modern American hunting, including nonslip marked retrieving and blind retrieves in water. On the other hand, being new, they have no traditions to guide them yet. Things are a bit chaotic right now. Judging is unpredictable. The rules are still being developed. Participants suffer all manner of frustration because of the inconsistencies from one test to another. The program is improving and will eventually stabilize as traditions set in. Right now, things are a bit confusing. But where does it say that making history should be easy?

Chapter 25 explains the Working Certificate tests conducted by the various national breed clubs. The American Water Spaniel Club has a challenging, four-level program designed for the unique needs of that versatile breed. The other clubs have identical (and very basic) tests designed to field test those breeds not eligible to compete in Field Trials plus those English Springer Spaniels that lack the "dogpower" to compete in trials.

The major complaint about all of these dog games is that they are too artificial. They "jest ain't 'nuf like huntin' fer me." In some ways that may be true.

However, people developed these dog games specifically to give us something to do with our dogs when we cannot hunt. How could they be just like hunting? Then, too, fairness to all participants demands rules—lots of rules usually—and rules introduce artificiality into any game.

The question then is not whether they are artificial, but whether they come close enough to hunting to entertain us and improve our dogs during the off-season. Any reasonable person would say, "Yes, they do. Indeed they do." So what's the problem?

In the musical *South Pacific*, some women-starved sailors sing a delightful song called "There's Nothing Like a Dame." In it, one line goes like this:

> *"It's a waste of time to worry over things that they have not,*
> *Be thankful for the things they've got!"*

Why not view dog games that way? Even if they are artificial, they are lots better than nothing during the off-season. They keep the dogs trained and in shape. They motivate and entertain the owners.

I've never heard anyone say dog games harmed his dog for hunting, but I've seen many dogs atrophy between hunting seasons for lack of work.

Besides, I've never heard anyone who has been successful in a dog game complain about its artificiality. No, it's the loser or, more often, the guy afraid to enter his dog. Either way, you can bet the complainer's dog couldn't find a pound of hamburger in the middle of the kitchen floor. That should tell you what such complaints are really all about.

Author accepts a prairie chicken from "Flick."

22
Hunting

YOU DON'T HAVE TO—in fact, you shouldn't—wait until your spaniel is fully trained before hunting him. No, within reason, the sooner the better. If he retrieves to you rather than running off, if he has been gunproofed, and if he will respond to the STOP and COME-IN whistles, he can help you a lot, even while he's still a pup. You will help him a lot, too, by taking him hunting as early as possible. His nose will tell him stories beyond your understanding about the ways of wild birds.

His first season may not go according to whatever script you have written for it. For example, Flick's first wild pheasant was such a disaster that I had to put him into "remedial untraining" to get him past it. He was only seven months old, but he had had a full summer's training. He had a decent ground pattern. He had flushed and retrieved many pigeons and a couple of store-bought pheasants. He responded to the whistle reliably and loved the sound of gunfire. So I took him hunting.

We started the day working a strip of cover along a fencerow. I didn't look too closely at the fence, which was a mistake. We hadn't gone a hundred yards when Flick alerted, dove in, and busted out a big, gaudy rooster pheasant. The bird barely topped the fence with Flick still leaping gamely after it. Flick crashed into the fence and bounced back. It was one of those "pig-tight" wire fences. He hit it within a couple of bounds of the flush. To Flick, it was a case of flush and *bam*! His canine logic was screaming, "The bird did it! The bird did it! Look out for birds!"

He wasn't injured, but he was stunned and frightened. He acted like a thirteen-year-old boy after being laughed at by the first girl he asked for a date.

An experienced dog would shake this episode right off, but this was Flick's first wild bird, the first one with absolutely no human scent on it. That could start him blinking birds. What to do? What to do?

First, I ended the day early, and went home to think about it. No sense staying out there and risking another disaster. At home, I decided to let him forget about it for a week, then take him pheasant hunting with no real intention to get any birds. I wanted to put him in places where he could chase runners for miles. Anything to make going after a moving bird fun again.

A week later, I took him to a birdy-looking cut grainfield, where pheasants should run forever but not flush. I turned Flick loose and stood there to watch. He raced up and down the rows, obviously trailing running birds, until he was ready to drop. Occasionally I saw one flush off in the distance. Flick went half a mile to the end of the field and back many times. Once he trapped a rooster between him and me, so it flushed—and I *missed*! (Expletives deleted.) This I attribute to my surprise . . . along with my usual lousy wing shooting.

Flick showed me that he had overcome any fear he might have had of wild birds. I loaded him up and went home. After that we hunted more conventionally all year.

Under normal circumstances a flushing spaniel should never be allowed to range to half a mile. However, that's exactly what Flick needed, so that's what I did. It did him no harm, either. The next time out, he responded to the whistle nicely and worked well for me.

Although hunting a green pup can be more training than hunting sometimes, hunting a trained spaniel should be mostly hunting. Fun. Exhilarating for both dog and man.

Don't overhandle your spaniel. In training, you have known where each bird was. You either planted it, rolled it in, or had an assistant roll it in. You may have had to work a bit now and again to get your dog to find it. This can become a habit that carries over into hunting, where you don't know where the birds are. If you overhandle here, your dog will not learn to seek out the birdy places on his own, as he should. Let his nose direct him, as long as he stays within the proper range. If he punches out too far, whistle him back in with the COME-IN whistle, or as a last resort, stop him with the HUP whistle and make him sit and wait until you catch up.

What if he's trailing a running bird? Still keep him in range with the STOP whistle. If he puts the bird up out of range, you won't get a shot. Dogs quickly learn this stop-and-go method of working runners. I remember trailing a rooster pheasant for half a mile once, with many stops along the way. Did the bird get away? No. My dog flushed it within fifteen yards of me, and wonder of wonders, I hit it. How do I know it was the same bird? Because the ground was covered with snow and I could see its tracks as well as my dog could follow its trail.

Don't be too fussy about ground pattern, as long as your dog hits all the good cover. If, for example, you are hunting one side of a hedgerow where the adjoining field is almost bare (like a freshly planted wheat field), you should encourage your dog to stay on the hedgerow side of you. Why waste his energy by insisting that he windshield-wiper out onto the bare field every cast?

Handle your dog only when he misses a particularly attractive piece of cover. And remember, he doesn't have to go through it to cover it. If the wind is right, he can learn all he needs to know by swinging past it. Make sure he covers the good spots with his nose. Don't fret about where he actually runs to do that. During training, you should come to understand how good his nose is, how close he has to get to wind birds. This varies from dog to dog.

While hunting, you must take care of all your dog's physical needs, just as you do at home and in training.

Conditioning should be a major concern. If you train frequently year-round, your dog should be in reasonably good shape for hunting. If you don't train all year, you should do it regularly for a month or so before opening day. Swimming helps bring the flabby dog into good shape quickly, but don't overdo it in any one session.

You need a suitable means for transporting your spaniel to and from the fields. Some let their dog(s) ride in the car with them. Some use crates inside station wagons or vans. Some use dog boxes on their pickup beds. Some pull trailers. All of these are fine, as long as the dog has adequate ventilation (especially in warm weather) and adequate protection from wind, moisture, and cold in colder weather.

Every year I see dogs running loose in the open beds of pickups. Veterinarians tell me they patch up a lot of dogs (the luckier ones) that have jumped out at inopportune times. More recently I have seen an occasional dog tied to a cable in a pickup bed. This prevents escape, but it leaves the animal vulnerable to weather and flying debris. I see no excuse for loose dogs in the back of pickups, whether tethered or not. Anyone who can afford a dog and a pickup truck can afford a suitable dog box or trailer.

In selecting your method of transporting your dog, you should consider the matter of "crime prevention." Every year I hear stories of dogs stolen from vehicles during hunting trips. Two years ago a man from Missouri called to see if I would sell Flick to him *right now* and for whatever price I asked. He said he had had a good spaniel until the previous weekend. He took the dog to Iowa to hunt pheasants. When he arrived at his hunting spot, he opened the dog box in the back of his pickup to find his dog was gone. Thinking back over his trip, he remembered leaving his pickup unattended only once, at a rest area. Someone must have stolen the dog while he was inside. Too bad. He was desperate for another spaniel with which to finish the hunting season. Somehow I think he would have paid whatever I had asked for Flick. But Flick is not for sale. I don't know whether the poor guy found another dog or not.

I usually let Flick ride in the front seat of my pickup with me to and from training sessions and hunting trips. Rocky rides in his side of the dog box in back. My dog box is chained and padlocked to my pickup, and each stall can be padlocked. When I hunt Flick, I lock Rocky in the dog box. When I hunt Rocky,

I lock Flick in the dog box. When I stop at a restaurant to eat lunch, I lock them both in. I have a two-dog fiberglass trailer I pull when hunting with more than two dogs. Each stall can be padlocked, and the trailer can be padlocked to the truck. Granted, none of these precautions would stop a determined dog thief—what would?—but they do protect me from casual thefts, which account for most hunting dog losses afield.

You should carry plenty of drinking water with you. Dogs do better on water from home, rather than whatever might be available where you hunt. Depending on how many dogs I take, I carry one or more two-and-a-half-gallon plastic containers of home water. I also carry a small plastic squirt bottle full of water in my game bag. I give my dogs drinks from this bottle when we're far from the truck.

I prefer to alternate dogs all day, working each one no more than an hour at a time before resting him. This is more work than my dogs get during training sessions, so I carry a small quantity of food to give them at midday.

Spaniels, having the kind of coats they have, and hunting the kind of places they hunt, can take on quite a load of burrs and stickers during the course of a day. It only takes a few minutes to remove these every time you return to the car. I have a special tool for this. It's called a mat rake. It has long teeth that are sharpened on the inside edges. I recommend that you get one and use it when your dog's coat gets loaded with burrs. One caution: Keep your fingers away from the sharpened edges of the rake. I forgot this once, and I sliced myself on them.

Some people simplify burr removal by applying oil to their spaniels' coats before each hunting trip. Dr. Gary Forshee told me he buys the cheapest, oiliest hair oil he can find, and it works great on his American Water Spaniels' curly coats. He said, "The cheaper it is, the greasier it is, so the better it works."

Another way to minimize the burr problem is by trimming a spaniel's coat very closely before hunting season. I don't recommend this. Except for floor-mopping show tresses, a spaniel's coat is meant to protect the dog in tough cover. I prefer pulling burrs to watching my dog get scratched up unnecessarily. I would, however, trim a show coat back to something more practical for a hunting dog.

Most dog-owning hunters do not carry canine first aid kits. I don't, partially because I frequently hunt with my son, Pat, who is a veterinarian. And partially for the same reason I don't I carry a human first aid kit: I wouldn't know what to do with it in an emergency anyhow. The patient, human or canine, will be better served if I hustle him to the nearest source of professional health care. In my several decades afield, I've never had to do this, and I hope I never do, but that's my plan.

If you want to pack a canine first aid kit, talk to your veterinarian about what to put in it. Different areas have different requirements. Remember, however, that accumulating all the right items is just the beginning. You have to learn when and how to use each item, too.

One way to lessen the probability that you will need a first aid kit is to help your dog through any fences you must cross, especially the barbed-wire kind. If it is low enough for your dog to jump, hold the top strand down for him. If it's too high for jumping, spread two strands for him to jump through. If it's too high for jumping and too tight for going through, lift him over.

Once last year, while hunting with Flick, I came to such a fence, or so I thought. It was another of those "pig-tight" affairs, only with a strand of barbed wire at the top. It looked too high for Flick to jump. I unloaded my gun, laid it down, picked Flick up, and hoisted all sixty-three pounds of him over the fence. He sprang from my arms to the ground lightly. Then I slid my gun under the fence and struggled over the top near a post. When I was astraddle of the barbed wire, and being appropriately careful, Flick jumped nimbly back to the other side! And then back again. I guess he wanted to show me that I had underestimated his ability as a high jumper.

If you hunt doves with your spaniel, do it sitting by a pond. Any other type of dove hunting—especially walking them up—involves too much danger of overheating. I almost lost a Golden Retriever that way once. Fortunately, we were near a river. When he got wobbly, I carried him to the river. He lay in the shallows for thirty minutes before he felt strong enough to get up. And he showed no signs of trouble until it was almost too late.

If you hunt ducks with your spaniel, even in the early season, give him plenty of time to run around and dry off after each bit of action. If you make him sit by the blind, he may chill from the water in his coat.

If you hunt late-season ducks—when the weather is really nasty and the water is topped with skim ice—either leave your spaniel home, or limit yourself to jump shooting. That is, unless you have an American Water Spaniel, in which case you can hunt them any way you like.

If you will take these simple precautions, hunting with your spaniel will be more fun than you have ever had hunting. I've hunted with many pointing dogs, and even more retrievers, and I have enjoyed every one of them. Still, spaniels are special, as you will see, first time you hunt with one.

Brenda Falkowski casts NAFC/FC Agatha's Morgan Broderick, as judge Ralph Palmer and an unidentified "shagger" watch.

Gene Falkowski's NAFC Orion's Arch Rival flushes a hen pheasant in a field trial.

23

Field Trials

ONLY ENGLISH SPRINGER SPANIELS may run in AKC Field Trials for spaniels. Nevertheless, every spaniel owner should learn to appreciate these trials, know what they accomplish, understand how they are conducted, and know how to enjoy them.

Purposes

These trials, initiated in 1924, exist to identify through competition the most capable English Springer Spaniels. The ultimate goal is breed improvement through selective breeding. To achieve this, Field Trial people have developed a challenging standard of performance. Supporting this standard are a long history, and rich traditions. Field Trials stand as a stable, predictable, understandable dog game.

Field Trialers seek fast, snappy spaniels, dogs that cover their beats quickly and completely, sweeping left and right ahead of their handlers at a blurring rate of speed. Some of these dogs float. Others bounce. But all successful trial dogs "pick 'em up and lay 'em down" with alacrity. They don't mess around.

Field Trialers prefer spaniels that flush birds hard, dogs that dive in with wham-bam-alakazam cockiness. They claim that such dogs give a pheasant no choice but to fly, that any softness on flush gives the bird another option, namely to scurry off on foot.

Field Trialers like spaniels that rock'n'roll on their retrieves. If the dogs hunt large areas around the falls, so what? As long as they find their birds in a reasonable length of time, who cares?

But Field Trials do much more than identify good breeding stock for a certain type of working spaniel. They provide opportunities for people with similar interests to gather and enjoy each other's company. They satisfy the competitive urges of English Springer owners. Some people are more competitive than others. For the noncompetitive, we have hunting tests (see chapter 24), and for the competitive, we have Field Trials.

Stakes and Placements

A Field Trial is divided into several stakes, or separate competitions among relatively equal dogs and handlers. The stakes are: Open All Age (more often called simply the "Open"), the Qualified Open All Age ("Qualified Open"), the Amateur All Age ("Amateur"), the Limited, the Novice, and the Puppy. Most trials have only the Open (or Qualified Open), the Amateur, and the Puppy. Those make a full load for one weekend.

The Open All Age Stake is the big one. It is "open" to all dogs, all handlers. Any dog over six months old, including those with all the Field Trial titles, may compete in the Open. Any handler, amateur or professional, may run dogs here. In this stake the four placing dogs earn points toward the "Field Champion" (FC) title. They also qualify for the Annual National Championship Trial, which explains why so many titled dogs continue to run in this stake trial after trial, year after year. These FC and AFC dogs keep the level of competition in the Open Stake high.

The Qualified Open All Age Stake is a specialized Open All Age Stake limited to dogs that have placed in any stake (except Puppy) in a previous trial. Clubs use this stake in place of the Open when they fear entries will be too large if they hold a regular Open.

The Amateur All Age Stake is similar to the Open. Only amateur handlers may run dogs in this stake, but no limitations are placed on the dogs themselves. Professionally trained dogs and titled dogs can compete, as long as amateurs handle them. In this stake, the four placing dogs earn points toward the "Amateur Field Champion" (AFC) title. They also qualify to run in the Annual National Amateur Championship Trial, which explains why so many titled dogs continue to run. These titled dogs keep the level of competition in the Amateur Stake high.

The (seldom-used) Limit Stake is for dogs that have never won first in an Open Stake or two firsts in any other stake (except the Puppy). They award no championship points in the Limit Stake. It is an advanced beginners' stake.

The (seldom-used) Novice Stake is for novice handlers who have never placed a dog in an Open, Amateur, or Qualified Open Stake, and who have never placed a dog first in a Puppy Stake and for dogs with similar qualifications. They award no championship points in the Novice Stake. It is a beginners' stake for those with older dogs.

The Puppy Stake is for dogs not over twenty-four months old (like the Derby Stake in retriever and pointing dog trials). Any handler, amateur or professional, can run a dog here, as long as the dog has not reached its second birthday on the starting day of the trial. Placing dogs earn no championship points. This is a beginners' stake, a warm-up for the big stakes, a place for both dog and handler to get trial experience.

In each stake, the judges award four placements to the top four dogs. They may also award a ''Judge's Award of Merit'' (JAM) to any unplaced dog that has done excellent work. In the Open and Qualified Open stakes, the placing dogs receive Field Championship points. In the Amateur Stake, the placing dogs receive Amateur Field Championship points.

Formats

The format of the Open, Qualified Open, and the Amateur stakes are identical. In each, the dogs run three quartering ''series'' on courses planted with game birds (usually pheasants). In the first two series, the dogs run in braces on adjacent beats. Typically, each dog runs until it has had a minimum of two bird ''contacts.'' Of course, it can eliminate itself at any time through some major mistake, like punching out too far, breaking, poaching on the other dog's beat, passing a bird without finding it, or failing a retrieve. In a contact, ideally, the dog flushes the bird, hups promptly, and waits to be sent for the retrieve. However, other things can happen. First, the dog may ''trap'' the bird on the ground before it can fly. That's okay, as long as he retrieves it to the handler. Second, the gunners may miss the bird. That's okay, too, as long as the dog remains steady.

The judges usually keep each dog on the ground until it has had at least one opportunity to retrieve, even if that means more than the minimum two contacts. A dog that traps a couple of birds, then has the misfortune to be running when the gunners make a couple of their rare misses, can be on the ground a long time.

Most judges keep each dog running until it has had an opportunity to ''honor'' its bracemate's retrieve. When its bracemate flushes a bird, the dog must hup and remain in place while its bracemate completes the retrieve.

In the first series, one judge follows all the dogs that run on the right-hand beat, the other judge follows those that run on the left. In the second series, the dogs change beats to run under the other judge. After each of the first two series, the judges make a list of ''call-backs,'' the dogs that did well enough to continue in competition for the next series. Dogs not called back are considered eliminated.

In the third and final series, each dog runs alone (without a bracemate) on a single beat. That allows both judges to evaluate each dog's work simultaneously. Field Trialers call this the ''show series,'' because in this series the handlers give their dogs their heads a bit, to allow them to show the judges what they can do with less control. Handlers can do this because, with no bracemate, they don't have to worry about poaching or breaking on honor.

After the third series, the judges announce their four placements and JAMs (if any). The winners celebrate while the losers vow to train harder next week.

If held, the Limit Stake's format will approximate that of the Open and Amateur.

The format of the Puppy Stake is much simpler. The dogs run individually rather than in braces. They only run two series, and typically get two contacts per series, more if necessary to get a retrieve. Although they may use game birds, most clubs save money by using pigeons. The Puppy Stake may be divided into "steady puppies" and "unsteady puppies." If so, each group competes separately, usually with different judges and on different courses. The unsteady Puppy Stake allows people with very young dogs to compete at their own level. Nice idea.

If held, the Novice Stake's format approximates that of the Puppy Stake.

At most licensed trials, the host club also offers a voluntary, noncompetitive water series. Each dog entered has to remain steady at the line while the gunners shoot a game bird (usually a pheasant) to fall in water some forty to eighty yards away. Then, when sent, the dog must swim out to retrieve the bird. Before a spaniel can earn the FC or AFC title, it must pass one of these water tests.

The format of the National Championship Field Trial is greatly expanded from that of the licensed trial Open Stake. It consists of seven series: four land series in braces, one individual land series, and two water series (similar to the test described above, but not voluntary). This trial is run annually, typically in late November or early December. Each year it moves to a different area of the country. To qualify for this trial, a dog must place in a licensed trial Open Stake during the preceding year.

The format of the National Amateur Championship Field Trial is the same as that of the National Championship, except that only amateurs may handle dogs in it. To qualify, a dog must place in a licensed trial Amateur Stake during the preceding year. This trial is conducted in conjunction with the National Championship Trial each year.

Titles

According to AKC custom, Field Trial titles, being competitive, go before the dog's name. These titles are as follows:

National Field Trial Champion, abbreviated as NFC, NFTC, or Nat.Fld.Ch., sometimes qualified by the year in which the dog won it, as "1992 NFC." To earn this title, the dog must win the Annual National Championship Field Trial.

National Amateur Field Trial Champion, abbreviated as NAFC, NAFTC, or Nat.Am.Fld.Ch., sometimes qualified by the year in which the dog won it, as "1992 NAFC." To earn this title, the dog must win the Annual National Amateur Championship Field Trial.

Field Trial Champion, abbreviated as FC, FTC, or Fld.Ch. To earn this title, the dog must win the National Open Championship Trial, or win two first places in Open and/or Qualified All Age Stakes, or one first place plus ten additional points in those stakes. Second place earns three points, third, two, and fourth, one. In addition, the dog must pass a water test.

Amateur Field Trial Champion, abbreviated as AFC, AFTC, or Am.Fld.Ch. To earn this title, the dog must win the National Amateur Championship Trial, or win two first places in Amateur Stakes, or win one first plus ten additional points in Amateur Stakes. Second place earns three points, third, two, fourth, one. In addition, the dog must pass a water test.

The Mechanics of a Field Trial

Each Field Trial is put on by a club formed for that specific purpose. Some clubs put on one trial per year, while others put on two (one spring, one fall). Either way the club works year-round on their trials.

They start shortly after the previous trial, when they meet for a postmortem review of the last trial.

Shortly after the postmortem, the club appoints a new Field Trial committee for the next trial. The committee has a chair, a secretary, and at least three other members. Together, they do the following things: schedule the next trial with AKC; select the site; select trial workers (bird planters, shaggers, field marshals, gunners, runners, traffic controllers); coordinate with a bird supplier; select and invite the judges, plus make their travel and lodging arrangements; select trophies and rosettes; prepare and mail premium lists; accept entries; conduct the drawing for running sequences; prepare and publish the catalog; handle all correspondence with AKC and other involved parties; plan the banquet and any other desired social gatherings; monitor the trial setup efforts before the trial; keep the actual trial running smoothly; act for AKC during the trial in any disputes or misconduct hearings; help award trophies and rosettes; clean up the site after the trial; and submit official results to AKC.

On the day before the trial, the committee goes to the trial grounds to lay out the courses. They mark them clearly, usually with fiberglass rods seven or eight feet high with flags on top. Each course is about forty yards wide. For brace work they mark two parallel courses, each forty yards wide, placing stakes on the outer edges and down the middle. Without these stakes, the judges and handlers would not know where each dog should quarter.

During the brace work series, three guns walk the course with the dogs. One gun walks the outer edge of each course. The third, typically the best shot, walks the centerline between the two courses. These must be good shots, and they must be familiar with spaniel trials. To give each dog as long a retrieve as possible, the guns ride out the birds as far as they can without letting too many get away. They do miss, but not often. If one dog gets ahead of the other, the center gunner goes with the leading dog. Since both dogs stop for each flush, the judges even them up again after each bird, so they don't ever get too far apart.

Quite a cast of characters walks each of the two parallel beats. First, a couple of bird planters works two hundred or three hundred yards ahead of the dogs, planting birds randomly. If they plant them too "hard," the dogs trap too many. If they plant them too "light," too many birds flush wild. Bird planting is an art as well as a skill. It is also hard physical work, for each planter wears a poncho full of birds, so he doesn't run out too often. He also doesn't get to see the trial. He's too far ahead of the dogs.

On each beat a handler works his spaniel. Immediately behind the handler is one of the judges. Immediately behind each judge is a "shagger," a person with a large basket on his back for dead birds. Each retrieved bird goes from the handler to the judge to the shagger's basket. Although periodically a runner brings the shagger a fresh basket and hauls his full one off, those baskets frequently get heavy.

Fifteen or twenty yards behind the center gunner, the field marshal walks along. He/she controls the gallery, which should stay behind the field marshal. He/she also queues dogs up for each judge, sends a runner after any dog that doesn't show up when needed, and generally acts as the interface between the judges and the rest of the world.

Every club can use plenty of runners. Some clubs handle many problems with walkie-talkie devices, but they still need runners.

Every club also needs traffic controllers, for both car and foot traffic. If people wander around too much, they can not only interfere with the trial, they can also pose a safety problem. The gunners may not see them at a critical time.

Spectating at Your First Trial

Whether you prefer the Field Trial–type spaniel or not, you will enjoy spectating at a trial. Of the three types of AKC Field Trials (pointing, retriever, spaniel), spaniel trials are perhaps the best spectator sport. The gallery stays close enough behind the dogs to see all the action. And there is plenty of action to see: dogs swishing this way and that; birds flushing every minute or so; the best shotgunners in the area dropping birds a long way off; dogs making spectacular retrieves.

At your first trial, you should be especially careful to stay with the gallery. Don't wander around aimlessly. Don't take a shortcut back to your car. Either could put you in harm's way when a bird flushes and flies in your direction. The gunners may not be able to see you. Or you could flush a planted pheasant. Or, or, or. Stay with the gallery.

In the gallery, stay behind the field marshal. He/she is there to establish the forward limit for the gallery. Even if others forge ahead now and then—and the most experienced trialers are the worst offenders—you should stay where you belong.

Ask questions of others in the gallery, but do it quietly. No loud talking and guffawing. This is no place to audition a new comedy act. Above all, don't be rude. If you prefer a slower spaniel for your personal use, you don't have to make a point of telling everyone around you about it. They really don't care. While on the trial grounds, accept the Field Trial performance standard and watch the dogs from that point of view.

If you go to a Field Trial to learn and to enjoy, you will succeed in both aims. If you go with any other agenda, you will fail. Be a good guest.

Canadian Field Trials

The Canadian Kennel Club (CKC) sponsors trials similar to AKC trials, except that they have no Amateur All Age Stake. The Canadian Field Trial titles, which dogs win much as they win AKC titles are: Canadian National Field Trial Champion, abbreviated as CNFC, CNFTC, or Can.Nat.Fld.Ch.; and Canadian Field Trial Champion, abbreviated as CFC, CFTC, or Can.Fld.Ch.

Pat Bramwell awaits a retrieve, as Judge Ralph Palmer watches.

Tawney Crawford lines her do-all English Cocker in a hunt-dead.
Bill Crawford

Elaine Lake handles her American Cocker to a Junior qualifying score under judge Chad Betts.

Lin Boucher accepts a retrieve from her English Springer in Junior.

24

Hunting Tests

AKC HUNTING TESTS FOR SPANIELS

Purposes

AKC initiated its noncompetitive ''hunting test'' program for spaniels in 1988. Many spaniel owners, unaware of the place of this program in the overall scheme of things, have misunderstood it. Many Field Trialers view the entire concept of hunting tests as the establishment of easy titles to rival in stature the challenging Field Trial titles. Not so, but that is the common perception of many.

To understand the spaniel hunting test program, view it as one front in a broad movement toward noncompetitive testing. This movement started with retriever tests during the early 1980s. AKC, yielding to enormous pressure from owners plus competition from the United Kennel Club (UKC) and the North American Hunting Retriever Association (NAHRA), initiated a retriever hunting test program in 1985. It immediately became, and remains today, the fastest-growing program in AKC history. Impressed by their success in retrievers, AKC initiated a similar program for pointing breeds in 1986. Another exploding success. They initiated the spaniel program in 1988. Another winner.

The concept of noncompetitive testing programs is still gathering momentum. AKC has implemented similar programs for Beagles, herding dogs, and sight hounds. They have even started a basic pet testing program, called ''Canine Good Citizenship'' testing. All of these programs have the same essential elements: noncompetitive testing, graduated testing levels, and after-the-name titles. Each has been more successful than anyone would have predicted.

Eventually, AKC (or some agency) will initiate similar programs for working breeds and terriers. Search and rescue dog testing is another possibility, with real humanitarian implications. Clearly, the noncompetitive testing concept has found a receptive audience in modern American society.

Why? Look at American society. Since the end of World War II, America has developed a massive middle class with sufficient leisure time and disposable income for hobbies. Before World War II the middle class (if you can call it that) had neither. The post–World War II middle class has expanded recreational pursuits in this country to a level unknown in any society in the history of the world. Purebred dog ownership is just one example.

Spaniel Field Trials, started in 1924, were not designed for our current middle class, which didn't exist then. Being purely competitive, Field Trials demand a significant commitment in both time and money. Even for those able and willing to commit the resources, Field Trials can be frustrating. Most dogs fail to earn the titles Field Trialers seek. Some of the best hunting dogs in this country are Field Trial washouts. Trials are an all-or-nothing gamble.

The noncompetitive testing programs are not all-or-nothing. They have many possible goals, several levels of achievement. That's why they appeal to such a broad spectrum of society. Since they came about forty years too late, many people are joining in en masse, playing catch-up, so to speak.

AKC has promoted its hunting tests as programs aimed at the hunter. True enough, but they appeal to a much broader range of dog owners: borderline Field Trialers, obedience trainers looking for a new challenge, dog show breeders wanting to test their stock in the field. In the spaniel world, hunting tests appeal strongly to the fanciers of those breeds for which AKC does not conduct field trials: Welsh Springers, English Cockers, American Cockers, Sussex, Field, Clumber, and show-bred English Springer Spaniels (which have no realistic chance in Field Trials).

For these folks, hunting tests offer the first opportunity to acquire AKC field titles. Such titles will become a substantial aid in breeding dogs with field ability.

The program is too new to be well stabilized yet. Unlike Field Trials, hunting tests have no traditions to fall back on. They are still building their traditions. That can be a painful process. The performance standard is not well defined. The rules are interpreted in different ways by different clubs, different judges. Field Trials went through these same growth pains many decades ago, only over a longer period of time and with fewer people involved. The very popularity of hunting tests adds to the confusion.

In 1989 AKC initiated a series of judges' clinics around the country. These have helped clarify and unify the perception of hunting tests nationwide. Over time review, revision, and clarification of the rule book will help even more.

Although Field Trials will always remain popular, especially among highly competitive people, hunting tests will become the more popular activity before the turn of the century. Hunting tests have something positive to offer everyone with a spaniel. And hunting test titles will become major factors in breeding programs. Placing puppies whose immediate forebears lack these titles will become increasingly more difficult.

Testing Levels and Formats

Hunting tests offer three graduated testing levels: junior, senior, and master. A dog does not have to complete its junior title before working for its senior, nor its senior title before working on its master.

At each level, dogs are tested on land and in water. Unlike Field Trials, dogs are not braced for the quartering work. Perhaps this is because so many different breeds participate. It would be difficult for the slower dogs to keep up with the faster ones.

In the junior level, the tests are land quartering and a nonslip water marked retrieve. While quartering, the dog should cover the ground but need not have a finished pattern. It gets two bird contacts (pigeons or game birds) and does not have to be steady. It must retrieve. In fact, if it traps a bird instead of flushing it, after the dog delivers it to the handler, one of the judges throws up a dead bird for it to retrieve. In the twenty-yard water test, the dog need not be line-steady. The dog need not deliver to hand.

In the senior level, the tests are land quartering, hunt-dead, and a nonslip water marked retrieve. While quartering, the dog must cover the ground reasonably well, flush and retrieve two birds (game birds only). If the dog traps a bird, the judge throws a dead bird for it to retrieve. The dog need not be steady but must not chase a flyaway uncontrollably. The hunt-dead varies widely from club to club. The dog is supposed to find and retrieve a bird that has been shot out of the dog's sight. In practice this may be a simple "stick your nose in the cover, doggie" test or it may be a land blind retrieve. Whatever I might say it is, it will be something else at the next test you attend. The nonslip water retrieve is about thirty yards long. The dog must be line-steady and must deliver to hand.

In the master level, the tests are land quartering, hunt-dead, nonslip water marked retrieve, and water blind retrieve. In the quartering test, the dog should show a finished pattern. It gets two bird contacts (game birds only), must be steady, must retrieve, must deliver to hand. The hunt-dead might be anything (as in the senior), but will more often be a land blind retrieve in master. The water marked retrieve is about forty yards long. The dog must be line-steady and must deliver to hand. The water blind retrieve must be a minimum of thirty yards. Different judges demand different levels of control. This is another area of confusion that will become more clear and uniform as the program matures.

Titles

Since the titles are noncompetitive, with specific requirements for completion, every good dog can succeed, given a reasonable number of chances. Further, dogs can succeed at three different levels, each with an identifying title. That makes reading a pedigree much more enlightening than it was when the only field titles were NFC, NAFC, FC, and AFC.

However, hunting tests do not allow dogs without ability to earn titles, as many Field Trialers seem to fear. The dog must do the work, even if it doesn't have to do it better than all the other dogs. The noncompetitive nature of hunting tests eliminates what poker players call the "good second-best hand" syndrome so common in competitive events.

Per AKC custom, hunting test titles, being noncompetitive, follow the dog's name. They are as follows:

Junior Hunter, abbreviated as JH: This is the lowest-level title. To earn it, the dog must qualify in four licensed junior level tests.

Senior Hunter, abbreviated as SH: This is the middle-level title. To earn it, the dog must qualify in five licensed senior level tests. If the dog previously earned the JH title, it only needs to qualify four times for its SH.

Master Hunter, abbreviated as MH: This is the highest-level title. To earn it, the dog must qualify in six licensed senior level tests. If the dog previously earned the SH title, it only needs to qualify five times for its MH.

The Mechanics of a Hunting Test

Field Trial clubs—more correctly clubs originally formed for Field Trials that have expanded their horizons to attract more members—hold most of our hunting tests. National breed clubs hold them, too, as do some local spaniel breed clubs, whose primary interest is conformation showing. A few all-breed hunting dog clubs also conduct spaniel tests.

A typical spaniel hunting test takes only one day. Consequently, many clubs hold "back-to-backs," that is, two separate hunting tests on successive days, usually Saturday and Sunday. A back-to-back draws a larger entry, because people will travel farther to run when they can earn two qualifying scores. While working toward Flick's MH, I twice traveled fifteen hundred miles round-trip to run in back-to-back tests conducted by Rice Creek Hunting Dog Club in Minnesota.

Different clubs run the testing levels in different sequences. Most of them start with the quartering tests for all three levels. Some start with the junior, followed by senior, followed by master. Others reverse the order. Since all dogs quarter individually, quartering takes only two gunners. Unlike Field Trial gunners, they do not ride the birds out. These are supposed to be hunting tests, so the falls should be shorter, more like the average spaniel encounters while hunting.

The judges should judge each dog according to the performance standard for its breed. Sussex and Clumber Spaniels just don't cover ground as rapidly as do field-bred English Springer Spaniels. That doesn't mean they shouldn't hunt eagerly and show appropriate style. I've judged Clumbers, and I found their style and animation delightful to watch. But I had to recalibrate my eyes, so to speak, so that I looked for what should be there with a Clumber running, not what I would see with my own Flick. Neither style is innately better or worse than the other. They are just different, and I pity the person who cannot enjoy watching a good one of either breed.

Some (usually inexperienced) people plead passionately for running in "real hunting cover." They want tall, nasty stuff, like the worst mess you might put your spaniel in during its lifetime. That's fine in theory, but it violates the most basic rule of judging, a rule that applies whether you're judging a hunting test or the Miss America Contest: *You can't judge 'em if you can't see 'em.* To evaluate a dog's performance, the judges must be able to see what it's doing most of the time. Just seeing an occasional bird pop up from the jungle isn't enough. Did the dog flush it or did it flush wild? Who knows?

Clubs have to run hunting tests (and Field Trials) in the cover to which they can gain access. That is seldom ideal. Even if it were gorgeous at 8:00 A.M., by noon it would lose its pristine beauty due to the many trips through it by dogs, handlers, judges, shaggers, gunners, and gallery.

Besides, what is "real hunting cover" anyhow? I once flushed a rooster pheasant from a plowed field. I was trudging from one strip of cover to another, and my dog was wandering off to one side. Yeah, I missed the shot, if you must know. When I hear someone making a case for "real hunting cover," I'm tempted to say, "I'm with you, pal. Let's run on a plowed field. Toughest shooting I've ever had."

After the quartering work, most clubs do the (unpredictable) hunt-deads for senior and master before going to water. Next, they go to water for the nonslip marked retrieves. Here, too, they may run juniors, then seniors, then masters, or vice versa. These are pretty straightforward. The bird may be a shot flyer or a thrown dead bird. For junior, it may be a pigeon, a pheasant, a chukar, or a duck. For senior and master, it must be a game bird (pheasant, chukar, duck). Those who know canine water work best prefer ducks for this test, especially when throwing dead birds. The feathers on upland game birds are not waterproof. They saturate with water and fall off. The skins are fragile, inclined to tear. Pigeons are even worse. Using upland birds and pigeons in water can create mouth problems—like the dog eating the bird as it swims—in the gentlest-mouthed dog. When rethrown and rethrown, which is typical in a water test with thrown dead birds, the birds deteriorate rapidly to mush. Ducks, on the other hand, stand up to reuse quite well. The feathers are waterproof and the hides tough.

The final test is the master water blind, the pièce de résistance, so to speak. This may be run alone or in conjunction with the water mark. The latter is much more difficult because the dogs may suck back to the mark when sent for the blind.

Some judges are extremely lenient in the water blind. I once saw a dog run around a pond, stumble on the bird, and return back around the pond. The judges gave it a qualifying score!

Some judges give the handler a time allotment (say ten minutes) in which to collect the blind, and they don't much care how it's done. Is that really a blind retrieve?

Some judges are extremely strict. Like the one who instructs the handler to send his dog in the wrong direction and then handle it to the bird when it reaches some point in the water. I've even heard of one who refused to let the handler know where the bird was!

Can you see why some handlers have become quite frustrated during these early days of the hunting test movement? However, the more farsighted participants shrug it off, knowing that time will settle things down. Traditions will evolve, as they have in Field Trials. Traditions will govern how tests are run, how they are judged. Everyone will understand what to expect when the entry form is sent in.

This is not Pollyannaish wishing. These are exciting times for those involved in the hunting test movement. We are making history every day. Those who are still young will tell their grandchildren about how hunting tests developed during their lifetimes.

Let me repeat here a prediction I have made often: The first AKC hunting test (for retrievers) was held in 1985. I was there. In fact, I was one of the master level judges. I would estimate that about 100 people were in attendance, certainly no more than 150. However, twenty-five years from now, 10,000 will claim to have been there. That's how important this movement will become by then.

Spectating at a Hunting Test

As I said in the last chapter, spaniel Field Trials are the best spectator sport among the three types of AKC trials. If anything, spaniel hunting tests are better. They have more breeds. They have the same basic quartering work, plus the hunt-dead (which could be renamed "judges' surprise," because no one else knows what it will be), the water marked retrieves and the master water blind retrieve. What else is there for a hunting dog to do?

When you spectate at your first test, follow the same commonsense rules I gave you for spectating at a Field Trial. Stay behind the field marshal, don't make unnecessary noise, and don't be vocally critical. Anyone can find fault with someone else's sport. Some Field Trialers are especially inconsiderate in their comments at hunting tests.

Ask all the questions you care to, take pictures if you like, and stay for the barbecue if they have one. Lots of fun.

NON-AKC HUNTING TESTS

UKC Hunts for Retrievers

UKC does not at this time sponsor hunting tests for spaniels. However, it does allow spaniels to participate in their tests for retrievers. Called "hunts" rather than hunting tests, these involve mostly nonslip retriever work on land and in water. Quartering tests are optional and quite popular in some areas of the country.

This program has three testing levels, named "started," "seasoned," and "finished." The titles available, which require successful completion of different numbers of finished level tests are: Hunting Retriever Champion (abbreviated H.R.Ch.) and Grand Hunting Retriever Champion (abbreviated Gr.H.R.Ch). These titles are noncompetitive but precede the dog's name, as do all UKC titles.

UKC nonslip retriever tests are on the level of AKC retriever tests. If they have quartering tests, they are significantly easier than AKC spaniel tests. After all, UKC tests are for retrievers. But for those spaniel owners who have earned the AKC MH title, especially those who do a lot of duck hunting, these UKC hunts can be quite a challenge. Spaniels do run in them, and do run successfully.

North American Hunting Retriever Association (NAHRA) Field Tests

NAHRA also conducts noncompetitive tests for retrievers. They call theirs "field tests." They allow spaniels to participate and earn NAHRA titles. NAHRA is not affiliated with any registry, which reduces the value of their titles in some eyes. But some spaniel owners do run their dogs in these tests, and do so successfully.

NAHRA has three testing levels, called "junior," "intermediate," and "senior." They are roughly equivalent to the corresponding levels in AKC and UKC tests for retrievers, with one exception that may interest you as a spaniel person: they require quartering in the upper two levels. Granted, they pass some pretty ragged imitations of true quartering, but at least they have it in every test at those levels.

NAHRA offers three titles: Working Retriever (WR) for dogs successful in the junior and intermediate levels; Master Hunting Retriever (MHR) for dogs that succeed several times in the senior level; and Grand Master Hunting Retriever (GMHR) for dogs that succeed many more times in the senior level. NAHRA titles precede the dog's name.

25

Working Certificate Tests

AKC WASN'T THE FIRST to recognize the need for some form of noncompetitive field testing program for spaniels. No, they were Johnny-come-latelies. The various spaniel national breed clubs began recognizing this need back in the late 1950s and early 1960s. These clubs, one by one, initiated their own "working certificate" testing programs. All clubs except the American Water Spaniel Club have the same format for their tests. I will treat the common format first, and the AWS format after that.

The primary motivation for these tests came from the dog show world. Breeders whose primary interest was conformation wanted some way to demonstrate and document the basic field ability of their stock. Except for the English Springer, none of these breeds had the opportunity to participate in Field Trials. The English Springer breed is so completely split between show-breds and field-breds that the English Springer show fancy had only a theoretical opportunity in Field Trials.

Tests for Spaniels Other Than AWS

These tests are quite simple. Some Field Trial people condemn them as useless. Not true. They serve a good purpose for the people who buy pups from show breeders with the intention to hunt a little and show a lot. Such people may be better off with a show-bred than a field-bred Spaniel. This is best determined by each individual dog owner.

Besides, simple as these tests are, they are light-years ahead of any effort by Field Trialers to measure the conformation of their stock. If that has ever been attempted, I haven't heard about it.

Because so many of the spaniel breeds are relatively rare, the national breed clubs depend on each other to conduct these tests. Any spaniel breed can run in the tests of any other spaniel breed. If such a dog qualifies, its parent club, not the sponsoring club, issues its certificate.

A Working Certificate test consists of two parts, one on land, the other in water. Each dog is run individually, not braced.

In the land test, the handler brings his dog to the line, removes the leash, and has the dog hup beside him/her until the judge tells him to cast his dog off. This may not happen for up to a full minute, for the judge must determine that the dog is under adequate control in this HUP-STAY as part of the land test.

When the judge so instructs him, the handler casts his dog off to quarter the ground. The judges do not look for a finished performance but do want to see the dog cover the beat and show some desire to hunt. About thirty yards down the course, the dog finds a planted bird (pigeon, pheasant, chukar). The dog should flush it and retrieve it when it is shot. The dog need not be steady, nor deliver to hand, but must retrieve and must not be gun-shy or hardmouthed.

In the water test, a set of gunners shoot a bird so it falls in water. Optionally, they may shoot and throw a dead bird (which gives them better control of the fall). The distance need not be long, but it must require a swim. The dog must retrieve the bird, but delivery to hand is not required.

Working Certificate titles are not officially recognized by AKC, UKC, or any other registry. The appropriate national breed club issues the certificates and maintains all relevant records. Breeders do put these titles on their pedigrees, and they are useful to puppy buyers, as long as they understand what level of work they represent.

The national breed clubs follow AKC title conventions by placing these noncompetitive titles after the dog's name. The titles are:

Working Dog (abbreviated as WD): To earn this title, the dog must satisfactorily complete both parts of a Working Certificate test once.

Working Dog Excellent (abbreviated as WDX): To earn this title, the dog must satisfactorily complete parts of a Working Certificate test once with all scores of "excellent."

American Water Spaniel Tests

The American Water Spaniel Club has a totally different format for its Working Certificate tests. The club has changed these tests almost every year. I describe here the 1991 tests.

The AWS format has four graduated testing levels (five counting the puppy test, for which it does not award a title): started dog, working dog, working dog excellent, and working dog superior.

The started dog level consists of three tests. In the "flushing test," the dog must quarter, find, flush, and retrieve a bird. It need not be steady, nor deliver to hand. In the "single land marking test," the dog must complete a thirty- to forty-yard nonslip retrieve. It need not be steady nor must it deliver to hand. In the "single water marking test," it must complete a nonslip water retrieve of no more than forty yards. It need not be steady, nor must it deliver to hand.

The working dog level consists of four tests. The first three are like the three in started dog, but a little more difficult. The dog must flush and retrieve (to hand) birds. It must be line-steady for both the (slightly longer) single marking tests, and must deliver to hand. The final test is the "delayed double marking test" in water, in which a second bird is killed as the dog returns with the first one.

The working dog excellent level consists of four tests. In the "flushing test," the dog must find, flush, and retrieve two birds. It need not be steady but must deliver to hand. In the "land double marking test," the dog does a nonslip double marked retrieve with the falls forty to sixty yards away and 90 degrees apart. It must be steady and must deliver to hand. In the "land blind test," the dog must complete a forty- to fifty-yard blind retrieve. In the "water double marking test," the dog must complete a nonslip double marked retrieve from water with the falls thirty to forty yards away.

The working dog superior level consists of four tests. In the "flushing test" the dog must find, flush, and retrieve two birds. It must be steady and deliver to hand. In the "water triple marking test" the dog must complete a short triple mark in water. It must be line-steady and deliver to hand. In the "long blind test," the dog must do a mixed land and water blind retrieve of approximately one hundred yards. In the "honor test," the dog must remain line-steady while another dog completes a nonslip retrieve.

These titles are not recognized by any registry. The American Water Spaniel Club conducts the tests, issues the certificates, and maintains all records. The titles are placed after the dog's name. The titles are as follows:

Started Dog (abbreviated SD): To earn this title, the dog must satisfactorily complete the started testing level twice.

Working Dog (abbreviated WD): To earn this title, the dog with an SD title must satisfactorily complete the working dog level twice. The dog without an SD title must pass it three times.

Working Dog Excellent (abbreviated WDX): To earn this title, the dog with a WD title must satisfactorily complete the working dog excellent level twice. The dog without a WD title must pass it three times.

Working Dog Superior (abbreviated WDS): To earn this title, the dog with a WDX title must satisfactorily complete the working dog superior level twice. The dog without a WDX must pass it three times.

Clearly, this is a very challenging program, tailored to the talents of this versatile spaniel.

The Future of Working Certificate Tests

Many wonder whether the new AKC hunting test program will eventually replace these tests. Maybe so, but I doubt it. The tests conducted by all clubs except the American Water Spaniel Club fill in the low end below the AKC program. True, the tests are similar to AKC's junior level tests, but the dogs need only pass a Working Certificate test once, not four times as in AKC tests. The American Water Spaniel tests are as challenging as AKC tests and address the specific needs of this spaniel, especially in the area of multiple marked retrieves (which happen more often in waterfowl hunting than in the uplands).

I feel the Working Certificate tests will remain in place and maybe even gain a little strength from the AKC hunting test program. The two will feed off each other, both in requirements and general interest. Hunting test hopefuls will try the Working Certificate tests first, and people who complete their Working Certificate titles will go into the AKC program as another challenge.

AM/CAN/ CH Tabaka's Tilt the Balance, CDX, SH, WDX, delivers a bird to Ruth Tabaka.
Courtesy Ruth Tabaka

26

Keeping Everything in Perspective

TRAINING, hunting, and exhibiting a spaniel can become an all-absorbing pastime. You train almost year-round, averaging maybe three times a week. You hunt almost every weekend during the season. You exhibit in hunting tests, Field Trials, Working Certificate tests (plus dog shows and Obedience Trials if you are so inclined) on weekends from the end of one hunting season to the start of the next. You can easily let this new hobby dominate your life.

But if you do, you'll burn out within five years. What's more, within that five-year span, the major areas of your life outside dogs may suffer irreparable harm. If you take too much time from work to play dog games, your career may stagnate. If you are married, you may slowly drift away from your spouse. If you have children, you may not be there for them (at least mentally) when they need you. In extreme cases, people have let their dog hobbies push them into unemployment, divorce, and custody battles. Extreme, but not rare cases.

No one is a more dedicated dog nut than I am. But even I see that dog games must remain in their proper place. A happy life, a successful life, is a well-balanced life. I don't know what the important elements were in your life before you bought your first spaniel. Probably spouse, children, friends, career, social and religious organizations, all in your own unique order of importance. Whatever they were, they should continue to dominate your mental, emotional, and physical energies. You had a place in your life for a dog before you decided to buy one. Otherwise, you wouldn't have started looking.

The trick now is to keep your dog and all related activities in that place. If you do that, you will stay happily "in dogs" the rest of your life. If you don't, you will burn out within five years, honest. And you may not have much to go back to, either.

Even within your dog activities, you should keep everything in perspective. The key question, which you should ask yourself often, is "Am I still having fun?"

If you let some particular dog activity dominate your attention, it can become self-defeating. Competitive activities tend to do this more than noncompetitive ones. Winning becomes everything to the overly competitive dog person. He/she stops seeing his/her dogs as companions. They become "pot collectors." If they don't bring home rosettes and trophies often enough, they lose their jobs to other dogs with "more potential." Ditto for the next batch of dogs, and the next, and the next. No one can win all the time. If nothing about your dog game pleases you except winning, you're off course.

Step back now and then and take inventory. Do you still like your dogs as dogs? Do you still enjoy training them, even when they are having problems that baffle you? Do you still enjoy buddying around with them at home? Do you still enjoy hunting with them, or are you too concerned that they might lose their competitive edge afield? Are most of your thoughts about your dogs and your dog activities positive?

In other words, are you still having fun?

If not, remember back to the day you decided to participate in the game that is frustrating you. Why did you start? Can you refresh and revitalize that motivation and stay in the same game? Would a month or two off help you straighten out your thinking? Or should you try another breed, another game?

A change in breed can help sometimes. I've worked with several breeds of pointing dogs, and several breeds of retrievers. Please understand: I don't just unload my old dogs and buy new ones. No, as an old dog becomes treasured memories, I fill his haunting kennel run with a dog of another breed. Each time I leave a breed, I know I will come back. When I do, I will not only be refreshed, but I will also bring new knowledge with me.

A change in games can also help. I've cycled and recycled through pointing dog Field Trials, retriever Field Trials, retriever hunting tests, spaniel hunting tests, Obedience Trials, and dog shows during my thirty-five plus years in dogs. When I start to burn out in one, I change to another, knowing I will come back refreshed someday.

Many dog nuts, especially those who haven't been around long, exhibit a curiously fierce loyalty to one breed and one game. Perhaps a perverted patriotism or a misplaced monogamy. Maybe just a taut (taught?) tunnel vision. Every time I have changed breeds and/or games, I have been amused by their reactions. They view me with suspicion. Those in the breed and game I leave look on me as a traitor. Those in the breed and game to which I change see me as a untrustworthy turncoat, or maybe a spy.

Most of these people haven't been in dogs 10 percent as long as I have.

Yet they are so "right" (righteous?), so dogmatic (no pun intended—well, maybe), and so very, very provincial.

I see their provincialism as a sign, not of their dedication to breed and game, but of their inexperience. I see their provincialism as something they will have to outgrow if they are to stay in dogs as long as I have.

One thing they never seem to see: *I'm still having fun.*

APPENDIX I

Glossary

N.B.: All titles found in pedigrees are listed in appendix 2, ''Reading Spaniel Pedigrees.''

Amateur All Age Stake: This is the stake in AKC Field Trials in which all dogs must be handled by amateurs. See chapter 23, ''Field Trials,'' for details.

American Kennel Club (AKC): This is the largest all-breed registry in the country, and the major registry for spaniels. With headquarters in New York, AKC regulates and oversees dog shows, Obedience Trials, Tracking tests, Field Trials, and hunting tests.

Arm Signals: When a handler wishes to redirect his dog that is moving some distance from him (normally on a blind retrieve but sometimes on a mark), he stops the dog with a whistle signal and waves his arm in the appropriate direction. This is also called ''casting,'' and it is a major part of blind retrieves.

Back-to-Back: Two hunting tests on a single weekend, one on Saturday, one on Sunday.

Beat: The area in which a spaniel quarters in a Field Trial or hunting test. Synonym for ''course.''

Belt Cord: A short length of stout cord used in line-steadying. It is about three feet long and has a loop on one end for attaching to the handler's belt.

Bench: This term is a synonym for ''dog show'' or ''conformation'' or ''breed.'' All refer to dog show competition. This term derives from the fact that it was once the custom at dog shows to keep all entered dogs on public display throughout the day on ''benches.''

Blink: When a dog locates a bird with his nose, but then avoids the bird, it is said to blink the bird. Bird-shyness (often a result of gun-shyness) occurs in both flushing and retrieving.

Blinker: A dog that blinks (finds and avoids) birds.

Blind: There are three possible meanings for this word in hunting circles (an economy of words we can scarcely afford!).

First, it can mean "blind retrieve," the type of retrieve in which the dog did not see the bird fall but is directed to it through whistle and arm signals.

Second, it can mean "duck blind," a form of concealment used in duck hunting.

Third, it can mean the "holding blind," in which dogs and handlers wait their turn to run a test in a Field Trial or hunting test.

Blind Retrieve: This is a retrieve in which the dog does not see the bird fall, so does not know where it is. The handler directs the dog to the bird through "lining," "stopping," and "casting" techniques. This involves whistle and arm signals.

Blind retrieves may be "cold" or "mixed." A mixed blind is one into which one or more marked retrieves have been incorporated. A cold blind is one run alone, without marks.

Bolt: When a dog runs off afield, refuses to return or even stop on command, he is said to bolt. This is a serious problem in a spaniel, because the dog will flush birds out of gun range.

Bolter: A dog that bolts (runs off).

Break: When a dog leaves instead of remaining steady, whether in a nonslip retrieving or a quartering situation, it is said to "break." A major fault in the more advanced stakes of trials and the higher levels of hunting tests. See also "controlled break."

Breed: Overlooking the obvious meaning of this word, namely a specific breed of dogs, such as the Clumber, consider for now only the meaning as the term is commonly used in the dog show world, where it is a synonym for "bench," "conformation," and "dog show." All refer to dog show competition. The term "breed," in this sense, derives from the fact that dogs are said to be competing in the "breed ring."

Breed Split: This term denotes the situation in a specific breed of dogs, such as the English Springer, in which there are two distinct types of dogs, one for dog show competition, the other for Field Trials and hunting.

Canadian Kennel Club (CKC): This is the major all-breed registry in Canada, similar to AKC in United States. It regulates and oversees Canadian dog shows, Obedience Trials, and Field Trials. It is the major registry for spaniels in Canada.

Casting: This refers to the manner in which a handler gives arm and whistle signals to redirect his dog to a bird. Normally, casting is done on a blind retrieve, but it can also be useful on a mark when the dog cannot find the bird.

CERF: The Canine Eye Registration Foundation, located at Purdue University in West Lafayette, Indiana. This organization reviews written reports by board-certified canine ophthalmologists about the conditions found in dogs' eyes. If they find the eyes of a dog one year old or older normal, CERF issues a clearance number. See appendix 2 (''Reading Spaniel Pedigrees'') for more details.

Chase: When a dog breaks and chases, especially after flushing a bird. This is the act of a spaniel that has not been steadied, or has not been steadied reliably. See also ''controlled chase,'' and ''uncontrolled chase.''

Clip-Winged Bird (Clip): This is a bird, usually a pigeon, with the flight feathers pulled from one wing. The bird cannot fly more than a couple of feet. Spaniel trainers use clips to encourage a hard flush. The dog catches the clip, so tries harder to catch the birds it flushes.

Conformation: This is a synonym for ''dog show,'' ''bench,'' and ''breed.'' All refer to dog show competition. The term ''conformation'' derives from the fact that in dog shows, the entrants are judged on how well they ''conform'' to the written breed Standard.

Control Bird: In a nonslip retrieving test, when they throw a dead bird instead of shooting a live one, they are said to use a ''control bird,'' so named because the throwers can better control the fall with a dead bird.

Controlled Break: When a breaking dog is brought under control quickly, it is said to have made a ''controlled break.'' While not a virtue, this is not as serious as a complete break.

Controlled Chase: If a quartering spaniel breaks and chases a flushed bird but is quickly brought under control, it is guilty of a controlled chase, which is much less serious than an uncontrolled chase (which see).

Course: The area in which a spaniel quarters in a Field Trial or hunting test. A synonym for ''beat.''

Diversion: In a double marked retrieve, the last bird down (normally the first retrieved) is the ''diversion'' bird while the first one down (normally the last retrieved) is the ''memory'' bird.

Dog Show: This is a formal competition in which dogs are judged on how well they conform to the written Standard of physical perfection for their respective breeds. Championship points are awarded in each breed according to the show location and the number of dogs in competition of each breed.

Double; Double Marked Retrieve: This is a marked retrieve in which two birds are thrown, one at a time, in different areas. The dog is expected to remain steady for both, and then to retrieve them one at a time on command. Normally, the dog will retrieve the last bird thrown first, since it is freshest in his mind.

Dummy: This is an artificial substitute for a bird, frequently used to train dogs in nonslip retrieving because of its easy availability and lower cost over the long haul. Dummies are always cylindrical and come in many sizes, from puppy dummies about two inches in diameter and six inches long to large ones four by fourteen inches. Some are made of canvas stuffed with cork or other material, but the most popular are hollow plastic affairs with knobby surfaces. These plastic dummies come in a variety of colors for a variety of visibility situations.

English Flush: The dog with an English (or ''soft'') flush hesitates before diving in to flush a bird. The dog may even flash-point or point solidly until told to flush. Preferred in England, this is faulted in American Field Trials, and to a lesser degree in hunting tests.

Field Marshal: The person who acts as the contact between the judges and the rest of the world in a Field Trial or hunting test. The field marshal walks a few yards behind the judges, controls the gallery (as best he/she can), queues the dogs up for judgment, communicates with the planters (sometimes by walkie-talkie), and does whatever else the judges request.

Field Trial: A competitive event held under AKC regulations (or CKC in Canada). See chapter 23, "Field Trials," for details.

Field Trial Club: A local or regional club formed to conduct AKC licensed Field Trials. Many of these clubs have also assumed responsibility for conducting AKC licensed hunting tests.

Flat Pattern: This is a quartering pattern in which the dog makes a windshield-wiper path back and forth before the handler.

Flyaway: This is a bird which is not shot, intentionally or not. It flies away, whether after being flushed or after being thrown (as in a nonslip retrieving test).

Flyer: This is a live, unfettered bird, one that flies freely. It is neither a clip nor a shackled bird.

Game Bird: In trials and hunting tests, the term "game birds" can mean pheasants, chukars, or ducks, since these are the only ones raised commercially. In hunting, any bird for which the state and federal governments allow hunting is a game bird.

Group: AKC has divided all the breeds it recognizes into seven "Groups": Sporting, Hound, Working, Terrier, Toy, Non-Sporting and Herding. All retrievers (as well as pointing breeds and spaniels) are classified as Sporting breeds. In dog shows, the Best of Breed winner for each breed competes in the "Group" for the four placements there. Then the winner of each Group (seven dogs in all) compete for Best in Show honors.

Gunner: This is a person who shoots birds for the dogs to retrieve in Field Trials and hunting tests.

Hand Signals: This is a synonym for "arm signals." It is part of "casting," which is part of "handling" a dog to a blind retrieve.

Handle: There are two meanings for this term (more unwanted economy).

First, it is a broad term used to describe everything a person does to control and assist a spaniel while training, trialing, or testing. Insofar as the person is the "handler," everything he/she does (good, bad, or indifferent) is "handling."

Second, in the more restrictive use of the word, a person only "handles" a dog when he works the animal to a blind retrieve. In other words, when he lines, stops, and casts the dog to a bird it hasn't seen fall.

Hard Flush: The dog with a hard flush dives in boldly with no preliminary hesitation when he flushes a bird. This is the preferred flush in American Field Trials, and to a lesser extent in hunting tests.

Hardmouth: When a dog damages a bird so that it is not fit for the table, he has hardmouthed it. A serious fault, this becomes an incurable habit in some dogs.

Honor: This has two related meanings. When two dogs are on the line in a nonslip retrieving test, one dog honors the other dog's work by sitting quietly at heel while the other dog makes the retrieve. The dog that retrieves is called the "working dog." The other is called the "honoring dog."

In a brace work quartering situation, when one dog flushes a bird, the other honors by hupping and remaining in place during the retrieve.

Hunting Test: This is the generic name for noncompetitive tests for Sporting dogs. AKC sponsors separate types for retrievers, spaniels, and pointing breeds. UKC (which see below) and NAHRA (which see below) conduct independent tests for retrievers, and allow spaniels to participate.

Hunting Test Club: This is any club formed specifically to conduct hunting tests.

HUP: This is spanielese for "sit." It is also the title of a perfectly delightful book on spaniels by James B. Spencer (which see, right here in front of you.)

Judge's Award of Merit (JAM): An award made in a Field Trial stake to an unplaced dog that has done excellent work.

Junior Testing Level: This is the lowest level in AKC hunting tests. See chapter 24, "Hunting Tests," for details.

Kennel Club: This term usually applies to those local and regional organizations which conduct dog shows.

Kennel Run: This is applied loosely to any type of canine living quarters, but I hope that when you speak of your kennel runs you will only speak of the finest concrete and chain link canine castle—which is no more than your hunting dogs deserve, right?

Limit Stake: This is a seldom-seen minor Field Trial stake, for dogs which have never won a first in an Open Stake or two firsts in the Novice or Amateur Stake. See chapter 23, "Field Trials," for details.

Line: This has multiple meanings (an unfortunate economy of words). As a noun, it can mean the starting point in a test (quartering or nonslip retrieving), or the path a dog takes to a blind retrieve. As a verb, it means the act of lining a dog to a blind retrieve. As a command word, it is the indication to the dog that he has the right "picture" in a blind retrieve.

Line-Steady: The line-steady spaniel sits quietly at heel until sent to retrieve in a nonslip retrieving situation or test.

Lining: This is the first of the three parts of a blind retrieve. The handler "lines" his retriever when he initially sends the dog from the heel position toward the bird.

Local Breed Club: This is a local or regional organization, normally affiliated with a national breed club, dedicated to furthering the interests of one specific breed.

Mark; Marked Retrieve: This is any retrieve in which the dog sees the bird(s) fall and is expected to retrieve them without handler assistance.

Master Testing Level: This is the highest level at AKC hunting tests. See chapter 24, "Hunting Tests," for details.

Memory Bird: This is the first bird down in a multiple marked retrieve. It is called the "memory bird" because it is normally the last bird retrieved, thereby requiring that the dog remember it while he retrieves the other bird(s).

National Breed Club: This is a nationwide organization of serious fanciers of one breed. This club is normally affiliated with AKC, and maintains the AKC-approved written Standard of physical perfection for the breed. My personal opinion is that every owner of a hunting spaniel should belong to his national breed club. It will keep him informed and involved.

No-Go: When a dog refuses to move from the spot it is sitting in on command, especially when initially lined in a blind retrieve, he is said to be guilty of a "no-go," which is a serious fault.

Nonslip Retrieving: This is a retrieve in which the dog starts sitting at heel while the bird is shot and falls some distance away. As a test, it simulates the retrieving done in waterfowl hunting (or prairie chicken hunting in Kansas).

Novice Stake: This is a seldom-seen minor stake at AKC Field Trials, limited to dogs that have never placed in any Open or Amateur Stake or won first in a Novice or Limit Stake. See chapter 23, "Field Trials," for details.

Obedience: A general term for a dog's proper responses to certain basic commands, like HUP, HEEL, COME, STAY, and DOWN. Obedience is the basis for all control training in the field. See chapter 12, "Obedience," for details.

Obedience Club: In all large and many medium-sized cities there are clubs devoted to formal obedience training and trialing. They offer the general public introductory courses in basic obedience training. These courses can be valuable to the first-time dog owner.

Obedience Trial: This is a formal activity for those involved in serious obedience training. Both AKC and UKC sponsor very similar trials. Both have three levels of noncompetitive titles. AKC also offers a competitive title for dogs which have won all three noncompetitive titles.

OFA: Orthopedic Foundation for Animals, located at the University of Missouri in Columbia, Missouri. This organization reviews hip X-rays submitted by veterinarians. If they find the hips of a dog two years old or older normal, they issue a clearance number. See appendix 2 ("Reading Spaniel Pedigrees") for more details.

Open All Age Stake: This is the stake in AKC licensed Field Trials in which all dogs and handlers may compete. See chapter 23, "Field Trials," for details.

Pattern: This is the generic term for the manner in which a flushing spaniel covers its ground while quartering. A pattern that covers the ground completely and efficiently is a good pattern. One that misses likely places or covers the same places repeatedly is not good.

Pattern Blind: This is a "practice" blind retrieve, in which the dog knows where the bird is, although he did not see it fall. This is a blind used to drill the dog in lining.

Picture: When a dog is properly lined up before being sent on a blind retrieve, it is said to have the "right picture." Dogs run blind retrieves with mental pictures gained through training and previous actual blind retrieves.

PIL (Poor Initial Line): In a blind retrieve, if the dog starts off in the wrong direction, he is said to be guilty of a PIL, which is an error.

Planter: A person who plants birds at a Field Trial, hunting test or Working Certificate test.

Pop: The dog running a blind retrieve is said to "pop" if he stops and looks for direction from his handler without being stopped by the handler's whistle signal. This is a fault, but not a serious one if not repeated too often.

Punch Out: A spaniel that ranges out of gun range is said to "punch out" too far. This is a serious fault in a flushing dog.

Puppy Stake: A popular minor stake at AKC Field Trials, limited to dogs no more than twenty-four months old. See chapter 23, "Field Trials," for details.

Qualified Open All Age Stake: An Open Stake in a Field Trial limited to dogs that have placed in any stake except a Puppy Stake. See chapter 23, "Field Trials," for details.

Quarter; Quartering: This is the spaniel's manner of hunting ahead of the hunter in the uplands. The dog searches the cover on both sides without getting out of gun range.

Refusal: This term is applied to disobedience in which the dog ignores the handler's command. A "whistle refusal" means the dog refused to stop when the handler blew the STOP whistle. A "cast refusal" means the dog didn't go in the direction the handler directed. And so on. When the dog refuses to move, it is often called a "no-go."

Rehearsing: This is a technique used in the early stages of multiple marked retrieve training. The dog runs the memory bird as a single before running the multiple mark. This helps him remember the memory bird during the multiple mark.

Roll In: When an assistant throws in a dizzied bird during training for quartering, he is said to "roll in" the bird.

Salting: A technique used in the early stages of nonslip retrieving training. The thrower scatters several dummies or birds in the general area into which he is throwing the mark. That way, if the dog gets to the area of the fall, he will find something to retrieve. This is a confidence builder.

Selecting: In a multiple marked retrieve, if the handler sends his dog for the retrieves out of their natural sequence (last down, first retrieved), he is said to be selecting. This requires an experienced dog.

Senior Testing Level: This is the intermediate level in AKC hunting tests. See chapter 24, "Hunting Tests," for details.

Series: The complete running of a single test in a Field Trial or hunting test stake. See chapters 23, "Field Trials," and 24, "Hunting Tests," for details.

Shackled Bird: A bird with its legs and/or wings secured in some manner. Sometimes pheasants are planted with only their legs shackled, and those loosely, to limit their ability to run. Ducks are sometimes shackled completely, wings and legs, to keep them from diving when the dog approaches. The most humane way to so shackle a duck is with a "duck sock," which fits over the bird's entire torso and ties around the neck and tail.

Shagger: The person who walks behind the judges in a Field Trial, hunting test, or Working Certificate test. His/her job is to accept and carry shot birds from the judges. Usually a shagger wears a large basket on his/her back for the dead birds.

Single; Single Marked Retrieve: This is a nonslip retrieving test in which only one bird is thrown for the dog.

Soft Flush: The dog with a soft (or "English") flush hesitates before diving in to flush a bird. It may even flash-point or point solidly until instructed to flush. Preferred in England, this flush is faulted in American Field Trials, and to a lesser degree in hunting tests.

Stake: This is a grouping of comparable dogs for judging purposes in Field Trials. This term is also sometimes used as a synonym for "testing level" in hunting tests.

Steady: The steady spaniel hups immediately after flushing a bird, sits to mark the fall, and doesn't leave to retrieve until sent. See also "line-steady."

Stickiness: The tendency to "stick" on (refuse to release) a bird. Such dogs are seldom hardmouthed. They just won't release birds.

Sticky: When a dog refuses to release a bird to the handler on command, we call the dog "sticky."

Stopping: This is a part of the blind retrieve, along with "lining" and "casting." After the dog has been lined toward the bird, he may drift off one way or the other. If he does, the handler blows a STOP whistle command (normally a single sharp blast), after which the dog should stop, turn to face the handler, and sit down (if on land) or tread (if in water) to await a "casting" whistle and/or arm signal.

Style: This term is used to describe a dog's manner of working, whether while quartering or retrieving. Each breed has a slightly different style, and should be judged accordingly.

Suction: In a mixed marked and blind nonslip retrieving situation, if the dog returns to the area of the mark when sent for the blind, it is said to have "sucked back" to the mark, to have been a victim of "suction." This is a serious error in blind retrieve work.

Thrower: This is a person who throws dead or live birds during a nonslip retrieving test in a hunting test. A person who throws a live bird (a "flyer") is sometimes called a "live thrower."

Tracking: This is a formal AKC-sponsored sport in which dogs earn noncompetitive titles by tracking human beings for considerable distances through the countryside and locating a dropped object (usually a glove) at the end of the track. There are two levels of tests: Tracking Dog and Tracking Dog Excellent.

Trap: When a spaniel catches a bird on the ground (especially in a Field Trial, hunting test, or Working Certificate test), he is said to "trap" it. Dogs with a hard flush trap more birds than do those with a soft flush.

Type: This is a dog show term which denotes the unique physical characteristics of a particular breed. "Type" is what makes an American Cocker, for example, physically distinct from the English Cocker.

Typey: This is an adjective applied, in dog show circles, to a dog that possesses plenty of its breed's distinct physical characteristics.

Uncontrolled Chase: When a quartering spaniel breaks and refuses to be brought quickly under control, it is said to be guilty of an "uncontrolled chase." Except for very young dogs, this is a serious fault, for the dog will disturb lots of cover and may flush birds out of range.

United Kennel Club (UKC): This is an all-breed registry located in Kalamazoo, Michigan. It has long been the major registry for Coonhounds, Toy Fox Terriers, American Eskimos, and American Pit Bull Terriers. It has recently become active in retrievers. Together with its member club, Hunting Retriever Club (HRC), UKC sponsors one of the three forms of hunting retriever tests. Spaniels are allowed to participate.

Working Certificate Test: This is a testing program established and sponsored by the various national breed clubs to test the working ability of the dogs of their specific breeds. See chapter 25, "Working Certificate Tests," for details.

APPENDIX II

Reading Spaniel Pedigrees

A PEDIGREE lists the dog's ancestors, usually for four to six generations back, in a schematic format. For each listed dog, the pedigree should give the registered name, all titles won, and all health clearances.

If you understand the meaning of the titles and health clearances, you can evaluate the dogs in a pedigree reasonably well. Pay little attention to the merits of dogs more than three generations back, for they contributed little to the dog in question. However, the parents, grandparents, and great-grandparents (in order of decreasing importance) contributed substantially. Study those fourteen dogs closely.

Trouble is, the titles and health clearances in which you are interested are all abbreviated, which makes them like hieroglyphs to the typical novice. Let me help you break the code with this brief explanation of each abbreviation you might find in a spaniel pedigree.

AMERICAN KENNEL CLUB (AKC) TITLES

The convention followed for AKC titles is to put competitive titles before the dog's name, noncompetitive titles after the name.

AKC Competitive Titles

AFC (also AFTC, Am.Fld.Ch.): Amateur Field Trial Champion, the title won in the Amateur All Age Stake in Field Trials for English Springer Spaniels, indicating outstanding field ability.

Ch: Champion, the conformation title won in dog shows, indicating good conformation, but saying nothing about field ability.

DUAL Ch: Dual Champion, the title indicating that the dog has won both the FC and Ch. titles. Currently available only to English Springers among spaniel breeds because of the Field Trial requirement. No English Springer currently carries this title, and because of the field/show breed split, it is unlikely that any will earn it in the foreseeable future. Be wary of any pedigree carrying this title.

FC (also FTC, Fld.Ch.): Field Trial Champion, the title won in the Open All Age Stake in Field Trials for English Springer Spaniels, indicating outstanding field ability.

NAFC (also NAFTC, Nat.Am.Fld.Ch.): National Amateur Field Trial Champion, the title awarded annually to the English Springer Spaniel that wins the National Amateur Championship Field Trial, indicating outstanding field ability.

NFC (also NFTC, Nat.Fld.Ch.): National Field Trial Champion, the title awarded annually to the English Springer Spaniel that wins the National Open Championship Field Trial, indicating outstanding field ability.

OTCh: Obedience Trial Champion, the only AKC competitive Obedience Trial title, indicating outstanding trainability, but saying nothing about field potential.

TRI-Ch: Triple Champion, the title given to a dog that has won the FC, the OTCH, and the Ch. titles. It is available only to English Springers among spaniel breeds because of the Field Trial requirement. To date, no English Springer has won this title. Because of the field/show split in the breed, it is unlikely that any will in the foreseeable future. Be very wary of any spaniel pedigree that contains this title.

AKC Noncompetitive Titles

CD: Companion Dog, the lowest-level title earned in Obedience Trials, indicating basic trainability, but saying nothing about field ability.

CDX: Companion Dog Excellent, the middle-level title earned in Obedience Trials, indicating significant trainability, but saying nothing about field ability.

JH: Junior Hunter, the lowest-level title earned in hunting tests, indicating basic field ability.

MH: Master Hunter, the highest-level title earned in hunting tests, indicating very significant field ability.

SH: Senior Hunter, the middle-level title earned in hunting tests, indicating significant field ability.

TD: Tracking Dog, the lower-level title earned in Tracking tests, indicating significant ability to trail human scent, but saying nothing about field ability.

TDX: Tracking Dog Excellent, the higher-level title earned in Tracking tests, indicating very significant ability to trail human scent, but saying nothing about field ability.

UD: Utility Dog, the highest-level noncompetitive title earned in Obedience Trials, indicating outstanding trainability, but saying nothing about field ability.

UDT: Utility Dog Tracker, the title given to a dog that has earned both the UD and TD titles.

UDTX: Utility Dog Tracker Excellent, the title given to a dog that has earned both the UD and TDX titles.

UNITED KENNEL CLUB (UKC) TITLES

Spaniels may run in UKC Obedience Trials and ''hunts'' for retrievers, both noncompetitive. All UKC titles precede the dog's name.

GR HR CH: Grand Hunting Retriever Champion, the highest UKC hunting retriever title, indicating very significant ability as a nonslip retriever.

HR Ch.: Hunting Retriever Champion, the second-highest UKC hunting retriever title, indicating very significant ability as a nonslip retriever.

HR: Hunting Retriever, the lowest-level UKC hunting retriever title, indicating significant ability as a nonslip retriever.

U-CD: UKC Companion Dog, the lowest-level UKC Obedience Trial title, indicating basic trainability, but saying nothing about field ability.

U-CDX: UKC Companion Dog Excellent, the middle-level UKC Obedience Trial title, indicating significant trainability, but saying nothing about field ability.

U-UD: UKC Utility Dog, the highest level UKC Obedience Trial title, indicating very significant trainability, but saying nothing about field ability.

NORTH AMERICAN HUNTING RETRIEVER ASSOCIATION (NAHRA) TITLES

Spaniels may run in NAHRA's noncompetitive field tests for retrievers, which include elementary quartering. All NAHRA titles precede the dog's name.

GMHR: Grand Master Hunting Retriever, the highest-level NAHRA title, indicating very significant ability as a nonslip retriever plus elementary ability in quartering.

MHR: Master Hunting Retriever, the second-highest NAHRA title, indicating very significant ability as a nonslip retriever plus elementary ability in quartering.

WR: Working Retriever, the lowest-level NAHRA title, indicating significant ability as a nonslip retriever plus elementary ability in quartering.

NATIONAL BREED CLUB TITLES (EXCEPT AMERICAN WATER SPANIEL CLUB)

The various national breed clubs (except AWSC) conduct identical noncompetitive Working Certificate tests. The titles follow the dog's name.

WD: Working Dog, the lower-level Working Certificate test title, indicating basic field ability.

WDX: Working Dog Excellent, the higher-level Working Certificate test title, indicating basic-plus field ability.

AMERICAN WATER SPANIEL CLUB TITLES

AWSC conducts four levels of noncompetitive Working Certificate tests. The titles follow the dog's name.

SD: Started Dog, the lowest-level title, indicating basic ability in both nonslip retrieving and quartering.

WD: Working Dog, the second-lowest level title, indicating basic-plus ability in both nonslip retrieving and quartering.

WDS: Working Dog Superior, the highest-level title, indicating significant-plus ability in both nonslip retrieving and quartering.

WDX: Working Dog Excellent, the second-highest level title, indicating significant ability in both nonslip retrieving and quartering.

FOREIGN TITLES

Most foreign titles found in spaniel pedigrees are either Canadian or English, both of which are almost identical in form and significance to U.S. titles. They are preceded by ''Can.'' or ''Eng.'' to indicate the country of origin. If a dog has earned identical titles in the U.S. and Canada, the titles are listed as ''Am. & Can. Ch.'' (conformation), ''Am. & Can. UD'' (Obedience) or ''FC/CFC'' (Field Trials).

HEALTH CLEARANCES

Currently only two health clearances are available to breeders: OFA (Orthopedic Foundation for Animals) hip clearances, and CERF (Canine Eye Registration Foundation) eye clearances. Both are placed beneath the dog's name in the pedigree. Spaniels, like most types of dogs, are subject to so many hip and eye problems that the buyer should avoid any litters not having good ''pedigree depth'' in OFA and CERF numbers. At a minimum, both parents should be certified. Two complete generations (parents and all four grandparents) would be better.

OFA hip clearances are in the form AA-NNNNANNA, where A = alphabetic and N = numeric. For example, ''ES-1234E25M'' means that an English Springer (ES) has been assigned OFA serial number 1234 as a result of scoring excellent (E) in its hip X-ray check when it was twenty-five months old. The ''M'' indicates the dog is male. A dog with ''good'' hips would have ''G,'' and one with ''fair'' hips would have ''F'' where the ''E'' is in this example. Dogs under twenty-four months are not eligible for OFA clearance numbers. Frequently only the breed identification and the serial number are listed in pedigrees: AA-NNNN.

CERF eye clearance numbers are in the form AA-NNN/NN-NN. For example, "WS-123/91-18" means that a Welsh Springer (WS) has been assigned CERF serial number 123 as a result of having been found to have normal eyes in a test performed in 1991, when the dog was eighteen months old. Dogs under twelve months are not eligible for CERF clearance numbers.

APPENDIX III

Important Contacts

ALL-BREED REGISTRIES

N.B.: AKC is the major registry for spaniels.

American Kennel Club (AKC)
51 Madison Avenue
New York, NY 10010

Field Dog Stud Book (FDSB)
222 West Adams Street
Chicago, IL 60606

United Kennel Club (UKC)
100 East Kilgore Road
Kalamazoo, MI 49001-5598

FIELD TRIAL AND HUNTING TEST SPONSORS

Spaniel Field Trials and hunting tests:

American Kennel Club (AKC)
51 Madison Avenue
New York, NY 10010

Retriever hunting tests in which spaniels may participate:

Hunting Retriever Club (HRC), a UKC affiliate
100 East Kilgore Road
Kalamazoo, MI 49001-5598

North American Hunting Retriever Association (NAHRA)
P.O. Box 154
Swanton, VT 05488

NATIONAL BREED CLUBS

N.B.: These contacts change from time to time. If you are unable to contact a particular through the person listed below, contact AKC and ask for the name and address of the club's current secretary.

American Spaniel Club (American Cockers)
Margaret M. Ciezkowski
12 Wood Lane South
Woodmere, NY 11598-2298

American Water Spaniel Club
Dick Suessens
P.O. Box 782
Sheboygan, WI 53082

Clumber Spaniel Club of America
Leslie Connell
14811 132nd Avenue East
Puyallup, WA 98374

English Cocker Spaniel Club of America
Mrs. Kate D. Romanski
P.O. Box 252
Hales Corners, WI 53130

English Springer Spaniel Field Trial Association
Marie Andersen
29512 47th Avenue South
Auburn, WA 98001

Field Spaniel Society of America
P.O. Box 187
Wales, WI 53183

Sussex Spaniel Club of America
Linda Legare
4488 280th Street East
Randolph, MN 55065

Welsh Springer Spaniel Club of America
Mrs. Pat Pencak
Old Forestburg Road
Sparrow Bush, NY 12780

Dogwood Welsh Springer Spaniel Club
Susan Hreha Healy
3655 Robin Road
Tallahassee, FL 32304

NATIONAL CONSERVATION ORGANIZATIONS

N.B.: These organizations promote conservation, especially through habitat improvement and management. Open to private membership, they publish magazines (for members) of interest to spaniel owners.

Pheasants Forever
P.O. Box 75473
St. Paul, MN 55175

Quail Unlimited
P.O. Box 10041
Augusta, GA 30903

Ruffed Grouse Society
1400 Lee Drive
Coraopolis, PA 15108

Ducks Unlimited
One Waterfowl Way
Long Grove, IL 60047

COMMERCIAL MAGAZINES OF INTEREST TO SPANIEL OWNERS

Spaniels in the Field
10714 Escondido Drive
Cincinnati, OH 45249

Gun Dog
Stover Publications, Inc.
1901 Bell Avenue, Suite 4
P.O. Box 35098
Des Moines, IA 50315

Wing & Shot
Stover Publications, Inc.
1901 Bell Avenue, Suite 4
P.O. Box 35098
Des Moines, IA 50315

CANINE TATTOO REGISTRIES

National Dog Registry
Box 116
Woodstock, NY 12498-0116

Tattoo-A-Pet
1625 Emmons Avenue
Brooklyn, NY 11235

CANINE HEALTH CLEARANCE ORGANIZATIONS

CERF (Canine Eye Registration Foundation)
Purdue University
1235 South Campus Courts, Bldg. A
West Lafayette, IN 47907–1235

OFA (Orthopedic Foundation for Animals)
University of Missouri
Columbia, MO 65211

Index